"Haider W... ...ettable journey. Warraich's quest is r... ...onfront the act of dying. A caring and thoughtful ....or, he also writes beautifully – drawing from his own patients and from statistics, medical ethics, literature and the sciences. He succeeds in humanizing a complex topic and gives us remarkable insights about the changing nature of 'modern death'"

Siddhartha Mukherjee, Pulitzer Prize-winning and bestselling
author of *The Gene* and *The Emperor of All Maladies*

"W... ch has written an extraordinarily informative and reflective book,
def... lancing historical facts, statistics, humanism and masterful story
tel... kudos to Dr Warraich for penning this gift to the reader – a truly
ill... ting book. It is a gem, one I shall treasure and share with many"

Professor Sanjiv Chopra, Harvard Medical School,
and bestselling author of *Live Better, Live Longer*

...itious review of how the end of life interacts with our modern
... of medicine... Warraich engages thoughtfully with some
...rsial topics... this book is needed for people experiencing and
...g with death throughout our modern medical system. It reminds
...he journey so far, the progress we have made, and the work that

Journal of the American Medical Association

... invites the reader to contemplate the art and science of death
.... [He] brings us through the 'medicalization' of death and returns
...p humanity... he does this lyrically and with brilliance, courage,
...lity" Eve Joseph, author of *In the Slender Margin*

...ry contribution to this important canon"

Ann Neumann, author of *The Good Death*

...art, contemplative, and appealingly humble voice, Warraich
...he mysteries... [and] ultimately guides us back to a place where
...home message remains the same, that at the end of life, being
...ith family, with community, with clarity – is what matters now,
...ver"

Dr Anna Reisman, Director,
Humanities in Medicine, Yale School of Medicine

"Warraich thoughtfully investigates the often alarming realities of death… [and] eloquently explores the act of dying"

Publishers Weekly (starred review)

"A sensitive review of a painful subject… an important contribution to a serious discussion of profound life-and-death issues"   *Kirkus*

"Warraich has looked at modern death with the cool eye of a scientist, and the heart of a humane doctor. It's a wonderful combination of history, anatomy, public policy, and storytelling. A warm and thorough guide to living well all the way to the end"

Ellen Goodman, Pulitzer Prize-winning columnist and *New York Times* bestselling author of *Paper Trail*

"An omnivorous, fascinating, free-range romp through the history and co-evolution of death and modern medicine"

Katy Butler, *New York Times* bestselling author of *Knocking on Heaven's Door: The Path to a Better Way of Death*

"A much-needed exploration of this treacherous territory, offering clear-eyed analysis of what it means to die"

Dr Danielle Ofri, author of *What Patients Say, What Doctors Hear*

"This book has something valuable to say to every person alive. Blending wisdom, research, and compassion, Dr Warraich shines a bright light into a dark reality of human existence. The result is nearly encyclopedic, with an illumination on every page"

Stephen P. Kiernan, author of *Last Rights*

"*Modern Death* tells the most compelling story: how something that once seemed so simple – the difference between life and death – became so complicated, and so important… Warraich takes on this mammoth subject and explains it with clarity, humor, intelligence and élan"

Daniel Wallace, author of *Big Fish*

MODERN DEATH

HOW MEDICINE CHANGED
THE END OF LIFE

HAIDER WARRAICH

Duckworth
Overlook

First published in the United Kingdom in 2017 by Duckworth Overlook

This edition first published in 2018

LONDON
30 Calvin Street, London E1 6NW
T: 020 7490 7300
E: info@duckworth-publishers.co.uk
www.ducknet.co.uk
For bulk and special sales please contact sales@duckworth-publishers.co.uk

A catalogue record for this book is available from the British Library

Printed and bound in Great Britain by Clays Ltd, St Ives plc

HB: 978-0-7156-5239-8
PB: 978-0-7156-5279-4

1 3 5 7 9 10 8 6 4 2

To my wife, Rabail,
for giving me the best years of my life

CONTENTS

ACKNOWLEDGMENTS

I was standing in a patient's room as he lay in bed dying, surrounded by family members. I was the youngest person in the room, yet everyone was looking to me for answers. It was like they were at a restaurant where they couldn't read the menu and had never tasted the cuisine. They knew so much more about life than me, but so little about death. That's when I decided that I wanted to write this book: for them and the countless others who let me be a part of the most agonizing moments of their lives. I also wrote it for myself and other healthcare providers, so that we would be better prepared to help.

I received a lot of inspiration at my hospital, the Beth Israel Deaconess Medical Center, in Boston, MA, where I was working when I wrote the book. It was there I learned what it took to deliver humane care. Much of what I know now to be true of what being a physician is, I learned there. Eileen Reynolds believed in me, offering me a spot in one of the most prestigious training programs in the country. I was selected to be a fellow in the Katherine Swan Ginsburg Fellowship in Humanism in Medicine, which was founded in the memory of Katherine Swan, a wonderful physician whose life was cut short at the age of thirty-four by cervical cancer. I never met Katherine, but I saw her humanity through her wonderful family, who continued her legacy through the program. It was during this time that I started to write regularly for the *New York Times*, where my editors including Toby Bilanow and Clay Risen, helped me improve my craft and reach an audience I could never have dreamed of.

Like anything in medicine though, it takes a small village to get anything done. This book has been no different. I presented the idea to my wife, who initially was skeptical. Between a busy medical training program and my research, it was ambitious to even think about writing a book. Yet as the words came and the stories formed, she gave me both the time and the confidence to keep going. I would come back from work and start writing in our tiny Boston apartment on our dining table for two. Without her, there would be no words, no pages, no chapters, and no book.

After I had written the book, I sought out an agent who would take a chance on a first-time author. I reached out to Don Fehr based on his previous work and though I had never met him, he got back to me within a day or so. He loved the manuscript and I knew my brief search was over.

I couldn't have found a better match in an editor than Daniela Rapp at St Martin's Press. Not only was she interested in the material, she was personally invested in telling this story, which is what mattered most to me. Even before we dove into finding a publisher, Don had already indicated that Daniela would be a great editor for me to work with and he couldn't have been more right. The entire team at St Martin's has been instrumental in making this process as streamlined and enjoyable as possible. I also have a lot of gratitude for all the wonderful authors who not only read the book but also offered their generous endorsements.

While I wrote the book in Boston, my new home at Duke University, in Durham, North Carolina, has been extremely supportive of my writing. Whether it is my faculty members within the Division of Cardiology and the Department of Medicine or the staff in communications, I have received my fair share of southern hospitality. These however are just some of the people who have been instrumental in helping turn this idea that I had on a solemn day in the hospital into a book that hopefully can tell one of the more important stories of our times.

MODERN DEATH

How Cells Die

It had been the longest of months—in both the best and the worst possible ways. Brockton is a small town about a half-hour drive south of Boston, but in many ways it seems a world apart. As you move away from Boston, you can actually see rust accumulate on bridges, signboards, and fire hydrants. Boston carries a tasteful level of agedness, akin to a hint of silver hair. The red brick Federalist-style apartments of Back Bay, many built in the colonial period, have just the right amount of decay, which gives them a deep and rich texture. With Revival- and Georgian-style buildings intermixed, Boston is just rough enough to be photogenic. Brockton, on the other hand, is a town falling apart. Crooked goalposts stand half erect in fields with tall grass that might not have seen a game of football in decades. The town is awash in violent crime and drugs.

The town of Brockton is served by a community hospital that mirrors many of the characteristics of the town it is located in. Medicine residents from my program would go to the intensive-care unit (ICU) in that hospital for an away rotation, and it was an experience of legendary proportions. Unlike the large academic referral center we were used to, with an abundance of nurses and doctors, the Brockton ICU was run predominantly by the residents even though the patients there were sicker in many ways. In the primary hospital where I was training, there was a surgical ICU, a neurological ICU, a cardiac ICU, a trauma surgical ICU, and a bevy of medical ICUs, but there was only one ICU at Brockton, leaving the care of patients with a host of acute conditions in the hands of the medical residents and the supervising physician.

It was a Sunday, Super Bowl Sunday no less, and it was my last day in Brockton. The Patriots had lost the week before, so my interest was somewhat muted, but still, it was Super Bowl Sunday. I was scheduled to be there until seven in the evening and it would take me an hour to get back to Boston with the traffic, which would mean I would miss a large chunk of the game. But this Sunday was an almost miraculously quiet day. My team was done with rounds by noon, and we got no new patients afterward. It was so relaxed that I did the unthinkable: I asked my team who was going to be there overnight, whether I could call the shuttle early if we continued to have a quiet day. We had a deal. When the clock struck three, the ED was not buzzing, all our patients were well behaved, and there was no one headed up from the wards, so after checking again with the team, I called the shuttle service to come pick me up at five. I called my wife, ecstatic that I would be done early, and asked her to call our friends so that we could actually have the Super Bowl party she had so wanted to host.

It wasn't long after I hung up that my pager buzzed. There was a medical emergency on one of the wards. I picked up my stethoscope and shuffled toward where the emergency was. When I got there, the whole ward stank of human excrement. One of the nurses directed me toward a room outside which a large crowd had gathered. I made my way through the throng and found that there were three nurses in the bathroom struggling with a patient who didn't seem to be fully conscious. He was slouched over on the toilet seat, totally naked, and the entire bathroom floor was covered in black and bloody feces. The bathroom was very small, and the patient was at least six and a half feet tall and must have weighed at least three hundred pounds. The nurses were trying in vain to lift him up, while a few others were attempting unsuccessfully to get his bed into the bathroom. There was complete chaos, and no one had any idea what was going on.

The man was barely breathing, but he had a pulse. I quickly realized two things: There was no way the bed was getting into the bathroom, and there was no way we could get the patient into the bed. I asked one of the nurse assistants to grab a wheelchair. He brought the wheelchair right up to the bathroom door, and I carried the patient with the nurses from the toilet seat to the wheelchair. Given how sick he was, I knew I didn't even have the time to fully examine him. I had the room emptied so that we could get the wheelchair out of the bathroom and roll the patient to the ICU. One of the nurses threw a bedsheet over his naked body, and we wheeled him up, his head slumped on his chest, to the ICU. He was drooling all over his chest, he was barely breathing, and in his wake he left a long trail of blood and stool that smeared the entire hallway behind him. The resident who was with me took a picture of the hallway with his smartphone. Neither of us had ever seen anything like it.

Once he was up in the ICU, it took about six people to transfer him from the wheelchair to the bed. One of the nurses who had been taking care of him on the ward and had accompanied him upstairs to the ICU told us that he was forty-something and had presented with some bleeding from his rectum last night, but it was only a small amount and he had never experienced similar symptoms before. The team on the ward had actually been thinking of sending him home later that day. The nurse had already called his wife, who was now on her way thinking she was taking him home.

The man, who had been very somnolent until now, started to wake up. But this was not a good thing. He was in shock and was completely delirious. He started thrashing around and pulling the IV lines from his arm. He was immensely powerful, and it took one person per limb to keep him from falling over. It became clear to us very quickly that his risk of choking was high and there was no way we could guarantee patency of his airways without intubating him and having him breathe with the ventilator.

I made my way to stand at the top of the bed and used one hand to keep his head planted down. He was looking me straight in the eye, grunting, with a towel in his mouth preventing him from biting down on his tongue. His blood pressure was in the tank and he had lost almost half his total volume of blood. He was in dire, dire straits. My eyes darted away from the patient's as I looked for the equipment I needed to be able to intubate him. A nurse on the other end of the room had a large green container, so robust it would fit right in at a bomb shelter, with all the tools I needed. With the supervising physician by my side, I picked out the appropriate-size laryngeal blade, which was basically a large tongue depressor made out of metal. I took the blade out and opened it up to be in its usual L-shaped configuration. All the while I was running through my head what I was going to do. I had intubated patients in the past, but never in such a boisterous environment. My attending, an anesthesiologist with Jedi-master skills, stood by me and didn't even hesitate in handing the blade over. Most attendings would get nervous and take over the intubation rather than wait for the trainee to mess around, but not him.

Sticking a tube down a person's throat is actually way harder than it may seem. The last thing you would want to do (although it happens frequently enough) is go down the esophagus and into the patient's stomach rather than down the trachea, which leads to the lungs. Blocking the way is the tongue, which extends much farther down than most people imagine. And then there is the small issue of the epiglottis, a trapdoor-like flap, which covers the trachea to prevent food from going down the windpipe when we speak or breathe. And then once you make your way past the epiglottis, you need to go past the vocal cords, which hang like fluttering curtains right at the top of the trachea.

Standing at the head of the bed, looking at his upside-down face, I signaled to the nurse holding a syringe full of milky propofol to inject the anesthetic. Even in the maelstrom, she was careful, flushing the IV with some saline, injecting the anesthetic, and then flushing again. After the propofol had been injected, we continued to hold the patient down, awaiting the relaxation of his muscular tone. Two minutes passed and we realized we needed something stronger, so we injected a paralytic. His head, which had been thrusting against my forearm, relaxed down;

his eyes, which had been staring at me with unspeakable grit, now just stared at the ceiling. Everyone let go and the patient became limp. He stopped breathing, and the respiratory therapist continued giving him oxygen through a bag mask. As soon as the patient's oxygen levels hit 100 percent, the race was on: I had only seconds to be able to intubate him before his oxygen level dropped.

I passed the laryngeal blade past his tongue and then used it to push the tongue down, lifting his chin up, in the hope that I would glimpse my goalpost—the vocal cords. But his tongue was beefy, and even when I flexed my wrist to the maximum, I could barely see them. I didn't want to just blindly thrust the tube down, which I was anxiously holding in my other hand. My supervisor, on the other hand, was now starting to get impatient. He told me that I wasn't flexing my wrist enough. I looked over my shoulder and saw that the patient's oxygen level was already down to 80 percent. I snaked my blade farther down his throat, almost lifting his head off the bed, and there it was—the thick rim of the vocal cords, pale like chapped lips, surrounded by membranes laden with small capillaries. I grabbed the J-shaped breathing tube, curved it down his throat, and jabbed it through the cords into the black beyond. I pulled out the metal wire that was maintaining the tube's form, and the respiratory therapist connected the bag mask and inflated the cuff in the tube that prevents air from leaking. Next, all of us looked for the telltale signs of the tube going down to the stomach instead of the lungs. The respiratory therapist squeezed the bag, and thankfully it was the lungs, not the belly, that inflated. A nurse put her stethoscope on the belly and heard no breath sounds there from the mask. This man was not out of the woods yet, not by a mile, but I looked up, my visor fogging up, my scrub cap sweaty; I was relieved that at least his airway was secure. I took my gloves off and saw the aides outside the room waiting to take over, with bags upon bags of blood, platelets, and clotting factor.

I didn't even make it out of the room before my pager rang, and before I could even look at it, the overhead speaker blared: "Code blue. Hospital lobby."

Torn, I looked at the other resident, who told me to run down and that he would hold the fort in the ICU.

There is an etiquette to running in the hospital; I avoid running under almost all circumstances, because it can make other people panic and can ruin one's composure. The rule I have for myself is that it's okay to run in stairwells where there are no patients or family members, but not in corridors. Which is why I went for the first stairwell I could find so I could just flat-out run.

I emerged from the stairwell on one end of the lobby and walked toward the entrance, where there was a large crowd of people gathered. Most appeared to be people who were visiting family members in the hospital and now were captivated by some kind of commotion. As I got closer I could hear a woman wailing and crying. A wall concealed the scene itself, and as I approached the entrance I became increasingly full of dread as to what I would find. Just before I caught a glimpse, a child cried out, "Is Mommy gonna die?"

Right in front of the double doors that led into the hospital, a young woman lay on the ground, seemingly unconscious. Next to her, a paramedic was kneeling, and as soon as he saw me, he told me that she still had a pulse but that she had just had a seizure. The woman, curled on her side, was very obviously pregnant. It had to be a seizure from eclampsia, I thought. I laid her flat on the ground to make sure she was breathing fine, which she was. But the commotion was still ongoing. Her mother was going completely berserk, pulling her own hair, screaming, and clearly scaring everyone around her. The crowd, now growing as more doctors and aides converged, was reacting more to the mom than they were to the woman, who was miraculously quite stable at present. The mom was even distracting the emergency-room physicians who had come to help the young woman, but then one of the aides told the mother more sternly than I would have, "Hey lady—keep it together."

I took the young woman to the emergency room, ensuring that she would have someone responsible for her, fulfilling my role as the emergency backup. With that settled, it was time for me to head back to home base. I looked at my phone; it was overflowing with unanswered texts and phone calls. On my way back to the ICU, I called the shuttle driver who was waiting outside and apologized, telling him that there was a patient in critical condition and that it would be great if he could pick me up once the patient was stable enough for me to go home.

As soon as I got back to the ICU, I made a beeline for the room of the patient I had intubated about fifteen minutes ago. The nurse promptly handed me the kit for placing a central line: there weren't enough IV lines to get him all the blood products he needed. The other resident was busy with other patients, so I grabbed the package and dove back into the vortex. We started with a large IV line in the femoral vein in his groin, then placed another in his chest and an arterial line in his wrist. It was as if I needed to perform all the procedures I had learned during residency in one day and on one patient. By the time I got done, it was clear that it was unlikely that the man would ever wake up again. While he was breathing on a ventilator and his heart was beating, we weren't sure whether he was alive anymore or whether he was brain dead or whether he was somewhere in between.

When I first started residency, signing off was very difficult. It was hard to shift responsibility for a patient I had been taking care of to someone who was just covering overnight. Any amount of verbal communication or any number of e-mail signouts would still leave me feeling that I had somehow left my patients hanging. When you are taking care of a patient, you feel that no one else might be able to manage the patient as well as you can, based on the fact that you know the patient the best.

By this time, though, in the third year of my residency, I had become seasoned enough to know when to ease off. I could stay there as long as I wanted, but that was probably not going to change the outcome. Looking at the man in front of me gave me perspective, though: he had gone from having a completely normal life yesterday to having ten additional points of entry in his body and his ability to make it through the night under question. It made my own worries almost comical in comparison. I was going to miss much of the Super Bowl, but as I looked at the patient's wife in the waiting room on my way out, it was clear that there were many, many people in this world who had a lot more riding on this night.

I walked down to the lobby, which was much quieter than when I was last there, and saw the shuttle, a black Lincoln sedan, waiting outside.

"Did he make it?" the driver asked, once I had gotten in and started eating the salad I had picked up from the cafeteria.

I looked in the rearview mirror, and the driver was looking back at me. I was a bit surprised, but not in a bad way. "Did who make it?"

"The guy you told me over the phone about, who was dying."

I suddenly remembered telling the driver on the phone that I was going to be late.

"I am not sure," I told him.

His eyes moved away from mine through the mirror and back to the road.

"Death," he said, "is such a primitive concept."

Doctors experience death more than any other professionals do— more than firefighters, policemen, or soldiers—yet we always think about death as a very concrete construct. It's a box on a checklist, a red bar on a chart, or an outcome in a clinical trial. Death is secular, sterile, and singular—and, unlike many other things in medicine, incredibly binary. So it was interesting to think of death more as a concept and a process than as a fact and an endpoint.

Looking back now, I can say that the driver was right on many counts. Perhaps the most primitive aspect of death is how we respond to it, how we spend most of our lives imagining it away, how we fear it as some sort of unnatural schism in space-time. Every time we talk about death, the food seems terrible, the weather seems dour, the mood sullen. Every time we think about death, we get so depressed we can't hold a meaningful thought in our heads. Many families talk about death only after their loved one is in the ICU, hooked up to more gadgets than Iron Man.

When I first thought about writing a book about death, I went up to my wife, a civilian, and told her about it. She seemed bemused. Just hearing the "d" word made her feel ghastly. I was surprised by her reaction, but since then I have become a bit more used to getting a similar reaction from others.

There are many things that, at any given moment, are deemed taboo subjects by society. Sex is perhaps the first thing to come to mind. Money, at least in some circles, is another. But even sex and money are things whose degree of tabooness varies from culture to culture and from time to time. Talking about death, though, has remained the hardest to pick of all forbidden fruit.

What makes death so difficult to talk about? The difficulty is due in part to social dogma and in part to tradition. The very nature of death, the mystery that surrounds it, breeds uncertainty. Uncertainty breeds fear, and contrary to general perception, never has death been as feared as it is today. The more medicalized death gets, the longer people are debilitated before the end, the more cloistered those who die become, the more terrifying death gets. The last century has given most people the gift of a prolonged life span, but the increased expectation of a long life has made an unexpected road bump all the more hard to digest. Those who know they are going to die early feel cheated of the promise of old age. The only way to make any real change is to tear away the vines of terror that creep up our legs whenever we talk about death and dying.

Conversations about death have become more ineffectual and detached from reality. Death is more commonly used as a political weapon to stir up fear among voters and constituents than it is accepted as an eventual fate of all living organisms. The fear of death has been used to instigate wars, form religions, and make a segment of society rich beyond their dreams, but before this century, we had almost no actual understanding of dying. This lack of understanding, however, has never stopped death from being extremely divisive, and to this day our comprehension of death remains stunted.

On the other hand, the driver couldn't have been more wrong. Death is as ancient as life itself, and you might even argue that death precedes life—for what was there before life, anyway. But the last century has seen death evolve and morph more than any previous time in human history. Not only have biomedical advances changed the ecology, epidemiology, and economics of death, but the very ethos of death—in the most abstract possible sense—has changed. Far from being clearer, the line between life and death has become far more blurry. These days we can't even be sure if someone is alive or dead without getting a battery of tests. While death may be a primitive concept, most people have very little idea what modern death is all about. There were so many things I wanted to say to the driver, but, at least that day, I chose to just sit back and listen.

AFTER REMAINING MORE or less static over many millennia, death changed on a fundamental level over the course of a century. Modern death is nothing like what death was even a few decades ago. The most basic aspects of death—the whys, wheres, whens, and hows—are fundamentally different from what they were at the turn of the last century.

To understand why we die, it's important to understand how we come to live at our most granular level. Human beings are made up of billions of cells of all kinds, each of which possesses life, but not conscious life. We also carry within us gazillions of bacteria that mostly reside in our intestines. In fact, the average human contains ten times more bacteria than human cells.[1] We know now that humans share at least forty genes with bacteria, and are thus distant cousins in a strange way.[2] Each of us, therefore, is like a mother ship carrying denizens, both human and bacterial, that together constitute an interdependent, fully functioning sentient colony with an identity that is not merely existential but physiological.

While death might certainly appear to be simpler than life, our understanding of how cells are formed predates our understanding of how cells die by at least a century. The process of cell division, wherein one cell divides, forming two identical daughter cells—mitosis—was first described in 1882 by the German physician scientist Walther Flemming. Meiosis, wherein one cell divides into two unique cells necessary for reproduction, was also discovered by two Germans, Theodor Boveri and August Weismann, in 1887.[3] Therefore, the process whereby a new cell forms was well appreciated as early as the late 1800s.

But not only was cell death not well studied until fairly recently, it was rarely witnessed. Pathologists, microbiologists, and people from all backgrounds peered down microscopes, but rarely saw a cell in the process of dying, although cells being formed were seen routinely on slides. It was conveniently assumed that cells were continuously dying to accommodate all the cells that were constantly being made. Recent advances in the field of cell biology not only have improved our understanding of how cells die, but have illuminated the life of cells more than almost any other recent discovery in this area.

The answer to one of modern biology's most vexing questions would come from the unlikeliest of sources. *Caenorhabditis elegans* is a nematode, the smallest of roundworms, transparent and only about a millimeter in length.[4] It minds its own business, staying mostly in the soil, feeding mostly on a diet rich in bacteria, and never infects humans. While it lacks a heart and lungs, it does have many organs similar to the organs of larger animals, such as a nervous system, and a fully loaded reproductive system with a uterus, ovaries, and even the equivalent of a penis. Interestingly, 999 out of 1,000 of these worms are hermaphrodites, with only 1 out of 1,000 being a "true male." The hermaphrodite doesn't really need a male for insemination, although given a choice it tends to prefer male semen to its own or that of another hermaphrodite. The typical *C. elegans* worm, barring any major catastrophe, lives for two to three weeks. This worm is a hardy being, and, in fact, *C. elegans* worms survived the *Columbia* space shuttle disaster, in February 2003.[5] When the end does arrive, in a scene with no small amount of drama, the worms emit a blue light just prior to their demise.

What makes these worms essential to science is their unique and relatively simple development. They demonstrate a phenomenon known as eutely, in that their adults have a fixed number of cells, and that number is specific to that species. Once a baby worm is born, it grows in size by cell division. When the cells reach a total of 1,090, they stop dividing. After this specific number of cells is reached, future growth is achieved just by enlargement of existing cells. In the hermaphrodites, though, a select few cells are automatically terminated. It is the genetically predetermined culling of 26 cells in a millimeter-long worm that has now elucidated how cells decide, or are nudged, to commit suicide.

The life cycle and cellular programming of this roundworm's cells was investigated first in Cambridge, United Kingdom, and subsequently in Cambridge, Massachusetts, in the United States. Sydney Brenner, a

South African biologist, set up his developmental-biology lab in Cambridge, UK, where, along with John Sulston, he analyzed the entire genetic makeup of C. elegans.[6] It was around this time, in 1972, that the name apoptosis was proposed by scientists John Kerr, Andrew Wyllie, and Alastair Currie for this "hitherto little recognized" phenomenon of cell death.[7] "Apoptosis" (pronounced "APE oh TOE sis") is a Greek word, used to describe the falling of leaves from trees, or petals from flowers. Brenner and Sulston were joined by Robert Horvitz, who later established a lab at the Massachusetts Institute of Technology, where he continued the work he had started across the pond. In 2002, Brenner, Sulston, and Horvitz were jointly awarded the Nobel Prize in Physiology or Medicine for their discoveries, which revolutionized our understanding of life as much as they did our understanding of death.

We know now that cells die mainly from three mechanisms: apoptosis, necrosis, and autophagy.[8] All three have important metaphysical implications.

The ugliest and least elegant of cell deaths is necrosis. The word is derived from the Greek word "nekros," which means "corpse," and the process occurs when cells are suddenly deprived of nutrients and energy. When blood flow is interrupted, as it is to the brain after a stroke or the heart after a heart attack, the affected cells undergo necrosis. Necrosis starts with the membranes of cells becoming increasingly permeable. Fluid enters the cells from outside, swelling up the cells and their contents in a grotesque fashion until the cells rupture, spilling their contents into the extracellular space. This wanton destruction is also purposeful, in that the first cells to necrose serve as sentinels, warning the rest of the body about the inciting event, whether it be an injury, extreme heat or cold, or a poisonous substance.[9] The human body is always being patrolled by the immune system, always looking out for foreigners. The contents of the cells represent the hidden self, given that they always remain cloistered within the cells, and they are perceived as alien if ever they emerge into the sera. Since the body is not used to seeing these molecules outside the cell, their release alarms the body, which promptly sends in immune-cell reinforcements.

Activation of the immune system initiates the salvage, rescue, and repair program. The cells that necrose are beyond help, but the immune system helps to keep the fire from spreading to unaffected parts. While necrosis was initially thought to be an accidental or uncontrolled form of death, recent advances have shown that it, too, is carefully orchestrated and can be selectively triggered and halted by molecular pathways.[10]

Autophagy is the process wherein the cell consumes ("-phagy") itself ("auto-") or parts of itself. A harbinger of death, autophagy is as essential for life as it is for death. Autophagy is used by the cell to convert its own defective or redundant components into useful nutrients during times of scarcity. Unlike necrosis, which occurs after a complete cessation of supplies, as in a heart attack, autophagy occurs in the presence of a relative scarcity, as in heart failure. When food is limited but still present (unlike when necrosis occurs), the cell tries to shut off unnecessary machinery or get rid of damaged goods by creating small autophagosomes. The autophagosomes are small bubbles that contain toxic materials. These autophagosomes engulf whatever machinery or materials the cell wants to dispose of and transform them into useful nutrients. Widespread autophagy, however, can result in autophagy-associated cell death.

If anything, autophagy is an essential means for the cell to stave off death, as it can be used to consume damaged cell parts such as mitochondria, which are the turbines that convert oxygen into pure energy for the cell and can induce cell death if they burst. An inability to perform autophagy actually accelerates the death of the cell instead of abating it.

Finally, then, we come to apoptosis, perhaps the most important and interesting form of cell demise. In necrosis, a defect in the integrity of the cell membrane is one of the first steps to occur, but in apoptosis the cell membrane remains intact until the very end. Apoptosis, in spite of its complexity, occurs much faster than mitosis—about twenty times faster—which might account for its less frequent sightings on microscope slides. The entire process takes place over hours.

When a cell is about to undergo apoptosis, it becomes more rounded and draws away from other cells. A cell is asked to terminate itself after it is tagged by the grim reaper of the cellular realm—tumor necrosis factor alpha, aka TNFα—which arrives by a cell's side and attaches to a receptor on the cell membrane. This is the molecular version of a kiss of death, activating the so-called death receptor pathway. The cell then dutifully follows its fate and triggers caspases. Caspases are enzymes that live within cells and usually help out with housekeeping, repairs, etc. But when activated by death signals, they initiate a cascade of events that results in a cell dying quietly within itself. Another way cells undergo apoptosis is when mitochondria, after detecting damage to the cell, release proteins from within the cell to signal the initiation of apoptosis. One of these proteins, aptly named "diablo," activates the killer caspases, ringing the death knell.

The cardinal feature of apoptosis is that the cell's organelles start to shrink. The cell membrane remains intact, never exposing the hidden self and therefore not taxing the immune system. Small blebs start breaking off from the membrane, and the cell disintegrates into smaller chunks. Apoptosis is frequently compared to the "controlled demolition" of a skyscraper, where it is very important to ensure that surrounding buildings are not damaged.[11] By a complex mechanism, when a cell is sentenced to die, phagosomes are alerted. Phagosomes are small cells that serve to digest cell components; they are unlike autophagosomes in that they target other cells rather than the cell they originate from. The signal emitted designates the apoptotic cells as separate from the true self and therefore kosher for consumption.

Life and death at our most basic, cellular level is much more complex, dynamic, and balanced than they are at a human level, which we view as a binary equation. At any breathing moment in our lives, we have cells being bequeathed life and cells that are signaled to die. So even as we live, parts of us are constantly dying. In fact, if apoptosis were to not occur, an average human being would accumulate two tons of bone marrow over their life span and possess an intestine fifteen kilometers in length. Even at an individual cellular level, there is a constant dynamic push and pull between factors that favor apoptosis and factors that block it. Therefore, every cell within our body is dancing to forces that move it closer to or farther away from death, and in a broader sense, we comprise cells that are both coming alive and dying at all times simultaneously. What pushes us as humans closer to death is when the net pull of apoptotic forces exceeds that of mitotic ones.

The various ways cells die reveal insights into the life and culture of cells. Presumably cells do not feel or exhibit emotions or dwell on ethics or morality as human beings do. But the ecology and mechanisms of death among cells denote how truly linked life is to death. In fact, when a cell "forgets" how to die, it ends up becoming something that threatens to bring the entire organism down. Those are cells that cause cancer.

Defects in apoptosis are responsible for half of all cancers. Normal cells all have a sentinel guardian called tumor protein p53 (TP53). TP53 initiates apoptosis whenever it detects cell damage in normal cells, releasing agents to do its bidding called Puma, Noxa, and Bax, among others. In response to damage by radiation, toxins, or other factors, TP53 allows Puma, Noxa, and Bax to orchestrate a death so clean that it allows other cells to live in harmony. But in cancers such as chronic myeloid leukemia, owing to mutations in TP53, pro-life proteins such as BCL2 are more active, which prevents the body from adequately carrying out its cleansing operation, resulting in immortal cancer cells. The chemotherapy for chronic myeloid leukemia, imatinib, actually works by blocking proteins that are part of the BCL2 family. Other cancer drugs promote appropriate apoptosis in cancer cells by other mechanisms. Some do so by activating death receptors; others block survivin, a cellular protein that normally disables caspases. Death is, in fact, so important in cells that efforts to avert cell death, while keeping cells seemingly alive, saps their abilities, with survivors often referred to as "zombie cells."[12]

Too much apoptosis, though, as one might imagine, is also not a good thing. In conditions such as Huntington's, Parkinson's, Alzheimer's, or amyotrophic lateral sclerosis, toxic misfolded proteins accumulate in nerve cells, prematurely activating cell death. However, chemotherapeutic agents that enhance autophagy improve the ability of cells to eliminate these vile proteins. Excessive apoptosis occurs in diseases, such as stroke, heart attack, HIV/AIDS, and autoimmune conditions, and therefore experimental treatments are being developed to inhibit apoptosis intelligently in these conditions.

Insights into apoptosis have shed light on the social lives of cells. Death is not a solitary event, and rarely occurs without it being indicated. In a piece in *Nature,* Gerry Melino wrote, "Such social control of life and death are vital in complex multicellular networks," and went on to ask, "Does social control inevitably imply navigation between conflicting signals?"[13] The society of cells, free of individualism, functions only to preserve the multicellular organism—which is the cell's home. Cells, as they age, are pegged, and acquiesce to a clean death. Our efforts at prolonging cell life often result in the cell surviving in a decrepit condition—referred to by Robert Horvitz in his Nobel lecture as "undead."[14] When I asked Dr. Horvitz what the existential and metaphysical implications were of our recently acquired understanding of how organisms actually die, he said, "Given the many years I've been studying cell death, it is perhaps surprising that only once before has someone approached me to discuss the existential questions that might relate what is known about cell death to human existence, including the issue of life and death." To Dr. Horvitz, programmed death is more than just an accident and contains lessons that we can infer about how best to persist as a species. "Biology is sophisticated and evolution has selected sophisticated evolutionary solutions. Perhaps one could make an analogy and say that if we as a species are going to survive, we have to ensure that we do not irreparably do harm that would make such survival impossible."

Many of the same tools that enact death are in fact extremely crucial for the life of not only the individual but the entire ecosystem. Falling leaves during autumn allow for renewal and constant reinvigoration of the trees that bore them. For the only thing worse than a cell that forgets how to live—is one that refuses to die.

AFTER IT BECAME clear that cells don't die merely by happenstance, the next quest that scientists embarked on was to understand just how cells fall off the conveyor belt of life and are nominated to die. Was it all just a cosmic coincidence or was there something greater at play? Were all cells prisoners of fate and destiny or were their environment and actions responsible for their outcomes? Did cells exhibit age the same way multicellular organisms such as humans did? And was there a way we could have cells stave off the fatal handshake of death?

Now, while immortality is a theoretical construct, it is intriguing to ponder what prevents us from being able to achieve it. The first obvious answer is disease. While human beings debate the purpose of their existence ad nauseam, most biological organisms are geared for one purpose alone—living. Disease is simply any deviation from the carefully choreographed dance that achieves the basic functions of life. As our never-ending war on disease marches on, disease still represents the low-hanging fruit in our quest to extend life. For while diseases are discrete and recognizable detours from normalcy, there is something in the background, something as intrinsic as life itself, that constantly pegs us back: senescence.

Benjamin Gompertz, a British mathematician, realized in 1825 that there were two distinct drivers of human mortality.[15] In addition to extrinsic events, such as injuries or diseases, there was an internal deterioration, which he called "the seeds of indisposition." Manifesting as silvering hair, deepening voices, and retarding reflexes, aging is the most persistent of human foes. As tireless as waves striking the bluffs, as effective as the river that shaped the Grand Canyon, age continues to eat away at us even as we find better ways to prevent, cure, and manage disease.

Our current knowledge of the lives of cells began under somewhat unusual circumstances. Alexis Carrel was but a medical student in Lyon when he saw the president of France fatally stabbed by an anarchist.[16] After the local surgeons' sutures failed to hold together the president's severed blood vessels, Carrel's passion for sewing blood vessels was born and he engaged one of Lyon's most deft embroiderers, Madame Leroudier, to teach him the art of suturing.[17] Carrel translated what held together the most ornate dresses into techniques that revolutionized how human blood vessels and organs could be put back together. After he applied his newly acquired skills to achieve amazing clinical results, instead of being rewarded over the course of his career, Carrel was passed over multiple times for promotion by those envious of his brilliance. Further frustrations mounted, and he decided to jump ship and move to Canada to "forget medicine and to raise cattle beef."[18]

Within months of his move to Canada, though, his talents were recognized and the University of Chicago recruited him. Over the next ten or so years, Carrel did more to advance surgery than almost any other surgeon during that time. A tribute in the *Journal of the American Medical Association* proclaimed some of his achievements: He "reunited vessels, inner lining to inner lining; he sutured artery to artery, vein to vein, artery to vein, and did this end to end, side to side, and side to end. He used patch grafts, autografts, homografts, rubber tubes, glass tubes, metal tubes, and absorbable magnesium tubes. . . . He transplanted the thyroid gland, spleen, ovaries, limbs, kidneys, and even a heart and so proved that, surgically, it was possible and easy to transplant organs."[19] Thus, much to the chagrin of detractors in his native France, Carrel was awarded the Nobel Prize in Medicine in 1912, the first to originate from the United States.

To Carrell, who had overcome so many challenges with his very hands, it seemed that nothing was beyond his reach. He had already repaired blood vessels thought previously irreparable and transplanted organs thought impossible to transplant. The natural progression of things led Carrel to study how to sustain human organs indefinitely—a necessary first step toward eradicating our mortal curse. Only recently had a way to culture cells outside the body been discovered, and Carrel was confident that the prevailing theory of cell division being finite— proposed by August Weismann, the previously mentioned discoverer of cell division—could be proven false.[20]

In his paper titled "On the permanent life of tissues outside of the organism," published in the *Journal of Experimental Medicine* in 1912, he described experiments that would go on to constitute a "complete solution."[21] In his most famous experiments, Carrel removed hearts from chicken embryos, placed them on slides, and incubated those tissue fragments at a set temperature in a specific medium. He showed that the externalized heart tissue, unlike the normal chicken heart plagued by mortality, kept pulsating for many, many years and was presumed to be "permanent."

According to Carrel, senility and death were preventable and resulted from "the accumulation of catabolic substances and exhaustion of the medium." In effect, Carrel was saying that aging and death were due to external stimuli rather than to some internal predesigned mechanism. In the right setting, he claimed, cells and tissue could be freed from the evil humors they were imprisoned in, and in a world free of scarcity, life could be made permanent. Funded by the world's then-richest man, John D. Rockefeller, and in conjunction with another man keen on re-defining the human experience, Charles Lindbergh, Alexis Carrel kept his chicken heart pulsating for thirty-four years—even beyond his own death, maintained by his lab workers.[22]

Owing to Carrel's experiments, eternal life appeared to be closer to attainment than it ever had been in the past, and in many ways, it hasn't been closer since. But not everyone was fit for such drastic life extension. To Carrel, there were many not even fit for life to begin with. In his best-selling book, *Man, the Unknown,* he wrote that all criminals and those who have "misled the public in important matters, should be humanely and economically disposed of in small euthanasic institutions supplied with proper gases."[23] Women, in particular, were both unworthy and unequal. "The mothers abandon their children to the kindergarten in order to attend to their careers, their social ambitions, their sexual plea-sures, their literary or artistic fancies, or simply to play bridge."

However, the Second World War derailed his future plans. He went back to France to set up a hundred-bed field hospital. Unfortunately, his French hosts surrendered, and thereafter he operated the hospital dur-ing the Vichy government's German-occupied rule and was assumed to be a collaborator. Even as he lived on war rations and operated this hos-pital, his health deteriorated, and he suffered two heart attacks before France was finally liberated. However, as soon as the Vichy government was overthrown, the new French government put him and his wife under house arrest. The American government tried to intervene, hop-ing to protect Carrel from what was seen to be an overaggressive reaction by the French. Yet before Carrel could be appropriately rehabilitated, he passed away, in November 1944 at the age of sixty-eight. Even though he died in his native land, he did so having been stripped of all titles in ignominy.

While eugenics died with him and in the defeat of Nazi Germany, Carrel had changed all prevailing thought about the life of cells. But his most enduring legacy would remain the sutures he had learned to sew so well from Madame Leroudier, as his advances in cell biology were unable to withstand the wear and tear of time.

WHEN THE PROMINENT biologist Leonard Hayflick was born, in 1928, the chicken heart pulsating in Alexis Carrel's lab was already sixteen years old and his ideas were widespread. Even when attempts to duplicate Carrel's experiment failed, the investigators themselves assumed that this represented a failure of the culture the tissues grew in.[24]

Such doubts crossed Hayflick's mind as well, as he was unable to get human embryonic cells to grow indefinitely in his cultures. In experiments he performed after completing his PhD at the University of Pennsylvania, he exposed human embryonic cells to extracts from cancer cells in the hope of inducing those cancerous changes in the human cells. However, he noted that after undergoing a specific number of divisions, the cells would stop proliferating. He wasn't sure whether this was because there was some resource in the culture that was getting used up or because there was a buildup of toxic materials. Yet when he combined two populations of old male and younger female cells, the older cells would still die earlier, while the younger cells would continue to divide in the same medium until there were only female cells left. The male cells, in fact, died at the same rate as a separate control sample consisting only of male cells. In a subsequent experiment, Hayflick showed that cellular age was not related as much to time as it was to the number of DNA replications. He cryogenically froze a sample of cells, and after being rewarmed they still replicated the same number of times.[25] This phenomenon was named "the Hayflick limit" by Australian Nobel laureate Macfarlane Burnet and proved once and for all that there was something innate in the cells that caused them to stop growing.[26]

Hayflick's work helped to reverse a dogma that had been introduced into science by Alexis Carrel's work since the early part of the twentieth century. While August Weismann had first theorized in 1889 that cell division was finite, Carrel's chicken-heart experiment wiped that out of the scientific lexicon. Further investigation revealed that Carrel's experiment was rigged and that he most likely knew that it was.[27] Every time he added a feed to the culture, it would include new embryonic cells. Each chicken heart was continuously composed of newly added embryonic cells, as opposed to the cells he started with, which lasted for only a few months. But now that the Hayflick limit had become an established phenomenon, the real question was why such a limit existed. The answer to this question could provide the answer to why cells—and, by extension, humans—aged.

DNA, the tiny double-helixed code that underwrites our cells, clumps together to form chromosomes. Each human cell contains twenty-three pairs of chromosomes; sperm and ova contain twenty-three single chromosomes, and form twenty-three pairs when they join. After Hayflick's discovery, scientists started to analyze the mechanisms underlying cell aging. When scientists first started to analyze cells to investigate the effect of aging, their attention was directed toward the very ends of the chromosomes.

Scientists noted that while central segments of chromosomes contained unique sequences of DNA that were similar across all cells within a species and were essential to program for the production of critical materials, the sequences at the ends of the chromosomes were quite curious. Firstly, the cell was unable to fully replicate the sequences at the end of the DNA strand.[28] The strand lengths also differed within cells, unusual because DNA was otherwise extremely consistent.

Elizabeth Blackburn was barely thirty in 1978, when as part of her postdoctoral research at Yale University she published her findings regarding the terminal segments of the chromosomes in protozoa, a family of single-celled organisms that use hairlike extensions to move.[29] What she found was very interesting: Unlike the rest of the chromosomes, which consisted of random sequences of DNA that could be used to print proteins and serve other cell functions, the terminal ends consisted of repeated sequences that were the same across species and served no specific programmatic purpose. The number of times the sequences were repeated varied from cell to cell[30] and was also represented in human cells.[31]

Subsequent research showed not only that the length of these terminal segments, called telomeres, varied from cell to cell, but, importantly, that these telomeres appeared to get shorter with each cell division.[32] These observations strongly suggested that telomeres were in fact responsible for the Hayflick limit after it was noted that when telomeres became very short, cells became unstable and apoptosis was induced.

In 1985, one of Elizabeth Blackburn's students, Carol Greider, along with Blackburn, discovered telomerase, the enzyme that both synthesizes and elongates telomeres.[33] By printing extra copies, telomerase can extend the length of telomeres in cells, and subsequent experiments showed that the addition of telomerase to otherwise normal cells could greatly extend their life span.[34] In fact, a recent experiment has shown that if telomerase is reactivated in mice that have aged prematurely from having telomerase previously silenced, many of the manifestations of aging can be reversed.[35] These terminal ends of chromosomes, which first caught the attention of scientists in the 1930s when it was noticed that the ends don't participate in fusion events that occur between chromosomes, are now thought to hold the key to maintaining balance between life and death in cells.

Telomeres are a very visual representation, like tree rings, of the constant struggle for life. As telomeres get critically short, cells are unable to replicate any further without losing essential DNA material. The result is an instability that promotes cell damage and eventual demise. DNA damage is the hallmark of cell aging, and in addition to telomere shortening there are several other mechanisms that cause cells to age. Damage to mitochondria, the cell's engines, results in the release of toxic materials that can hasten apoptosis.

Caloric and dietary restriction are now also known to promote longevity.[36] Growth hormone and insulin growth factor, both responsible for growth in humans and many other organisms, have reduced activity as we age. However, purposefully down-regulating their activity by reducing dietary intake by about 20 to 40 percent puts organisms into survival mode. Sensing a reduced supply of nutrients, cells reduce their growth, metabolism, and replication, reducing the chance that errors will occur. This results in longer life spans. As we age, we also suffer from an exhaustion and depletion of stem cells, which otherwise provide a constant supply of fresh cells to join the ranks.

Cellular senescence appears to be as well regulated as every other aspect of cell life, making it clear that senescence is achieved and doesn't merely happen. The reason cells age and are then replaced, like everything else in the microscopic world of cells, is to perpetuate life. While cells battle age, much as we do, with very robust repair mechanisms, they also recognize when cell damage begins to accumulate to a point of no return. It is at that point that cells weed out aging cells to protect the organism at large from uncontrolled death and necrosis. While telomerase, the enzyme that helps cells grow to perpetuity, may seem like a modern philosopher's stone, it has a dark and twisted legacy. Far from being a purveyor of life, it is a harbinger of death and is found in nearly all immortal cancers.[37] To remain in a state of never-ending growth, cancer cells use telomerase to constantly elongate their telomere segments, pushing death away and growing endlessly.

At a cellular level, immortality already has a name and a face: It's called cancer, and it's not particularly comely. The telomerase paradox—that telomerase is essential both for longevity and for sustaining malignant cells—is represented in many other attempts to prevent cellular demise. Our attempts to increase human life expectancy have had effects similar to those attempts at a cellular level and have changed the ecology and landscape of death in modern times. Our ongoing battle with aging, disease, and death has had profound effects on social and economic constructs.

How Life (and Death)
Were Prolonged

Before he became the first person to systematically study everything that killed people in seventeenth-century London, John Graunt, born in 1620, lived many lives, including as a haberdasher, soldier, and councilman.[1] The London he grew up in was not much different from the one of the present day: overcrowded, teeming with traffic, and flooded with immigrants. Much as economics made it necessary to chart the demographics of the living, economics was the reason it became necessary to understand the dying. When Moses was asked by the Lord to perform a census of adult Israelite males in the book of Numbers (1:1–3), it was to collect donations that would be allocated to constructing the Tabernacle, the mobile residence of the Lord which the Jews carried with them during the Exodus, as well as an accounting of the arms that the Jews would come to bear if battle were to become necessary. Similarly, when Thomas Cromwell, the vicar-general of Henry VIII, introduced parish registers, it was to inform merchants curious as to whether potential customers in a particular region were increasing in numbers or dying off from the plague.

It wasn't until 1661, more than 120 years after these parish registers were first introduced, that John Graunt systematically analyzed these publicly available registers and published his findings.[2] In *Observations on the Bills of Mortality,* Graunt collected data from several decades' worth of parish registers, available as bills of mortality. Graunt—a "practical intuitivist" at best, with little or no mathematical knowledge— created the first modern cross-sectional record of death. He was the first and only accidental statistician to be enrolled in the Royal Society and has been called both the father and the Columbus of statistics.[3]

Graunt's description of death in seventeenth-century London is at once both vivid and mysterious, written at a time when the scientific method was only coming of age. The causes of death recorded in *Observations* run the gamut from terrifying and morbid to darkly amusing. People were eaten by wolves and worms and stopped in their tracks by fear and grief. Some were "found dead in the streets," while others were "starved," "shot," and had "fainted in bath." In fact, many diseases mentioned in the report are merely a historical curiosity at this point. "King's evil" was the preferred name for tuberculosis of the lymph nodes of the neck, which often manifested as weeping cheesy exudate from the neck that could purportedly be cured by the king of England. It is said that Henry VIII would touch up to four thousand people suffering from King's evil a year. "Headmouldshot" occurred when the bones constituting the skull overlapped in infants, and was frequently followed by convulsions and death. Many things listed as the cause of death, such as impotsume, livergrown, dropsy, and thrush, were merely symptoms of possibly some other undiagnosed disease.

Some diseases had different names; tuberculosis was called consumption, epilepsy called falling illness, venereal disease called French pox, psychosis called lunatique, stroke with paralysis called apoplexy, and pertussis called rising of the lights.[4] And some major killers, such as "teething" or "stopping of the stomach" . . . well, who knows what those poor people had. Fortunately, many diseases, such as smallpox and the plague, have been eradicated since, and others, such as scurvy, rickets, and marasmus, have been eliminated in developed countries owing to better nutrition.

In the course of his work, Graunt showed that women lived longer than men, and that the highest risk of death was actually during childhood. An interesting observation he made was that the probability of dying leveled off during adulthood and the risk of a twenty-year-old dying was the same as the risk of a fifty-year-old dying. Thus the risk of dying did not increase with age during adulthood, denoting that people were not dying of age-related diseases.

At the same time, on the other side of the Atlantic in North America, newly arriving European colonists were faring no better.[5] Immigrants were falling like pins to a condition called "seasoning." Up to a third of immigrants moving to the New World would fall sick during the initial period after moving, while acclimatizing to the new environs. The disease could last for up to a year, and many immigrants would continue to feel aftereffects for a long time. It is now postulated that seasoning might in fact have been malaria, which can have a wide variety of manifestations. Migrants suffered from a host of other infectious diseases, such as "the bloudie flux" (bloody diarrhea), which probably represented typhoid from salmonella infection. These seventeenth-century Europeans had much shorter life spans in North America than their counterparts did back home, and the African slaves they brought with them fared no better. Such was the terrible price of freedom.

Although the eighteenth century was one of great upheaval, especially in North America, it seemed that medicine and the understanding of death remained at a virtual standstill. In 1812, during the inaugural year of the *New England Journal of Medicine* (then called the *New England Journal of Medicine and Surgery*), an annual bill of mortality for the town of Boston was published.[6] Boston was only then coming of age as a hub of science and intellect, emerging from a period of stagnation. Ralph Waldo Emerson stated, "From 1790 to 1820 there was not a book, a speech, a conversation, or a thought in the state of Massachusetts."[7] With a population of only around 33,250 back then, Boston was a smallish town with better days ahead.

Poring over the causes of death in Boston in 1812, I find that most of my favorites from the early 1600s make return appearances. Vague disorders such as decay, debility, intemperance, and spasms killed a substantial number of people among them. Amongst the 942 deaths, the heaviest hitter was consumption (221), followed by flux infantile (57) and stillbirth (49). People continued to die of lightning, "childbed," drinking cold water, insanity, worms, mortification, and the mysterious white swelling. Less than 3 percent of people died of "old age," and about half a single percent died of cancer, presumably since they never got old enough to develop it. At birth, the mean life expectancy was only twenty-eight for males and twenty-five for females, and even if you made it past five years of age, the life expectancy was forty-two and increased incrementally only to forty-five if you made it past twenty years of age. Death remained sudden and mired in superstition.

Fast-forward another hundred years and it seems that enlightenment had finally started seeping into medicine. Gone were the vague syndromes and symptoms of previous reports. In the January 1912 issue of the *New England Journal of Medicine* (then the *Boston Medical and Surgical Journal*), the death rate in the United States had nearly halved from a hundred years before, to about fourteen per thousand.[8] People now died of diseases, not symptoms—i.e., pneumonia not cough, typhoid not bloudie flux, and tuberculosis not King's evil or consumption. Current staples such as cancer and "organic heart diseases" started to appear on the list, albeit in much smaller numbers. In an associated article, titled "Past, Present and Future," the prior accounts of intemperance and teething were looked at with amusement and it was noted that the medicine of even three generations before was "not yet out of its swaddling clothes." But this was followed by a bold and disturbing proclamation: "Perhaps in 1993, when all the preventable diseases have been eradicated, when the nature and cure of cancer have been discovered, and when eugenics has superseded evolution in the elimination of the unfit, our successors will look back at these pages with an even greater measure of superiority."

Reading reports about how people died in the seventeenth and eighteenth centuries, I feel more humility than any great measure of superiority. At any given time, we always find it easier to look back and comment on how wrong people were in the past. Our ability to assess the future, and therefore the wrongness of our present ways, is much more flawed. Death was cloaked in as much obscurity in the mid-nineteenth century as it was millennia or more ago. But all that changed by the mid-1800s, with the germ theory of disease, the institution of hygiene, and the development of anesthesia and vaccines. Coupled with dramatic improvements in living conditions and nutrition, medicine finally became a science fundamentally changing the human experience, and has shown no signs of looking back since.

WHILE INFECTIOUS DISEASES wielded the sharpest scythe at the start of the twentieth century, their blade has been blunted with advances not only in treatment, with the development of antibiotics and vaccines, but also in the understanding of the relationships among hygiene, sanitation, and vectors of disease. Improvements in managing infectious diseases have especially impacted pediatric health, resulting in vast reductions in the burden of childhood mortality. These improvements are the primary reason for the increase in life expectancy over the past century.

While tuberculosis, diarrhea, measles, and pneumonia continue to exact a telling toll in developing countries, they account for increasingly fewer deaths in developed countries.[9] Pneumonia, ranked at number eleven, is the most fatal infectious disease in the United States. The next most fatal infectious disease, at number twenty-three, is HIV/AIDS, which since 1990 has seen a 64 percent reduction in the number of years people lose to it. With improvements in HIV/AIDS care ongoing, it may go down even further in rank.

Instead of death by infection, violence, or other discrete processes that yank life right out of one's nostrils, most Americans are robbed of their lives by chronic diseases, which don't just strike like a lightning bolt but sap the body and the mind long before the eventual end. Eight of the ten top causes of premature death in the United States are heart disease and stroke, lung and colon cancer, chronic obstructive lung disease, diabetes, cirrhosis, and Alzheimer's disease. Damningly, most of these are on the rise, with diabetes increasing by 60 percent and Alzheimer's by a whopping 392 percent just since 1990. By 2005, half of American adults had at least one chronic illness[10] and a fourth of these suffered from at least one limitation in daily activities because of it.[11] One in three Americans born in the year 2000 will go on to develop diabetes.[12] Therefore, even as we have made great advances in improving life expectancy around the world, the number of years that people live disabled with chronic diseases is actually on the rise.

And to what can we attribute this vile game of whack-a-mole, where we knock back some diseases only to confront the rise of others?[13] Certainly, some of these diseases are rising in incidence because of poor dietary choices and the acquisition of bad habits such as tobacco smoking and drug use. Some of them are newly appearing because of new diagnostic criteria, such as depression and other mental-health disorders, hypertension, and high cholesterol. Some of them, such as HIV/AIDS, represent truly new diseases. But perhaps most of these new chronic diseases represent not so much the failure of medicine in staving off death as much as its success, since people actually live long enough to acquire them.

A study of this phenomenon must start with the death of Warren Gamaliel Harding in room 888,[14] the presidential suite of the Palace Hotel in San Francisco, on August 2, 1923, after just two years of serving as the president of the United States. Warren Harding is considered by many the worst president in US history. This distinction, while contested, was earned by Harding through a combination of wanton corruption, adulterous affairs, and uncontrolled alcoholism. Warren Harding's political career started, quite inauspiciously, when he was sitting next to Harry Daugherty getting his shoes shined. Daugherty, a Republican insider in Ohio, was convinced that Harding *looked* presidential,[15] and would not only shepherd his campaign to the Senate, but hold Harding's hand all the way to the White House. Both men's story, recently depicted in HBO's *Boardwalk Empire,* would end in shambles. Daugherty's term as attorney general was marred by controversy, culminating in his indictment for bribery and attempting to defraud the US government of millions of dollars. History would not be kind to Harding, either. [16]

Harding was also one of the unhealthiest American presidents.[17] For many years prior to his death, Harding suffered from the telltale signs of heart disease—chest pain, shortness of breath, swelling in his legs—and yet he continued to smoke, drink, and overeat. While he had an army of physicians, his most trusted voice was his homeopath, Charles Sawyer, who was convinced that crabmeat poisoning was responsible for the symptoms leading up to his untimely demise.[18] According to the memoirs of Ray Lyman Wilbur, then the president of Stanford University, a physician who had been involved in Harding's care during his final days and was present at his side when he died, "A quick shiver suddenly went through the frame of the President, and without a groan he died instantly."[19] While the official cause of death was apoplexy, the most likely cause of Harding's death was cardiac arrest, either from a heart attack or from an abnormal heart rhythm. After his wife declined an autopsy, on Sawyer's advice, the ground was ripe for a conspiracy theory, which in this case was that Harding's wife had poisoned Harding on account of his infidelities.

Yet the truth is that Harding's death, even though he was entitled to the most state-of-the-art care, would almost never happen now. With the advent of medications, lifesaving interventions, and broad public-health initiatives, even though heart disease remains the most common cause of death in the United States and the world, that burden is coming down sharply.[20] A modern-day president, on the first hint of chest pain, would get stress testing and cardiac imaging, have his vital signs and labs checked out and acted on appropriately. While nowadays a systolic blood pressure below 120 is considered optimal, Harding's average blood pressure was around 180 millimeters of mercury—unacceptably high by any standard. But even if all of these measures failed to prevent Harding from having a heart attack, these days cardiac catheterization and surgical procedures are fairly effective at preventing death from a heart attack if treatment is immediate, and he would have lived on with what is now the most common cause of hospital admissions in the United States amongst the elderly—heart failure.

The evolution of medicine and the resultant change in the nature of disease is charted in the medical history of another politician, who lived through not one but five heart attacks. Dick Cheney is the owner of what is probably one of the weightiest medical charts in the country and in many ways exemplifies how advances in medical care have revolutionized both life and death.[21] With a family history of premature heart disease, he had already smoked twenty-plus years of multiple packs of cigarettes a day before his first heart attack, when he was just thirty-seven. He quit smoking, but there wasn't much doctors could do for him beyond that. He had his second heart attack in 1984, and after his third, in 1988, surgeons performed cardiac bypass surgery, in which they took four veins from elsewhere in his body to provide alternative courses for blood to supply his heart, given that his own vessels were all diseased and blocked. After he had his fourth heart attack, in 2000, he underwent cardiac catheterization, a procedure in which cardiologists snake catheters up to the heart through either the wrist or groin, and he got two metallic stents to keep his heart vessels propped open.

It was around this time that Cheney's heart, having sustained innumerable hits, became too weak to support the needs of his body. Heart failure, the final reckoning for all sick hearts, is caused by the heart's inability to course blood forward and to prevent blood from pooling behind it in the lungs, abdomen, and legs. Failure of the heart to pump blood to vital organs results in dizziness and confusion, low blood pressure, cold arms and legs, and kidney failure. Failure of the heart to prevent blood from pooling up behind it results in collection of fluid in the lungs, causing difficult breathing; in the abdomen, causing a swollen belly and a feeling of fullness; and in the legs and arms, causing swelling and edema.

Heart failure kills via two main mechanisms: a malignant irregular heart rhythm that throws the heart into standstill, called cardiac arrest, which can occur suddenly; or pump failure, which results from a progressive weakening of the heart and escalating symptoms of heart failure. To prevent an arrhythmia from killing him, Cheney had an "implantable cardiac defibrillator" placed in his chest, which could shock his heart out of a malignant arrhythmia. Sure enough, in 2009, as he was backing his car out of his garage, his heart went into ventricular fibrillation. Under any other circumstances, Cheney would have died of this, but not that day, as his defibrillator shocked his heart out of that rhythm even as he rammed his car into the garage door. But even as he dodged a lethal arrhythmia, his pump was failing. He went on to receive a left ventricular assist device, a mechanical turbine that sat in his heart constantly pumping blood. Unlike a normal heart, which pumps blood with rhythmic contractions, the turbine pumps blood continuously. Therefore, for the time that he had the device as he waited for a heart transplant to become available, Cheney didn't even have a pulse. His wait for a heart transplant would be over in March 2012, when, after being on the transplant list for about two years, he received a brand-new heart in Virginia.[22]

Reaping almost all the cumulative benefits of advances in cardiovascular care meant months in the ICU, several weeks of which Cheney spent on a mechanical respirator, as well as countless more months in rehab. Unlike Warren Harding, whose death was swift and supposedly painless, Cheney, like many Americans, has battled with chronic diseases for years. Heart failure, which didn't even show up on any bills of mortality a hundred years ago, now shows up on the death certificates of one in nine Americans and accounts for a million hospital admissions a year, more than any other disorder.[23]

Cancer, perhaps the most storied disease of our times, has also benefited immensely from advances in both prevention and treatment. Despite this progress, cancer, which appeared to cause less than half a percent of deaths in Boston in 1812, is now the second-leading cause of death in the United States.[24] Improvements in cancer screening and treatment, however, mean that many more people have cancer diagnosed at an earlier stage or achieve full remission with treatment. There are eleven million people living with cancer in America, and this number is on the rise. Treatments for congenital heart disease, which is the most common type of birth defects and used to practically be a death sentence, have resulted in more adults living with congenital heart disease (about a million in the United States) than there are children born with it.[25]

The rise in chronic diseases has indelibly changed death for human beings. Death, in most cases, is no longer a sudden conflagration, but a long, drawn-out slow burn. In fact, doctors grappling with this change named the time of debility before death "pre-death."[26] In a paper published in the *Lancet* in 1971, the authors indelicately wrote, "It seems that many of those who survive into old age enter a phase of 'pre-death' in which they outlive the vigor of their bodies and the wisdom of their brains. The century which followed Darwin has yielded a new biological phenomenon: the survival of the unfittest."

BEFORE ALEXANDRE-GUSTAVE EIFFEL built his famous tower and Alexander Graham Bell invented the telephone, before we had even discovered how cells came to life, Jeanne Louise Calment was born in the French town of Arles, on February 21, 1875.[27] She was only thirteen when she sold coloring pencils to Van Gogh and twenty-one when she married her second cousin. As a housewife, she lived a life of great comfort. As she grew older, she started losing those around her. She was fifty-nine when her only child, Yvonne, died of pneumonia; sixty-seven when her husband died, after consuming a dish prepared with spoiled cherries; and eighty-eight when her only grandson died, in a road accident. Even as she continued to smoke, eat chocolate, have meals drenched in olive oil, and ride her bicycle, she kept growing older and older, and in 1988 she was declared the oldest living person in the world. For another nine years and seven months, Jeanne remained the oldest living person in the world, during the course of which she became the first person to turn 115 and then 120. When she passed away, on August 4, 1997, she was, and remains to this day, the oldest documented human being to have ever lived—at 122 years and 164 days.

Stories of men and women who defied death abound in history books. Perhaps the most famous of these figures is Methuselah, Noah's grandfather, who recently made an appearance in pop culture, played by Anthony Hopkins in Darren Aronofsky's film *Noah*. Methuselah, whose legacy remains as a synonym for longevity, is said to have lived for 969 years, and his death prompted God to unleash the great Flood.[28]

More recently, though, not only have the why and the how of death changed, the *when* has changed, too, and perhaps changed the most. The last four of humanity's roughly eight thousand generations have experienced an extension in longevity that has been noted for no other organism in history.[29] Not only has change of this extent, which mostly started after 1900, never been observed for any living thing outside a laboratory, it has never been achieved even with cells or organisms in an experimental setting. Over the past 125 years or so, we have evolved so far beyond our hunter-gatherer predecessors that a thirty-two-year-old hunter-gatherer had the same probability of dying as does a seventy-two-year-old man in modern Japan. In fact, our ancestors' life spans now more closely resemble those of chimpanzees than ours. Let this sink in as I explain further.

Human longevity has stayed more or less stable over human history. While we, specifically the genus *Homo,* have been around for about 2,000,000 years, *Homo sapiens* did not emerge until about 200,000 years ago, in Africa.[30] For the first 190,000 years or so, we lived as hunter-gatherers in small groups and tribes, before we learned the arts of agriculture and rearing livestock. These folks, in spite of the advent of civilization, could do little to change the true nature of their health. Their lives were much more exciting, much less predictable. If they made it past childhood, which few did, they had about the same chance of dying whether they were young teenagers or fifty-somethings. Childbirth was one of the most dangerous things that could happen to a person, and resulted in women dying at a much higher rate than men.[31]

However, in spite of this, people did make it to older age:[32] the average age of the kings of Judah between 5000 and 1000 BC was in the fifties, and that of Greek poets and philosophers between 450 and 150 BC was in the sixties.[33] Yet this was a product more of statistical chance than of any meaningful intervention on their parts.

Around the year 1800, the average age of people worldwide was in the late twenties.[34] But this was little different from the average age of people around the time agriculture was developed, ten thousand years ago, which was between twenty and twenty-five years. Prior to this, the average age varied significantly from year to year, the graph rising and falling like strokes on a seismogram during an earthquake. Death was truly random, not only on a personal level but also on a population-wide level. Even being rich didn't matter, as life expectancy did not demonstrate any relationship with income, and richer countries fared no better than poorer ones.

Starting around this time, the average life expectancy began rising steadily at a rate with no historical parable. Each year, around three months is added to the average human life expectancy.[35] This effect is seen in all countries, although some, such as Japan and Scandinavian countries, have performed better than others. Since about 1840, this represents an impressively linear change. Not only is the average age increasing, there is also an increase in the maximum life span achieved.[36] At this rate, the distribution of the human race by age, which has traditionally been pyramidal, with lots of young people at the bottom and fewer older people at the top, is going to turn rectangular in the upcoming decades.

So how were we able to achieve this? Well, the greatest spur to life expectancy has been the dramatic reduction in childhood mortality. Sanitary birth practices, hygienic practices, public sanitation, improved nutrition, increased maternal education, and improved maternal health are some of the public-health initiatives that have helped reduce childhood mortality. Coupled with antibiotics and vaccines, in developed countries they have all but eliminated the great burden of infectious diseases that used to endanger children on a daily basis. The second major change has been the reduction in morbidity and mortality in middle-aged people, with a large reduction in cardiovascular mortality as well as violent fatalities. This reduction has been so dramatic that if we were to completely eliminate all deaths in people less than fifty years of age at this point—which accounts for about 12 percent of all deaths in the United States—the average life expectancy would increase by only another 3.5 years.[37]

Only more recently, since the 1970s, have we started making major headway in reducing the risk of death and disease in more elderly people, resulting in the fact that the rate of increase in maximum life span has almost tripled since 1969 compared with previous decades.[38] The debate plaguing biologists, demographers, and biodemographers in recent times has really been whether we can sustain this exponential rise in life expectancy and, importantly, whether there is a human equivalent to the Hayflick limit.

Some within the scientific community believe that the unabated rise of the human life span is itself proof of the absence of an upper limit. But the camp that posits an upper limit on the human life span is much more populous and includes in its ranks Leonard Hayflick himself, who wrote recently, "Because the aging process is a universal property of all molecules (and most atoms), intervention in the aging process borders on the likelihood of violating fundamental laws of physics."[39] Many in the scientific community are now starting to believe that we may be approaching the plateau of life extension. It is estimated that even with the elimination of all heart disease, cancer, and diabetes, average life expectancy would still not exceed ninety years.[40] Therefore many scientists hold that the average life span of a completely disease-free human being would be eighty-five years,[41] and mathematical modeling estimates that the maximum attainable life span for human beings is 126 years.[42]

Jeanne Calment broke the previously decided limit on the human life span of 120 years and came close to this new hypothetical limit set after her death as well; yet there are many others who are hoping to test it. Centenarians are the fastest-growing age group in the world; the United Nations estimates that there were about 300,000 centenarians in the world in 2010 and their number would grow tenfold by the year 2050.[43] Interestingly, the current paradigm shift in longevity has exclusively been achieved by improvements in external factors, such as improvements in our environment and improved management of diseases. It is as if we have been purifying the culture a cell is growing in without actually changing the cell itself. The doubling of human life expectancy from forty to about eighty over the course of about 150 years means that a change in genetics has little role to play in the plasticity that we have demonstrated in our lifetimes.[44]

Widespread old age is a relatively new experience for our species and has some interesting evolutionary implications. For long swaths of our history, women never experienced a postmenopausal life. From an evolutionary aspect, this can be thought of as a great failure of reproductive fitness: to an evolutionary biologist, what good is an organism that cannot reproduce and cannot help perpetuate the species? For some time scientists actually thought that a postmenopausal life was unique only to human beings, a notion we now know is false.[45] Like female humans, who have a bell-shaped fertility curve that lasts through their menstruating years, killer whales, the worm *Caenorhabditis elegans,* and Bali mynah birds also have a postreproductive life.[46]

However, that modern women live a significant portion of their lives after menopause owes both to the dramatic increase in human longevity and also specifically to a great reduction in deaths associated with childbirth. Furthermore, women consistently outlive their virile male counterparts, with the gap between male and female survival increasing as age increases. In fact, among supercentenarians—people older than 110 years—women outnumber men a whopping thirty-five to one.[47]

Evolutionary biologists have shown that the very postmenopausal women thought to be an evolutionary aberration are the key to human longevity and that we may owe our long lives to our grandmothers. By freeing young mothers from the pressures of gathering resources for their newborn children, grandmothers in hunter-gatherer (and even more recent) societies allowed their daughters to get on with the business of having babies while they helped rear the children. Mathematical simulations have in fact demonstrated that the Grandmother Hypothesis, first posited in 1966,[48] is one of the primary reasons human life spans moved from an apelike pattern to our modern human life span.[49] Further research also credited grandmothering in enhancing the life spans of killer whales, the other mammalian species that enjoys a humanoid life span.[50]

Progress in offsetting death has prolonged elderly life, which has also had profound effects on the opposite end of the spectrum—childhood. Certainly, demographers have noted that the number of children whose parents died prematurely has gone down.[51] Orphanages were not only pervasive in Dickensian England, they were a historical necessity, owing to the high rates of death throughout life. The peculiarly long childhood of humans has always fascinated biologists, particularly as the time that offspring remain immature and dependent in humans is longer than in perhaps any comparable species. Humans take fourteen or more years between weaning and reproduction, compared with their closest evolutionary relatives, chimpanzees, who take around eight years.

Initial theories formulated by scientists postulated that given the larger size of the human brain and the complex tasks that human beings undertake, such as hunting, humans just needed more time to develop the skills required to undertake these tasks. However, when anthropologists analyzed the hunting and foraging behaviors of hunter-gatherer communities around the world, their results were surprising. Observations of remote tribes like the Meriam on the island of Mer,[52] close to Australia, and the Hazda people, in Tanzania,[53] showed that children differed little from adults in their ability to forage. Differences that did exist were attributed more to the smaller size and lesser strength of the children than to intellectual skills required for subsistence. In fact, the role of practice was also not clear, as Hazda children with less practice appeared to do as well as the well-regimented ones, indicating that there was no relationship between a longer childhood and better survival skills.

Thus the theory currently favored is that the length of human child dependency has derived from our longer life spans. Research across species has shown that a longer life is associated with an older age at conception. This means that the older a mother is when she conceives her first child, across species, the longer a life will be experienced by the progeny. Sociologists chalk this up to the inherited-capital theory, which states that skills and assets acquired by the parents over time translate into a better quality of life for their children. Another reason childhood and dependency in humans are much longer than in other species is less altruistic. The restriction of children from adult life and tasks means less competition for older individuals in society, who can therefore exhibit their evolutionary fitness. The grandmothers might be coddling children to offset their maturity more for their own benefit than for the children's.

Even as scientists discuss the pros and cons of radical life extension, not everyone benefits even from the extension of life we have come to take for granted as an entitlement of subsisting in a developed socioeconomy. Even within the United States, there continue to exist great disparities in life expectancy, with the fruits of modern science and healthcare vastly misdistributed. Compared with other countries that are part of the Organization for Economic Cooperation and Development, the United States has lower average life expectancy, and this gap is growing. American women live shorter lives on average than Chilean or Slovenian women, both of whose countries spend less per capita on health and have lower per-capita incomes as well.[54] What is interesting is that this is not for want of resources; while both men and women in the United States die before their Canadian neighbors, the city of Pittsburgh—only America's sixty-first-most-populated city—has more MRI machines than all of Canada combined.[55]

Within the United States, some counties experience life expectancies greater even than those of Japan and Switzerland, while others are more similar to third-world countries such as Algeria and Bangladesh. In fact, only about three hundred miles separates Fairfax, Virginia, and Mc-Dowell, West Virginia, the counties with the longest (eighty-two years) and the shortest (sixty-four years) life expectancies for men in the United States. Socioeconomic disparities may explain this gap; the median household income is $109,383[56] in Fairfax and $22,972[57] in McDowell. Race remains a significant driver of disparities: In 2010, African Americans lived for 3.8 fewer years than white Americans, and even though this gap is down from 7.6 years in 1970, it remains unacceptable.[58] Importantly, though, income and race are inextricably tied, and while one can debate which factor is more significant, it must be noted that McDowell County is overwhelmingly white, 89 percent, compared with Fairfax County, 53 percent white.

The most startling fact about these socioeconomic disparities impacting healthcare is that they are an artifact of modern times. Research that looked at life expectancies in countries starting in the 1800s showed that in the nineteenth century, how long you lived had little to do with how many gold bricks you had stashed away.[59] In fact, this gap started to emerge only in the twentieth century, and has grown wider not only between rich and poor countries, but within single countries, as disparities in the United States have shown.

A primary feature of modern death, therefore, is its inequity. In Brockton, a destitute town just a half hour away from Boston, many people still die the old-fashioned way. They show up to a hospital without any prior medical history or any prior testing, on no medications, and they leave covered in white linen drawn up to their eyebrows. The experience of modern death is shaped as much by social and economic change as it is by medical advances.

Perhaps what we have learned about death from a microscope is as important as what we learned from analyzing the bills of mortality. To me, there are lessons we can learn from cellular dynamics that go beyond just making the new targeted therapy or age-defying wonder drug. Cell death demonstrates an extraordinary amount of social awareness. A cell never dies in isolation, but in clear view of its peers. A cell also rarely dies of its own volition; a wiser force that is in touch with the greater organism understands when a cell is more likely to harm itself and those around it by carrying on. A cell also understands better than we humans do the consequences of overstaying one's welcome. While we humans aspire to immortality, to a cell, immortality is the worst fate possible.

As the battle to avert death and prolong life rages on, the consequences of this constant tug-of-war still aren't fully known. The one facet of modern death that is most well understood is not why people die or when people die—it is *where* they die. The vast majority of people die in places where inert tones provide the palette, disinfectant the aroma, alarm bells the soundtrack, and open-back johnnies the wardrobe. At no time in our history has death been farther from home than in the last few decades.

Where Death Lives Now

Martha told the pastor that she had lived a great life. She had lived a long life, seen both poverty and comfort. She had five children, who all now had families. Like many other women, she had outlived her husband, but never stopped *living.* Her medical history was long and winded; she had lived through colon cancer and a stroke. She had almost every chronic disease you could imagine: chronic kidney failure, peripheral vascular disease, diabetes, hypertension, coronary-artery disease, and severe heart failure. But she had not let any of these slow her down. Not until now, at least.

The rash had become visible quite innocuously a few months ago. It had started around her neck and along the lining of her clothes. She went to her primary-care physician, who thought that she had eczema, a common skin reaction, and prescribed her a steroid cream. Martha used the cream for a few months, but instead of getting better, the rash only got worse and spread to her chest and abdomen. The itch that kept her up at night did not at all respond to the steroid cream, which is usually a safe bet for most rashes. Exasperated, she went to a dermatologist, who thought that the rash was a reaction to her cholesterol medication and advised her to stop it immediately. But the rash spread further, invading her face. She went back to the dermatologist, who was alarmed by its evolving appearance. He took a skin biopsy and, concerned about infection, started her on an antibiotic for a week. Unabated, the rash spread all over her body, including her arms and thighs.

When her son went to see her at home, a week after the antibiotic had been started, he found her on the floor. She told him she had been sitting in the chair but had slumped down and was so weak she could not get herself back up. The son called an ambulance, which drove her to her primary-care physician's office. Astutely, the doctor obtained an ECG, and it showed that she was in the throes of a heart attack.

In the emergency room, the heart attack was confirmed. She was admitted to the cardiology floor. As we debated whether the best way to treat her heart attack was with medications or with an invasive procedure in the cardiac catheterization lab, the dermatology team was called in to figure out what was causing her terrible rash. Their diagnosis left the team beyond bewildered: it was a rare form of blood cancer.

We promptly started treatment, yet her hospital course continued to get more complicated. One night in the hospital, after I had left for home, the covering intern was called to check up on her. Martha was the chattiest patient on the floor and all of a sudden she had gone mute. The intern ordered a CAT scan, which showed that she had suffered a massive stroke. When I came in the morning to take signout from the night team, I felt the ground vanish from beneath my feet as I learned about these events. Martha was sent to the neurosurgical ICU but came back to the cardiology floor after a few days with some of her function, but none of her vigor, back.

Meeting the family was always a treat. All five children, wearing lime-yellow gowns, with their spouses in tow, came to the hospital to meet us and discuss her course. The team's main concern was about how aggressive we would want to be with her treatment. Should we go ahead and do everything humanly possible, including the cardiac catheterization, or focus more on palliating her symptoms? Throughout the many meetings we had, the only thing she had to say was "Doctor, when can I go back home?"

I certainly didn't have a crystal ball. I had my own guesses about which one of her heart's arteries was blocked, what was causing fluid to build up in her lungs, and what was causing her to be too weak to even lift herself off the floor. I was comfortable having an open discussion with her about her ailments, but the one thing I knew but had little stomach to tell her was that the moment she got into the ambulance, she had embarked on a one-way trip to the hospital, with little hope of going back.

THROUGH MUCH OF time, writers and poets and philosophers have found parallels between life and death, and between birth and dying. The mirroring of life and death does not just provide lyrical flourishes, it is reflected in history. Back when human beings gave birth to their young'uns in caves, they also passed away in caves. And ever since we built homes, it seemed natural that the very function of a home, other than providing daily shelter, was to provide a place where life can come and life can go. In ancient Greece, families would pin an olive wreath to their doors after the birth of a boy and wool for a baby girl. Like birth, death continued to occur at one's home for centuries. Up until the twentieth century, all births took place at home.

Death, too, unless it was sudden or violent, also occurred at home. Taking one's last breath in one's own bed, a sight ubiquitous in literature, was the modus operandi for death in ancient times. In the book *Western Attitudes toward Death,* Philippe Ariès wrote that the deathbed scene was "organized by the dying person himself, who presided over it and knew its protocol" and that it was a "public ceremony . . . [at which] it was essential that parents, friends and neighbors be present."[1] While such resplendent representations of death continue to be widely pervasive in both modern literature and pop culture, they are mostly fiction at best. Dying in one's own bed is a rare privilege, an outlier in the calculus of modern dying.

Even up until the first quarter of the twentieth century, people tended to die more commonly in their own homes. In 1912 in Boston, where the number of hospitals was and remains much higher than in almost any other part of the country, around two-thirds of people died in their homes.[2] This trend was also found in other countries; around 56 percent of Australians died at home in 1912.[3] However, the advent of medical technology and the increased age and complexity of patients, shifted this phenomenon to the hospital. By the 1950s, a majority of people died in hospitals and the likelihood of this happening increased with age.[4] By the mid-1970s, a complete reversal had taken place, and upward of two-thirds of patients died in hospitals.[5] One study that analyzed where cancer patients died in Cuyahoga County, Ohio, from 1957 to 1974 found that the number of cancer patients who died at home went down further during this time, from 30 percent in 1957–59 to just 15 percent in 1972–74.[6]

These days, not only are people dying more often in hospitals, they are seeing a lot more of the hospital in the time before they die.[7] In 1969, about 1 percent of people were admitted to the hospital in the last year of their life; this number went up to 50 percent by 1987. Nowadays, barely one patient in five is able to die in their own home, down from all five not all that long ago. This trend closely shadows the trend in births: While 80 percent of women gave birth at home in 1930, that number fell to just about 1 percent in 1990.[8]

This purported hospitalization of death was not looked upon kindly by commentators. In his book *Medical Nemesis: The Expropriation of Health,* the social commentator Ivan Illich wrote, "Society, acting through the medical system, decides when and after what indignities and mutilations he (man) shall die."[9] In a letter published in the *British Medical Journal* in 1972, a physician relayed the comments of a dying man's caregiver: "We wanted him to die in peace, rather than in the hospital."[10]

While initially it was hospitals that tractor-beamed patients out of their homes and into their grasp, more recently nursing homes have seen the greatest growth in the number of patients who live out their end of days there. In the same study looking at deaths in Cuyahoga, deaths in nursing homes almost tripled, from 7 percent to 20 percent, while hospital deaths remained stable. Scientists now estimate that by 2020,

40 percent of Americans will die alone in nursing homes.[11] Nursing homes and their immediate predecessors, geriatric units in hospitals, were also not looked on kindly, with one doctor in 1960 describing them as "forbidding when viewed from the distance," going on to say, "the long wards with their regular lines of closely placed beds, oddly mimic the silent mounds in the neighboring cemetery."[12]

The hospitalization of death is not a uniquely American phenomenon and is common to most other industrialized economies. The United States is not even the worst offender, as it is by many other metrics of overmedicalization. To this effect, both the World Health Organization and the United Nations have identified the lack of people passing away at home as a priority. In one analysis that compared the final resting place for people in forty-five countries, Japan topped out, with 78 percent of their deaths occurring in hospitals, while China was second to last, with 19 percent of people there dying in hospitals and the rest dying at home.[13] Norway, at 44 percent, had the highest percentage of people dying in nursing homes. However, similar to the United States, as people got older their chance of dying in a nursing home increased. Overall, though, exactly two-thirds of people around the world in this analysis died in institutions, with this percentage going up to about four in five for people older than sixty-five years of age.

One in five people die at home in the United States, too, but there are some interesting differences compared with the United Kingdom. As patients grow older in London (reflective of trends across England) they are more likely to die in a hospital, as opposed to New York, where older patients mostly die in nursing homes, especially those older than eighty years of age.[14] Given current projections, it is estimated that by 2030 only one in ten people in the United Kingdom will be able to die at home.[15]

What determines whether someone is going to die at home, in a nursing home, or in a hospital? The answer is a complex interplay, with an overlap of factors indigenous to the individual, to their support system, to the economic and health-care environment they exist in, and to the disease that is hurtling them toward the end. Even though patients want to die at home, the question is whether that desire can actually budge any of the large tectonic plates that crash into each other, vying for supremacy, as an individual approaches death.

EVEN AS THE debate about institutionalized death raged on, patients and their wishes were left out of the entire discussion, as had become the norm in medicine. Surveys of patients, both in the United States and around the world, have now conclusively shown that, overwhelmingly, patients want their homes to be the place they die.[16] One exhaustive study that pooled results from eighteen studies showed that all but one of those surveys showed that a majority of patients desired to die at home. These results were consistent regardless of whether the people surveyed represented the general public or patients with terminal cancer. The only study in which home was not the desired place of demise was one from the United Kingdom, in which more patients appeared to prefer a hospital-based hospice facility.

One interesting phenomenon that has been noted is that patients' preference for a home death seems to go down as they age and approach death. Even though home remains the preferred majority destination, the increasing demands of care make patients think twice about where they would want the end to unravel. As death approached, even as the enthusiasm for home care dropped for some patients, it was replaced not by hospitals but by hospice as a preference. In studies that asked patients to forecast whether they would prefer to die in hospitals, no more than a third of patients ever felt that a hospital would be a preferred place to pass.

So it appears that the majority of patients desire to experience death at home. This, however, is at odds with a reality in which few patients have the *opportunity* to die at home. Even when patients do die at home, they have only just been discharged from a hospital. One study from New Hampshire showed that of patients who did die at home, a third had been discharged from a hospital seven days or less before they died.[17]

The dynamics behind the rampant institutionalization of death are manifold, and only a few of them are related to medicine, health, and disease itself. Like so many things under the umbrella of death, the drivers of this surge are equal parts economic, social, demographic, environmental, psychological, and geographical.

The nature of a patient's disease and disrepair can have an influence on the eventual place of death.[18] Interestingly, patients with cancer are more likely to die at home than patients with heart disease or respiratory disease. One study showed that patients with heart disease or stroke were twice as likely to die in a hospital compared with patients with cancer.[19] This is reflective of the fact that physicians are much better at assessing the severity and prognosis of cancer, especially more common types, such as lung, breast, or prostate cancer, which follow a somewhat predictable course. A cancer that is small and has not spread to regional tissues or metastasized to distant parts of the body is much more likely to be treatable than one that has. Patients also respond to the word "cancer" and are likely to take cancer more seriously than other conditions. Patients with terminal cancer are also much more likely to be referred to palliative care services, which often opens the door to a home death. Outside the United States, though, patients with cancer are more likely to die in a hospital.

Among types of cancer, "liquid" cancers that affect blood cells, such as leukemia and lymphoma, are less predictable, and because patients with these cancers can still have some treatment options left even at a terminal stage, they are more likely to die in the hospital than at home.[20] Patients with a more protracted and taxing course are also more likely to die at home. However, patients with increasing nursing needs, those who require twenty-four-hour supervision or special equipment such as breathing-assist devices, are less likely to die at home.[21] Patients with Alzheimer's disease, who suffer from a prolonged period of dementia and confusion prior to dying, are most likely to die in a nursing home rather than at home or in a hospital.

What is less clear is what role age has to play, but most rigorous studies show that most patients greater than eighty-five years of age tend to die in nursing homes rather than at home or in hospitals. Women, who incidentally tend to live longer and thus be older than men when they die, are also more likely to die in a nursing home rather than in a hospital, strengthening the stereotype of nursing homes overflowing with old ladies.

The role of family is possibly one of the most important predictors of allowing someone the opportunity to die at home. Over the twentieth century,[22] the family nucleus has been pummeled several times,[23] and one of the greatest hits has been provided by geographic dispersion.[24] At the start of the twentieth century, around 60 percent of American widows lived with their adult children. Now two-thirds live alone. As might be easily inferable, and has been demonstrated by data, having robust social support doesn't just allow for a more comfortable death, it makes it more likely that one can die at home. Another factor that has been brought out to be important is not just the patient's own preference for dying at home, but the caregivers'. Both perceptibly and imperceptibly, where the caregivers feel death is appropriate ends up affecting the final destination. In fact, studies that asked caregivers retrospectively where they thought their loved one wanted to pass, caregivers were much *less* likely to designate that place as home than the patients themselves. Exhaustion and fatigue certainly play a huge part, and the desire to have one's loved one die at home dwindles as death approaches.

Marital status is another important determinant. Surprisingly, a lot of research shows that patients who are married are more likely to die in the hospital than at home. This finding seems to grate with common sense and research showing that social support correlates positively with dying at home. Yet when one studies the question more closely, one notes that patients who are widowed are actually much more likely to die in a nursing home than patients who are married. To me, and to other observers, what this means is that patients who are married are more likely to remain at home longer than those who are widowed. Married patients exist in a home-hospital dyad rather than the home–nursing home–hospital trifecta.

Access to healthcare and the diversity of services are important aspects to consider. Even though most patients desire to die at home, and it is widely recognized that there needs to be an international drive toward allowing people to die at home, not all deaths should occur at home. Many patients with chronic lung diseases, like COPD and interstitial pulmonary fibrosis, can be well otherwise but cannot breathe without getting maximal support from a breathing machine. There are very few mechanisms that would allow a patient such as this to die comfortably at home. One study in Washington State showed that patients from rural areas were more likely to die at home, raising the concern that people in areas with poor access may die at home even when they have unmet medical needs.[25]

Access in medicine, however, is a double-edged sword. Healthcare is an unusual industry, the patient is an unusual consumer, and health is an unusual commodity. One disturbing aspect (in a long list) is that supply creates demand in medicine. In Boston, there are thirteen major teaching hospitals in a five-mile radius of where I used to live. And all of them are bursting at the seams with patients, desperately fighting for space, competing for an ever-larger piece of a lucrative pie. This introduces us to the concept of demand elasticity. In a field such as, say, air travel, increasing the number of airports and reducing the cost of flying might encourage people to prefer flying over, say, taking the train. But what if the number of airports increased but the price of air travel remained sky-high, and a plane got you to your destination no faster than the train? Would people still be incentivized to partake of a TSA pat-down and opt for air travel? Well, in medicine the standard laws of economics break down.

Take the example of ICU beds, which the United States has more of per capita than almost any other country.[26] The consequence of this supply has been that patients in the United States who are admitted to the ICU are much less sick than patients admitted to the ICU in other countries. Patients in the United States get admitted to the ICU because that's what the market demands, since ICU beds reimburse higher than standard hospital beds. Why this can work in healthcare is because of the indirect relationship between the consumer and the bill; if you go to a restaurant to have dessert after dinner and the restaurant offers you a four-course meal at an exorbitant price that you may never complete, you might politely refuse their offer. It is because of this paradox that even though patients in American ICUs are less sick than those in, say, the United Kingdom, Americans are more likely to die in ICUs than people in other countries are. While a paucity of beds might push physicians to move patients toward a more comfortable and less acute place when they have reached the end, an excess of beds makes that moot.

Demand elasticity also affects where people die. People are more likely to die in a hospital in areas where there are a large number of hospital beds; the higher the per-capita density of nursing-home beds, the more likely one is to die in a nursing home. This is also seen in other countries: Japan, the country with the highest rate of people dying in hospitals, at 78 percent, also has the highest number of hospital beds per capita (13.7 per thousand people), as well as the longest average length of stay (18.5 days).[27] Supply also drives demand at a more granular level: One's likelihood of dying in a hospital bed is directly related to how far one lives from a hospital and whether one has been previously admitted to a hospital. Similar forces draw patients toward dying at home; availability of home care and hospice services at home are strong predictors of dying at home.

With all these forces pushing patients toward or away from their homes, what remains to be figured out is how much of a factor a patient's own wishes are in this milieu. Are patients hostage to their environments, their family situations, and the characteristics of their debility, or do they have any semblance of control in this algorithm?

Turns out that a patient's "preference" does not represent words etched on a tablet, fixed and set in stone. Interviews with physicians and nurses delving into their experiences regarding their patients' wishes revealed that their patients ran the gamut from "adamant that she was dying at home" to those who would never want themselves to be debilitated at home, saying, "Get me into the hospice. I don't want my family to see me like this."[28] Most patients, though, are cognizant of how demanding their illness is becoming on themselves and their caregivers, and are open to discussing options. Physicians can also shape these preferences as they see appropriate. While physicians are very comfortable talking about place of death when it is brought up, they are not comfortable raising the subject themselves. Some physicians even feel that it is unethical to talk about place of death with those patients who want to

"fight till the very end." In most cases, though, circumstances surrounding a patient end up taking precedence over the patient's own wishes,
which, it seems, are malleable to the contingencies of reality.

The overwhelming wish of patients to die at home has not gone un-
noticed by policymakers. In fact, dying at home, and allowing for that
to happen, is a major marker of quality healthcare. This recognition that
patient wishes ought to be respected has trickled down to actual change.
After decades of dwindling numbers, recent years have seen a small,
steady, and consistent rise in the number of people passing at home. But
before we pop the champagne, I prescribe a pause, because there is much
more to that turnaround than meets the eye.

ON MAY 11, 1751, Benjamin Franklin and Thomas Bond laid the foundation for Pennsylvania Hospital, the United States' first hospital, with
a mission to care for the poor, sick, and mentally challenged who were
wandering the streets of Philadelphia. Hospitals continued to pop up
slowly across the United States, but it was the introduction of Medicare
and Medicaid, in 1965, that provided perhaps the biggest stimulus for
growth in hospitals and hospital utilization. Just between 1965 and 1970,
medical expenditures rose 23 percent, and the industry hasn't looked
back since.[29] The surge in usage, however, resulted in a seismic shift:
People had been dying in their homes since the dawn of civilization, and
now a wide majority of people were breathing their last in hospital
rooms.

This movement was followed by a backlash, not just among the public but also among physicians, one of whom wrote in the *Journal of the
American Medical Association* in 1976, "Hospitals should not be for
dying. . . . Only the homeless need die in a hospital."[30] While this was
certainly an extreme sentiment, it was reflective of a notion that hospitals were doing less to treat those more likely to benefit from medical
care than to just serve as overly invasive cemeteries.

The medical community was not deaf to these voices of dissent,
and while many terminally ill patients were diverted into the burgeon-
ing nursing-home industry, a small but steady reversal also started.[31]

Between 1990 and 1998, the percentage of Americans dying at home increased from 17 percent to 22 percent, with a simultaneous increase in nursing-home deaths from 16 percent to 22 percent. Furthermore, between 1983 and 1998 hospital deaths fell from 54 percent to 41 percent. By 2007, the number of Americans under sixty-five dying at home increased to 30 percent, and the number older than sixty-five to 24 percent.[32] While this trend deserves to be celebrated, buried in the numbers is the sad truth that, now more than at any prior time, being able to die at home is an inequitably distributed privilege.

In 1980, race was not a determinant of where one died. Both whites and African Americans died at an equal rate in the hospital. Since then, those two curves have started to diverge. Today, minorities of all ages are much more likely to die in a hospital than whites.[33] Among those younger than sixty-five, non-Hispanic whites are much more likely to be able to die at home than any minority, and among those older than sixty-five, they are much more likely to die in nursing homes. Coupled with this racial disparity, there is also a class disparity.

One of the strongest predictors of dying in a hospital is one's socio-economic status; the poorest patients are the ones most likely to die in hospitals. While poorer people in other developed countries, such as the United Kingdom, are also more likely to die in hospitals, the effect of income is much more pronounced in the United States: the difference in home deaths between the poorest and richest quarters in New York is three times more than that in London.

People trying to understand why this is the case have come up with several theories. One very plausible reason is that minorities may have fewer resources. Whites are almost four times more likely to receive home care than African Americans or Hispanics. African Americans are also much less likely to use hospice services even after accounting for other factors such as socioeconomic status. Minorities are also more likely to be uninsured or underinsured, another predictor of dying in a hospital. There could be other reasons, too; minorities tend to live in urban areas dense with hospitals. The effects of these disparities don't just affect those they afflict; they affect the entire health-care landscape.

Care in the last six months of life already accounts for a huge chunk of overall medical costs in the United States, but the cost of this care is not evenly distributed.[34] African American patients accrue 32 percent more costs in the last six months of life than similar white patients. End-of-life care is even more expensive in Hispanic patients, who account for 56 percent more expenditure than matched whites. Most of this additional cost is not due to age, gender, socioeconomic status, geography, the burden of underlying disease, or even whether hospice was used or not. About 85 percent of this additional cost is due to greater use of aggressive treatment measures, such as ICU care, and invasive procedures, such as mechanical ventilation, cardiac catheterization, surgical procedures, dialysis, and cardiac resuscitation.

There are many countries in the world where care in a hospital remains an aspiration for many. In a place like Pakistan or India, being admitted to and getting cared for in a hospital remains a right of those who have made it. But the disparities in developing countries are easier to understand. For one, in developing countries your chances of being overfed and obese go up as you get richer, a much more intuitive relationship than in developed countries, where poor people are more likely to be overweight and obese.

The phenomenon in industrialized countries of the poorest and most disadvantaged people dying in hospitals and therefore accruing more costs is also not unique to the United States. Such is true of our friends across the pond, too; the poorest are much more likely in the United Kingdom to die in hospitals than the most affluent.[35] Yet, as mentioned earlier, the variation there is much less compared with here in the United States. Therefore, while death, in its very own self, is in many ways the same as it has been, modern death means different things to different people. The grim reaper has never been known to be kind, but at least he used to be egalitarian: How he wielded his scythe was blind to the affluence of the victim. Death today is more heterogeneous than it has ever been in the past.

MARTHA, THE MOST free-spirited patient I knew, was stuck in the hospital. It took some time for her and her family to understand that life would never be the same again. She had been independent before coming to the hospital, had lived by herself in an apartment complex for senior citizens. As the team, we had made it clear that there was little we could do to reverse much of what ailed her. At this point, I took it upon myself to honor one final wish: to let her die at home.

It had been difficult to get the family into the hospital because of their work schedules. By the time they came, she had been in the hospital for a few weeks. Unlike in previous meetings, Martha was quiet, weakened beyond measure, and now starting to get confused and delirious. She had five children, all of whom loved her, took care of her, and lived close by. But even with all this going for her, they couldn't arrange for someone to be with her at home day and night. I suggested they come up with a rotating schedule, but even that was not possible. None of them could keep her at their home either.

The only way we could pave a way back home for her was if we could have her build up her strength until she could regain enough function to be somewhat independent. But it was hard to get her the rehab she needed in the hospital. Hospitals, designed as they are for acute care, do have physical and occupational therapists, but the ratio of therapist to patient is nowhere near what it is in a nursing facility. I worked with the case managers on the floor, but we got rejected by each and every nursing facility. As soon as someone heard about her case and her rash, Martha became anathema even though she was not really contagious. I spoke with many of the nurse managers at these facilities personally, but nothing I could say would reassure them. Days continued to pass, and her once-bustling room became increasingly bleak. We kept trying until one day, as I was punching away on a keyboard in the workroom, a nurse came up to me and told me that Martha had stopped breathing. She never breathed again.

The data would indicate that no one checked more boxes of being able to die at home than Martha. She was white, she was female, she had great family support, she had good insurance, and, most of all, she really wanted to pass away in her own home. And yet with everything I could muster on my end, I could do little but delay the inevitable. She died with not one familiar person or fond household item around her.

Martha's story and the stories of millions around the country almost make me think that a death at home is nothing more than a mirage, an unattainable relic of the past. Many of the forces that have pushed people out of their deathbeds and onto a gurney are here to stay and will only keep getting worse. Economic pressures will keep driving families farther apart geographically as their members go out in search of sustenance, moving to where they can get jobs. There are fewer people at home to take care of elderly parents and relatives. Economic inequalities are only getting worse.[36] As medical care gets better, people live longer and through more chronic diseases, and are likely to be much less independent during their twilight years than people of previous generations.

Allowing people to die at the place of their choosing, however, remains extremely important, and Martha's story to me crystallizes why. The one thing that people lose more as they grow older, grow sicker, and inch closer to the end is control. Patients realize that dying at home doesn't just mean that they can sleep in their own blanket, get out of bed without alarms going off and an army of nurses running into the room, or have breakfast without a phlebotomist pricking them in the morning to check their blood glucose. As people age, their schedules become increasingly governed by their medical appointments and hospital admissions, their diet is affected by their diseases and their medications, they become increasingly enslaved. In bygone times, dying didn't leave people this helpless. In fact, people orchestrated their own last speeches and their own deathbed scenes. Only they were the experts on themselves.

In his first novel, *The Cement Garden*, Ian McEwan told the story of a family that falls apart.[37] After the father dies suddenly, the four young children are left at home with their mother, who is ailing from a mysterious disease. When she finds out what she has, she decides to not pursue any aggressive treatment. She decides to spend her last days at home. Things unravel after she passes: to avoid foster care the children bury her rotting corpse in the courtyard, one of the boys regresses to the point of acting like an infant and sleeping in a cot, and Jack, her older son, has sex with his seventeen-year-old sister. It all takes a macabre turn.

Now that I think about it, the biggest leap from reality was not what followed, but that Jack's mother was allowed to die surrounded by her magazines, propped up by her own pillows. The exodus of dying people from homes has broadly resulted in them being exiled from our neighborhoods and communities. Nothing makes both adults and children learn more about life and living than death and dying. Not too long ago, death was not something that happened in hospitals or cloistered facilities; it happened in real neighborhoods surrounded by real people. When someone was dying, neighbors would come check up on them, and when they passed, they were grieved for not just by loved ones, but by all in their vicinity. The erosion of this communality of death, however, first started when people moved from villages to cities. Sir David Smithers, a famous British cancer physician, who recognized the missing pieces in terminal care much earlier than those around him, wrote about death in the village he had grown up in: "In a village everyone dies, it is normal practice, everyone knows about it. . . . In a block of flats in town somebody may die alone on the other side of a wall a few feet away from you and you may know nothing of it."[38]

How We Learned Not to Resuscitate

Scientific advances have made the experience of dying, one that was undertaken in a fairly uniform manner, very different from what it has been throughout history. Many of our expectations of what death ought to be like have been wired into our brains over hundreds and thousand years of evolutionary learning. This is precisely what makes modern death such a jarring and alienating experience. In innumerable ways, medicine has made life better, and certainly longer. But death itself is more harrowing and prolonged today than it has ever been before.

My maternal grandmother—Nano, we called her—was a woman of wondrous spirit and bountiful strength. Yet when she was barely in her early sixties she was considered ancient. Married as a teenager, Nano bore eight children. The only time she ever left Pakistan was when she went for the annual Muslim pilgrimage, the hajj, in Saudi Arabia. She was having dinner at my uncle's house recently when she started to feel a burning in her chest. Nano thought it was probably acid reflux and tried to brave her way through it. She felt nauseous and threw up, but that didn't make the burning any better. My uncle grew increasingly concerned and rushed her into the backseat of his car. By the time they reached the hospital, she could barely stand up, so he carried her into the emergency room. Nano died within minutes.

Her death, which occurred while I was writing this book, hit me like a thunderbolt. I had no inkling that she was very sick and that she was as close to passing away as she probably was. No one really had any clue just how or why she passed away. And such is true of most people who die there. Perhaps by recent standards, what was the most striking thing about how she passed away was this: Her first day in the hospital also happened to be her last.

How people die in the third world today is how people in the modern world used to die before the advent of advanced medical technologies. Witnessing death in Pakistan when I was growing up was akin to getting into a time machine and traveling back to earlier times, where death was still a mysterious agent. Disease was defined by narratives and stories rather than diagnostic codes. People's cabinets were filled with ornaments, prayer books, and herbs rather than prescription medications and medical devices. Of the few who experienced it, pain was fought with faith rather than opiates.

Not only was medicine different in the past in rich countries, how people lived and how families were structured was also different. Given the lack of life-sustaining therapies, most people could receive care at the home. Families were more geographically cogent, and given the less stringent nature of work and the higher proportion of young people, there was more help available for the elderly. Much of this remains true to this day in developing countries, which is why there is almost no concept of nursing homes and rehabilitation facilities there.

While it is easy to romanticize how death occurs in third-world countries, that would represent but one side of the picture. While I lost many loved ones during the process of writing this book, my entire life has been touched by the demise of someone I have never met or seen. Abdullah would have been my eldest brother, had he lived. My mother was barely twenty years old when she became pregnant, and everything seemed to be going well. She had seven brothers and sisters, who were waiting for the first baby in that generation of the family. Moments after he was born, before anyone could even take a picture, for entirely unknown reasons, Abdullah stopped breathing, and never breathed again. To this day, I imagine what it would be like were he around.

Deaths like Abdullah's are common in poor countries today and were common in the United States and Europe at the turn of the twentieth century. It is these unlived lives and preventable deaths that are the truest reminder of the heavy debt we owe to all of the physicians and scientists and public-health experts who have provided us more cures than we know what to do with.

Another big reason so much of the culture around dying has changed in most developed countries is health insurance. Not too long ago, all health-care services were fee-for-service in the United States and much of the industrial world. This meant that being in a hospital was like being in a hotel. The longer you stayed, the more you indulged, the more you paid. This would result in some heartbreaking choices. Back when I was in Pakistan, I remember taking care of a child in the ICU with debilitating malnutrition. The child's father was a laborer of little means. As the number of days in the ICU multiplied, the father started getting concerned more about his healthy children. With the hospital bill climbing every day, he had to make a choice between starving his other children or trying to save his sick child. He ended up deciding to discontinue intensive care, and the child passed away almost immediately.

Health insurance allows patients to receive life-prolonging and life-sustaining therapies and interventions in the hospital without having to worry about astronomical out-of-pocket bills. This change is one big reason there is even time for the aforementioned conversations about where we die to occur and for many of these issues to arise.

Both for better and for worse, death has changed dramatically. There are things that we have gained and there are things that we have lost. We have delayed death but have also made getting there more difficult. Nothing encapsulates the diverging directions we have taken better than the complicated story of cardiopulmonary resuscitation, or CPR as it is commonly known as. Akin to being the antihero of modern medicine,

CPR is at once a reminder of how far we have come and a reminder of how much we have left behind.

IT WAS ONE of those days when morning rounds extended well into the early afternoon. We had so many patients on our ICU team that they were spread across other ICUs. Morning rounds in the ICU are a way for the team who have been on call since the morning before to present all the information pertaining to each of the patients to the team coming on. During rounds, though, the team operates like air-traffic control, with clear roles designated to everyone, trying to get as many as possible of the designated tasks done in the morning so that the team can concentrate on major tasks like procedures or taking care of new admissions in the afternoon and evening.

This particular rotation was one of the most demanding in our program. Unlike any other ICU team, our team had no real upper limit of patients. We could assume care of patients outside our native unit, and therefore served as a pop-off valve as other teams hit their caps. And yet I don't remember a time when I had more fun working. My team comprised some of my best friends from residency. Our attending was one of the smartest, most laid-back physicians in the hospital. It's difficult to overemphasize how a cohesive team not only helps team members enjoy what they do, but also improves the care patients receive. With the sun shining bright, and rounds approaching an end, as our team entered the room of the very last patient on our list there was no apparent indication that a catastrophic turn of events would soon be upon us.

The patient, a man in his sixties, was one of the youngest patients under our care at the time. His life had taken an unfortunate turn recently when he had a large bleed in his brain that had rendered him unable to communicate in any meaningful fashion. One sentinel event had sent him from his regular life to lying mute in a hospital bed. But given the acute nature of events, there was still some chance that his brain would be able to recover a reasonable amount of functionality. After we had examined him and were about to step out of the room, it seemed that he was lying too low in his inclined bed. So before we finished up we decided to give him a boost.

A bed boost, while sounding simple enough, is still something that needs to be carefully choreographed.[1] The bed needs to be leveled, the bed brakes need to be applied, pillows ought to be removed, two (or four) people need to grab the draw sheet underneath the patient, and then on the count of three those people pull the patient toward the head of the bed. Only at the last minute did I realize that the bed brake had not been locked, and I planted it down with my foot. With the boost successful, we exchanged imaginary high fives, and had started milling out of the room when out of the corner of my eye I noticed that the patient appeared to be choking and his face was turning blue.

My eyes darted toward the bedside ECG monitor, and instead of showing the finely organized activity characteristic of a normal heart rhythm, it showed that he was in a malignant fast heart rhythm with wide peaks and troughs indicative of ventricular tachycardia. I rushed to his side and placed the tip of my index and middle fingers over his left wrist. I could feel his pulse going fast—bobblebobblebobblebobble—until there was nothing. Only later would it dawn on me that I had palpated the very last pulse of a patient for the very first time in my life. But there was no time for such rumination; the patient was in cardiac arrest. I yelled out to the nurse at the reception desk, "Call a code blue!"

Hospitals have many "codes" that convey some sort of emergency. Code red usually means there is a fire, but mostly happens after someone leaves a sandwich for too long in the microwave. A code black can indicate that the hospital computer system has crashed, a truly modern medical emergency. Nothing, however, gets people's attention like a code blue, which means that someone has had a cardiac arrest.

What follows in a hospital after a code blue is called is why so many people, in spite of all its challenges, go to medical school and train through residency, accrue debt and stress and incapacitate their social lives, and work tirelessly, filling out mountains of paperwork, waiting for elevators and then taking the stairs because the elevator always takes too long, and so on. Such is the zeal of response that the focus has now changed from getting more people to respond to a code blue, commonly referred to only as a code, to having *fewer* people respond to avoid overcrowding. At some codes in the hospital, more than a hundred people responded.

Yet before any of that could happen, the other resident on the team informed me that the patient was DNR/DNI, indicating that he or a proxy had expressed a Do Not Resuscitate and Do Not Intubate directive. The nurse issued an overhead announcement canceling the code call. So instead of the rumble of an approaching army of doctors arriving to resuscitate him, there was but stillness. We all looked on as his heart remained static and all color left his face.

Questions bombarded me then, as they do now when I think about how that man passed. Some questions were specific: What circumstances led to his passing? What was his life like before he ended up here in the hospital? Was there anything we could have done to prevent him passing away? And most importantly was there anything reversible about how he died? Some questions, though, were much broader: How did we learn to resuscitate the dying? What were things like before we knew what we know now? And, perhaps most importantly, how and why did we learn not to resuscitate?

IT WAS NOT too long ago that CPR did not even exist. Hitherto, up until the 1940s and much of the 1950s, the treatment of choice for patients whose hearts went into arrest and stopped beating involved a surgeon cutting open the chest and massaging the heart with his gloved hand.[2] Other crude and ineffective treatments included the direct injection of medications into the heart. Broadly speaking, cardiac arrest comprises two main entities. In "ventricular fibrillation" or "ventricular tachycardia," the heart's normal organized contraction is lost and the heart quivers rapidly, causing no meaningful blood flow. The brain, the organ most dependent on continuous blood flow, the bringer of valuable oxygen, can be irreparably damaged within moments after cardiac arrest. The other form of cardiac arrest is referred to as "asystole," during which the heart just halts to a standstill and the heart rhythm is ominously reduced to that dreaded flatline. "Pulseless electrical activity" is a dastardly cousin of asystole, in which even though the heart is not contracting meaningfully, and the patient has no pulse, there is deceptive activity on the ECG.

The principles of modern CPR first started with the management of victims of drowning. The first report of a successful attempt at resuscitation was noted in the Old Testament: The prophet Elijah went up to a dead child and put "his mouth upon his mouth, and his eyes upon his eyes, and his hands upon his hands . . . and the flesh of the child waxed warm."[3] Mouth-to-mouth breathing was first established as an acceptable treatment for victims of drowning by the Paris Academy of Science in 1740. After a span of time in which physicians went in several incorrect directions, the foundation of modern mouth-to-mouth resuscitation was laid by Peter Safar, a Viennese physician who completed surgical training at Yale and subsequent anesthesiology training at the University of Pennsylvania.[4] In an experiment that would surely never be approved by an ethics review board nowadays, he took eighty young volunteers, mostly women in their twenties and thirties, put them to sleep with anesthesia, and analyzed which position caused the least amount of obstruction in their breathing tubes. He concluded that the best way to open up someone's airways was to have them lying on their backs with their chin tilted backward. With this experiment he reversed previous thought that having patients lying on their bellies was the best way of ensuring that their airways remain open. The development of machines such as the iron lung, which could be used to maintain the delivery of oxygen to the lungs (i.e., "mechanical ventilation"), allowed us to overcome the failure of at least one major organ system—the lungs.[5]

In parallel to progress in helping patients maintain breathing, research initially performed in animals studying how to restart a still heart was making its way to human beings. To revive the heart in cardiac arrest, there are two main pathways—mechanical and electrical. The heart is as close to an electrical machine as any organ in the body. Electrical signals, generated by the body's native pacemaker, called the "sinus node," spread in an organized fashion, first through the smaller upper chambers called the atria, and then downward to the muscular ventricles, which, when activated, cause the flow of blood through the body. In ventricular fibrillation or ventricular tachycardia, the electrical activity of the heart goes into complete disarray, with the sinus node no longer in control. The ventricles, instead of contracting forcefully, merely flutter, and effectively cease to function.

The first documented report of using an electric shock to "reset" the heart into a normal rhythm was presented in 1774, titled "Electricity Restores Vitality."[6] A three-year-old girl, Sophia Greenhill, fell from a window in Soho, London, and was declared dead by surgeons at a local hospital. Twenty minutes after this declaration, a Mr. Squires applied electricity to different parts of the dead child's body, and upon application of electricity to the chest, the girl started breathing and had a return of pulse. However, this case was poorly documented and remained forgotten in the annals of history until recently. The next step in this discovery did not occur until 1899, when Swiss researchers discovered that small bursts of electricity could induce dog hearts to go into ventricular fibrillation, while larger surges could actually shock the heart out of these malignant rhythms.[7]

It wasn't until 1947, though, that electricity was first successfully used in a human being.[8] Surgeons in Cleveland were wrapping up an otherwise uneventful surgery in a fourteen-year-old boy when suddenly they noticed that his blood pressure had bottomed out and he went into ventricular fibrillation. The surgeons immediately opened up his chest again and started to massage his heart and gave him medications. After about thirty-five minutes of cardiac massage, the boy still remained in ventricular fibrillation. It was then that the surgeons placed one electrode behind and one in front of the boy's open heart and applied an electric shock. They had tried this on five previous patients, none of whom had made it. Like those patients' hearts, the boy's heart continued to fibrillate. They applied the shock a second time, and this time the heart just stopped. Within moments, though, the surgeons noticed "feeble, regular and fairly rapid cardiac contractions." The surgeons continued to massage his heart for another half hour, and after all was said and done, the boy walked out of the hospital, alive and well.

Paul Zoll, a physician after whom the cardiology floor in the hospital I did my medical residency in was named, first successfully demonstrated the use of "defibrillators" that could be used without the need to open the patient's chest and could simply be applied onto their skin.[9] In his case series, published in the *New England Journal of Medicine* in 1956, he devised an algorithm to describe the steps required to attempt to revive an arrested heart.[10] However, shocks are useful only for ventricular fibrillation or ventricular tachycardia and show no benefit in patients with asystole or pulseless electrical activity, which account for two-thirds of all patients with cardiac arrest.[11] Newer defibrillators actually take the thinking out of this by automatically letting first responders know if the cardiac arrest is shockable or not.

For all its complexity, the heart has just one function: pumping blood. Therefore, the third and final principle of CPR, after air and electricity, is squeeze. Moritz Schiff, an Italian physiologist based in Florence, is credited with pioneering artificial circulation.[12] An account of his experiments published in 1874 by Dr. Hake, a visiting physician, provides an interesting insight into not only the experiments but the public view on animal cruelty in the late nineteenth century.[13] "Much curiosity has been awakened here of late by some ill advised parties having commenced proceedings in the law court against the Laboratory of Physiology," Hake writes in the opening paragraph of his report describing Schiff's experiments, but adds that "the process has been withdrawn, the accusation of cruelty to animals made against the eminent Professor having proved utterly based only on ignorant rumors." After sedating the animals and paralyzing their hearts with chloroform, Schiff would compress the heart with periodic motions of his hands until "the organ finally resumes its spontaneous action." Having demonstrated his ability to restore function, Schiff, curiously, refrained from restoring life. After the animal started to recover some of its neurological function, such as the eyelid reflex, Schiff would withdraw his hand: "The animal is now capable of being brought back to cerebral consciousness; it would, however, be both cruel and useless to extend the experiment so far."

It was in 1878 when the German professor Rudolph Boehm, in present-day Estonia, would induce cardiac arrest in cats with chloroform and then squeeze their chests from side to side for up to thirty minutes until they were revived.[14] This form of "closed-chest cardiac massage," a precursor to modern CPR, would be overtaken by open-chest cardiac massage, which was first attempted in a human being in 1898 by the French surgeon Theodore Tuffier. He was rounding on a twenty-four-year-old patient of his, five days removed from his appendix, when the patient became unresponsive and pulseless. Tuffier cut through his chest and compressed his heart with his fingers; while the patient's pulse returned fleetingly, he eventually died.[15] Because of its more invasive and direct nature, open cardiac massage became very popular and was considered the therapy of choice for patients with cardiac arrest, especially those who didn't respond to defibrillation.

It wasn't until 1960, in a paper published in the *Journal of the American Medical Association* by William Kouwenhoven, James Jude, and Guy Knickerbocker from Johns Hopkins, that the three cores of modern CPR—ventilation, external defibrillation, and chest compressions—were combined as one.[16] This seminal advance would turn out to be one of the defining moments of modern medicine. Soon, thousands upon thousands of health-care workers around the world were trained to do CPR. CPR is now one of the most visible medical interventions in popular culture, almost as ubiquitous as the Heimlich maneuver.

MODERN RESUSCITATION WAS the culmination of work that took place in parallel over hundreds of years, across continents, and changed how death itself had been viewed. In many ways, these measures of resuscitation challenged the supposition that death was final and absolute. Before the era of resuscitation, one of the most well-established means of attempting to revive the apparently dead or victims of drowning was the insufflation of tobacco smoke in people's rectums.[17] In fact, this modality became so common that it was endorsed by the Royal Humane Society, and tobacco enemas would be found along the Thames River to resuscitate drowning victims, much as defibrillators are placed in public places these days. This practice was sustained well into the nineteenth century in Western countries.[18] Therefore, Kouwenhoven's, Jude's, and Knickerbocker's paper in 1960 that first combined all three aspects of resuscitation—air, electricity, and squeeze—not only changed emergency medical care, it changed the way life would end for most human beings. The authors of that paper could not have foreseen the consequences of their study even in their wildest dreams.

The importance of CPR and resuscitation was quickly realized around the world. The 1960s were also a time of great change for the entire medical system. An emergency response system was developed with trained paramedics manning ambulances. This greatly improved access of patients to the health-care system. This was also a time when, because of an increase in procedures and testing, physicians started to move out of small offices and clinic practices into hospitals, and brought their patients with them. Improvements in treatments of the biggest killers, such as infectious diseases and heart disease, prolonged life. But as medicine became more adept at keeping people alive through their heart attacks, the sum total of patients alive with heart disease multiplied. Many of these patients would go on to develop chronic conditions such as heart failure. As patients got older, the incidence of cancer also increased, further increasing the number of people requiring intensive medical care. This exponential growth in sickness, and in the sheer amount of *stuff* that physicians were able or willing to do to treat it, resulted in the development of the modern medical-industrial complex.[19]

Mechanical ventilation was first developed to treat what is now a disease on the verge of eradication. Poliomyelitis is a virus-transmitted disease that can cause paralysis. Not only did polio afflict an American president, Franklin D. Roosevelt, but at its peak in the 1950s it also caused twenty-one thousand cases of paralysis annually in the United States.[20] Paralysis in polio would start from the legs but in severe cases would ascend and immobilize the muscles needed for breathing. Imagine, then, thousands of children who suffocate to death with all their senses intact. The only means of treating these children was to hook them up to mechanical ventilation devices such as the iron lung. The iron lung, developed by two researchers from Harvard in 1929, Philip Drinker and Louis Agassiz Shaw, was a cylindrical chamber in which the patient was placed.[21] The iron lung supported breathing by creating negative pressure outside the body, helping to expand the chest and lungs. However, it wasn't as effective for patients afflicted with polio paralysis, as their chest muscles lacked any strength to respond to the pressure changes created by the iron lung.

Scandinavia was particularly violently hit by the polio epidemic in 1949–50. Children from all over Denmark were moved to the Blegdam Hospital in Copenhagen. In spite of traditional ventilation, almost 85 percent of children with polio and breathing difficulty would die.[22] Desperate to improve outcomes in his young patients, Bjorn Ibsen, the senior anesthesiologist in the hospital, designed a new way to help these children breathe, with machines that more closely mimicked what the body did physiologically.

To cause air to enter the lungs, the body creates negative pressure inside the lungs to suck air in. Ibsen therefore created a tube with an inflatable cuff (which would prevent air from leaking) and inserted that down the throat through an opening in the front of the neck called a tracheostomy. The tube created negative pressure inside the lungs, causing air to be sucked in and used for oxygen delivery. This would be the first direct ancestor of modern ventilation devices. What he lacked at that time was an ability to keep these machines running on a continuous basis. To overcome this he required a person to stand by the bedside and manually inflate and deflate the pump, causing air to be delivered to the patient. With up to 75 patients with polio being mechanically ventilated at any given time, 250 medical students were required to be at patients' bedsides at all times, taking turns as they manually ventilated the patients. This new advance, reported by Ibsen in the *British Medical Journal,* was adopted worldwide very soon and became the standard by which patients with breathing difficulties would be managed in ICUs.[23] With the integration of CPR in the 1960s, and the introduction of cardiac monitors, the modern ICU was ready for prime time.

MEDICINE HAD BEEN an art for thousands of years and was only now becoming a science. With the marriage of technology and medicine, the number of interventions that physicians could perform began to rise exponentially. Almost in parallel, discoveries started to be made that fundamentally altered humanity's conception of life. The development of X-ray imaging and CT scans allowed the diagnosis of diseases that would have almost certainly been missed without cutting open the body. The basic element of life, DNA, was first described by James Watson and Francis Crick in 1953 in their classic paper in the journal *Nature*.[24] Not only were we treating diseases with new medications such as antibiotics, we were also developing vaccines that would prevent diseases from occurring in the first place. The polio vaccine has in fact eradicated polio from all but two countries. But as medicine strengthened our ability to live, it started to encroach on people's right to pass.

A sixty-eight-year-old English physician was diagnosed with stomach cancer in the late 1960s.[25] Having already retired from practice after a previous heart attack, he did not enjoy great health to begin with. He had his stomach surgically removed, but to no avail, as the cancer had already spread all over his body. The tumor, compressing his spinal nerves, caused so much pain that even high doses of morphine brought him no relief. Ten days after his surgery, he collapsed and was found to have a large blood clot in his lungs. A young physician heroically removed the clot from his arteries surgically, but on his recovery, the physician, while thankful for the care he had received, implored that if he were to have a future cardiac arrest that he not be revived. The degree of his pain was such that he almost never found any relief. Such was his conviction that he even wrote a note in the medical chart, and communicated with the hospital staff, that he not be resuscitated in the future. But even with this knowledge, after two weeks, when he went into cardiac arrest, this time after a large heart attack, he was resuscitated four times that very night. A hole was made in his neck to help him breathe, but his condition after the cardiac arrests was almost subhuman. His brain ceased to function in any reasonable way; he kept having convulsive vomiting and seizures. And yet the staff continued to give him antibiotics and other measures to sustain his life until eventually his heart just stopped.

Tales like this became the norm during the late sixties and early seventies. The prevailing attitude during that time was summed up in a communication from another British physician in 1969:

Death, it seems, must be prevented whenever possible, whatever the ultimate costs, no matter how painful the period of repayment by the patient and his relatives. The fear of death is normally divisible into two parts: the fear of death itself, and the fear of the suffering that may have to be endured before death. Have we now to add a further dimension, the fear of resuscitation?

Many doctors used to feel that the greatest of our professional hazards was the mistake that kills. Has it now been usurped by that which keeps the patient alive?[26]

Physicians found themselves in a situation they had never been in before at any point in history. With medical advances in just about every specialty and field, it seemed that medicine was finally beginning to translate dreams into reality. They had striven to buy their patients more time since the inception of their profession, but no one had anticipated what the long-term outcome of these advances would be.

Technology also greatly changed the patient-doctor relationship. Before the post–World War II boom in medical science and technology, physicians and doctors interacted mostly either at home or at the clinic. However, with a spike in interventions, testing, and the ability to manage sicker patients, medical care shifted to hospitals. Instead of reducing the distance between patients and their doctors, hospitals muddied the relationship. Technology drew physicians away from patients, as more and more physicians started to rely on lab tests, scans, and procedures to learn about their patients' pathology. This coincided with the signing of Medicare into law, in 1965, which exponentially improved patients' access to healthcare. Hospitals thus increased the number of patients that each physician had to take care of, and with the rising demands of documentation, the time that doctors spent with their patients dwindled.

The infusion of science in medicine also provided doctors with a knowledge base that they previously did not possess. But like many other professionals who were privy to a body of complex information, physicians became particularly arrogant. Especially in the 1960s, the gulf had never been wider between doctors' and patients' preferences. In fact, one study conducted in 1961 showed that 90 percent of all physicians did not believe that it was right to disclose a cancer diagnosis to a patient.[27] This finding was reflected in other studies conducted at that time as well.[28] Most physicians believed that the main reason to not disclose this information to patients was to sustain hope. However, when it came to moving patients toward having a procedure or radiation, physicians were more likely to use terms such as "tumor" or "precancerous lesion."

Interestingly, this attitude was completely divergent from that of patients, a vast majority of whom reported in studies that they would want to be privy to that information.[29] Medicine also remained a deeply patriarchal profession, reflecting the rest of society at that time. One physician, writing in the medical journal *Lancet,* stated that "the different career prospects of men and women doctors are due to psychological and physiological factors as well as social ones."[30] He then went on to quote Steven Goldberg's 1977 book, *The Inevitability of Patriarchy,* suggesting that lack of male hormones in females deprived them of the drive needed for dominance.

This authoritarian and paternalistic attitude had serious and deleterious effects on patients, particularly those at the end of life. Most physicians made unilateral decisions about how aggressively to treat patients. These decisions could be anywhere on the spectrum, from extreme to minimal care. Physicians would either continue to aggressively treat patients in spite of their stated wishes otherwise or would decide by themselves that further treatment was futile. In fact, some hospitals had standardized this practice long before a national conversation about the ethics of resuscitation had occurred. For example, at a hospital in Queens, New York, physicians stuck purple dots on charts of patients who were deemed to be too sick for resuscitation or unlikely to derive any benefit.[31] What this amounted to was a gross judgment call that physicians made on their own accord, deciding which patients deserved resuscitation and which patients didn't. These decisions were rarely shared with patients or their families.

Another practice that became increasingly prevalent was that of "slow codes."[32] These resuscitative attempts, also referred to as sham, show, light blue, or Hollywood codes, were performed on patients that physicians had deemed too feeble or terminally ill to derive any real benefit from the full-on assault, which is a code blue. While some of these assess-ments were born out of a humane attempt to prevent any unnecessary harm coming to the patient, frequently such decisions were made if the patient or their family were not on the same page as the doctor. Given the murky nature of this whole practice, slow codes were something never openly discussed, only whispered about in hospital corridors.

In the middle of this legal and ethical void, patients and their relatives would sometimes meet at a middle ground with their physicians. In pa-tients with intractable pain, terminal illness, and a poor prognosis and quality of life, on the patients' or families' advice, physicians would prac-tice "judicious neglect." In private conversations, physicians would con-sult with the families and decide if "heroic measures" (another oft-used but highly charged and controversial term) were to be pursued or not. This mostly meant cardiac resuscitation and mechanical ventilation.

For some time, all the above practices became quite the norm, until a twenty-one-year-old girl from New Jersey, losing weight to fit into a dress, collapsed after taking a few pills and drinking gin while partying with her friends. Karen Ann Quinlan had lived a painfully normal and unremarkable life up until that moment. From then on, in a space be-tween life and death, she would come to define modern death, more so than any other person in history.

KAREN ANN QUINLAN was born March 29, 1954, in St. Joseph's Children's and Maternity Hospital in Scranton, Pennsylvania.[33] The hospital pro-vided facilities for unwed mothers to live in. A month after her birth, Julia and Joseph Quinlan filed adoption papers and took her in. Karen lived two lives. Her first life was that of a regular middle-class girl: she swam, she skied, she dated, she attended mass with her family, she went to high school, and she worked at a local ceramics company. However, this life of hers changed after she was laid off from her job at the ceramics company. Soon after, she found herself moving from job to job, and increasingly found comfort in the company of sedative pills and alcohol.

There was nothing unusual about the night of April 14, 1975. Karen was partying with her friends at Falconer's Tavern, a bar close to Lake

Lackawanna. In the days prior to this night, she had barely eaten or drunk, trying as she was to fit into a dress. In the bar, she had some gin and also took some tranquilizer pills. At some point during the night at the bar, she collapsed. One of her friends took her back to the house where she had been living with a group of friends. It was there that it was noted that Karen had stopped breathing.

In many ways, what ensued in the moments after she was noted to not be breathing showed just how far medical care had come over just a short period of time. Her friend performed mouth-to-mouth resuscitation in an attempt to have her start breathing again and to get oxygen to her brain. However, it was later determined that her brain lacked oxygen for at least two fifteen-minute periods.

Emergency medical services were then called—another recent advance. In fact, a universal emergency response telephone service, "911," had only been instituted in 1967, based on a recommendation by the President's Commission on Law Enforcement and Administration of Justice. An ambulance then took her to a local hospital, where she was hooked up to a mechanical ventilator. On physical examination, her pupils were fixed, in that they did not constrict or dilate in response to light—a very basic human reflex. She also didn't respond to any painful stimuli.

Three days into her hospitalization, the doctors consulted neurology, and the neurologist on call, Robert Morse, examined Karen. In the court documents, he described that he found Karen to be comatose and with evidence of "decortication"—a condition that represents extensive damage to the higher parts of the brain—reflected in a telltale posture with the legs stiff and straight and the arms flexed tight.

Karen's condition did not improve. If anything, it became worse. When she first presented to the hospital, she weighed about 115 pounds. To help feed her, a nasogastric tube, going down her nose and into her stomach, which could be used to provide her food and medication, was placed. Yet in spite of this, she dropped to less than 70 pounds within the next few months. Her parents, the Quinlans, were both devoutly Catholic and continued to struggle with the situation as she stayed in her comatose state.

Karen, while not the first patient to wind up in this situation, would certainly become the most high-profile. Generally, families and physicians would come to a decision among themselves, or physicians would unilaterally decide that they wouldn't proceed with resuscitation. Five months after Karen first came to the hospital, Joseph Quinlan requested that the physicians withdraw care and take Karen off the ventilator. Karen's doctors, Robert Morse and Arshad Javed, refused. To allay the doctors' fear of having a malpractice lawsuit brought against them, the Quinlans even drafted a document freeing them from any liability. But the doctors insisted that they were not willing to remove Karen from the ventilator.

It was here in a hospital bed, breathing with a ventilator, a skeleton of the person that she was when she was brought into the hospital, that Karen began her second life. Ostensibly, her state was not unique. In fact, countless other patients were in her condition. And yet, as events would transpire, she would go on to shape the landscape of death more than any other.

All the physicians involved in Karen's care agreed that her prognosis was extremely poor. They also agreed that the chances of her reverting out of her coma were next to nil. Many physicians at that point might have gone with the Quinlans' wishes, yet the doctors in this case did not do so. In retrospect, it is still difficult for me to imagine what I would have done had I been in their position. On the one hand, Karen was in a state where her quality of life was almost subhuman. She was dependent on a machine to help her breathe. She needed artificial nutrition, in spite of which she weighed only about seventy pounds. And it was clear that there was no available technology or intervention that would help her regain any of her normal function. Subjecting her to a continuation of all these interventions was not making her feel better in any conceivable way, and keeping them going was not going to make her feel different either.

And yet on the other hand, this space was a complete ethical and legal vacuum at that time. Physicians are trained to think autonomously and to manage the patient in front of them. Several times a day, physicians face ethical decisions that they have to make. Most of the time, they do what is congruent with their own moral compass. Particularly during that time, they rarely looked over their shoulder and second-guessed a decision. Frequently they would go ahead and write their own rules. Variability in medical practice increases as one moves into a data-free zone, and ethical decisions at the end of life were about as data- and legislation-free as it got.

In this case, while the physicians agreed that Karen's outlook was terrible, they also realized that they had no legal right to be able to withdraw care that was sustaining her. At the same time, they were wary of what consequences they might have to face if they went ahead with that decision. In this case, though, the doctors claimed to the media that they were warned that prosecutors could bring murder charges against them if they went ahead and disconnected the ventilator, a plausible claim given the lack of legal precedent in this situation. That they paused to think about what their decision would mean on a more global level is commendable.

For the Quinlans, this decision had not been easy. They had spent several months pondering the situation. Joseph Quinlan conferred with his local priest, who also agreed with withdrawing care given the low likelihood of her having any meaningful recovery. But once they came to a decision that continuing what they thought were "extraordinary" measures was against what Karen would have wanted, their conviction was set in stone. It was then that they decided to file a suit and take the matters to court.

The Quinlans probably had no idea that they had just initiated one of the most significant lawsuits of their time. But precedent was not on their side. Just a few weeks earlier, a New Jersey Court sitting in Newark had not allowed a thirty-nine-year-old woman with terminal leukemia the right to refuse a feeding tube.[34] This was also a time when paranoia regarding possible removal of support for terminally ill patients was very high. Indeed, in his opening statement, Dr. Morse's lawyer compared the Quinlan suit to Nazi atrocities during the Holocaust and gas chambers during World War II.[35] The small town of Morristown in northern New Jersey had rarely been the center of attention since George Washington encamped his armies there in the late 1770s. Hundreds of reporters from national outlets thronged the streets, hunkered down outside the Quinlans' home, and occupied most of the seats in the court-house. In her book *The Mansion of Happiness*, Jill Lepore, a professor of history at Harvard and a staff writer for the *New Yorker*, wrote, "*In the Matter of Karen Quinlan* marked a fundamental shift in American political history. In the decades following *Quinlan*, all manner of do-mestic policy issues were recast as matters of life and death: urgent, uncompromising, and absolute."[36]

THE KAREN ANN Quinlan case was the first step in what is now known as the "right to die" movement. While the initial thoughts of the state prosecutor and attorney general were that this case was a challenge to New Jersey's established definition of death, it was disclosed just before the trial went to court that Karen did not have an entirely flat EEG and that she could breathe spontaneously from time to time without support from the ventilator. Therefore, the one thing that everyone agreed upon in this case was that Karen was *not* dead. While this is an area of great interest and controversy, the definition of death was one thing that did not hinge on the results of this case. Yet this was the first time that the courts had formally analyzed the myriad complexities that had arisen in the care of patients at the end of life after advances in technol-ogy had made those discussions even possible. End-of-life care posed such vexing and intricate facets, with substantial overlap between med-icine, theology, and laws pertaining to human dignity, privacy, and autonomy, that it was understandable that none of the courts had pro-actively sought to delve into this area.

The trial started on October 20, 1975, at the New Jersey Superior Court, presided over by Justice Robert Muir Jr., and lasted for just about two weeks. In many ways, this trial would lay the template for future high-profile trials. The Quinlans received thousands of letters and pack-ages, including many from faith healers, many of whom claimed to be able to cure Karen of her ailments. Joseph Quinlan's assertion was fairly straightforward: that he be appointed Karen's guardian and subsequently be allowed to move forward and disconnect Karen from the ventilator and allow her to die.

At the time the trial went to court, Joseph Quinlan was not the designated guardian. In fact, the court had disallowed him from holding that position, given that they knew he would want her removed from life support, and had appointed a part-time public defender, Daniel Coburn, as Karen's legal guardian. Coburn also disagreed with disconnecting the ventilator. The decision to be removed from the respirator, Justice Muir stated, "is to be left to the treating physician. . . . I am satisfied that it may be concurred in by the parents but not governed by them." In other words, he merely reinforced the existing notion—the doctor knows best. This was also reflected in the respect and endearment that society had traditionally placed on doctors' shoulders, feeling that a doctor would always make the best decision.

It was the court's refusal to grant Mr. Quinlan guardianship that brought the case to trial.

When the Quinlans arrived at the Morris County Courthouse, they were accompanied by three Catholic priests. One of those was Thomas Trapasso, the Quinlans' parish priest, who also knew Karen well. He, along with the other priests, had conferred with the Quinlans over the past few months and had come to the conclusion that they had the right to not continue her life in her then-present state with artificial means. This was largely based on an address by Pope Pius XII to a group of anesthesiologists in 1957 in which he clarified that physicians had no duty to prolong medical treatment in the face of no hope of recovery against a patient's wishes.[37]

After two tumultuous weeks, though, Justice Muir's ruling came down and it came down hard. On November 10, 1975, he announced that Joseph Quinlan was not to be the patient's guardian and placed the burden of decision making on the physicians taking care of Karen. In his ruling, he stated:

> There is a higher standard, a higher duty, that encompasses the uniqueness of human life, the integrity of the medical profession and the attitude of society toward the physician, and therefore the morals of society. A patient is placed, or places himself, in the care of a physician with the expectation that he [the physician] will do everything in his power,

everything that is known to modern medicine, to protect the patient's life. He will do all within his human power to favor life against death.[38]

The ruling by Justice Muir emphasized the role of the physician, as not only an expert in medical matters but also as an exemplar of the ethical and moral standards of society. "What justification is there to remove it [the nature, extent, and duration of care] from the control of the medical profession and place it in the hands of the court?" he asked.

If anything, the debate in the ruling was about whether the courts should have any influence in the medical management of patients in any spectrum of their care. But this thought process was only reflective of a much wider phenomenon that had stood the test of time: that the preferences of patients and their caregivers and guardians had little to any impact on matters of health.

The court also opined on what many had thought was the central focus of this case—to define what exactly were the rights of patients. While *Roe v. Wade* had focused more on the right of life, the Karen Quinlan case, to many observers, pertained to the so-called right to die. In his statement, though, Justice Muir unequivocally stated that "there is no constitutional right to die" and that in this case, a decision to terminate the ventilator would amount to homicide and an act of euthanasia. Whether the removal from the respirator was considered an affirmative action or one of omission, it was beside the point: "There is no constitutional right to die that can be asserted by a parent for his incompetent adult child." In fact, Justice Muir stated that it was in the state's best interest to preserve life.

The other patient right that came into question was the right to privacy. The Quinlans' lawyer, Paul Armstrong, argued that the state's decision to adjudicate the Quinlans' decision to withdraw their child from the respirator was an incursion on their right to privacy. The Quinlans argued that by way of the right to privacy, they had a right of self-determination to decide whether to withdraw any "extraordinary measures" that would appear to be futile in this case. While not expressly stated in the Constitution, the right to privacy, and by extension self-determination, has well-established legal precedent in the law. In fact, in his judgment on the case *Union Pacific Railway Company v. Botsford* (1891) Justice Horace Gray echoed the words of an earlier ruling when he stated, "The right to one's person may be said to be a right of complete immunity: to be let alone." While the Quinlans argued that this right of privacy could be exercised by a parent for their child, the court disagreed, and argued that the state's interest in life outweighed the parents' wish for the respirator to be removed. But just like so much else in the Karen Quinlan case, this just raised more questions than answers. For at this point in time, no one really knew what a patient's rights were.

JUSTICE MUIR'S DECISION was a setback for the Quinlans, but it only strengthened their resolve. They realized that they had brought in front of the court a milieu so dense with the complexities of science, religion, and the law that expecting a lower-level court to rule on it might have been ambitious. As Karen lay in the hospital, without any further evidence of recovery, they went ahead and appealed the ruling in New Jersey's Supreme Court.

The public and the media continued to remain engaged with the case. Increasingly, the public's sentiment was moving toward the Quinlans' position. The story had started off in a fairly straightforward fashion. Karen was the brown-haired, hazel-eyed girl—"Snow White," she was called by the newspapers—who had fallen asleep, and now her fate was being fought over by her (adoptive) parents, her doctors, and the courts.

Much attention was placed on her physical transformation. The picture that had come to define her was one from her high school, in which she embodied a wholesomeness that drew rampant interest in her ordeal. That picture, however, was dated, and what was available of her current state made for furious speculation. Her decorticate posture was frequently described in the court as "fetal" and "grotesque." Perhaps the most vivid description came from Julius Korein, a neurologist who at one point during his testimony described her as an "anencephalic monster."[39]

Anencephaly is an exceedingly rare congenital malformation in which fetuses do not undergo the development of their brains. Anencephaly had come under focus recently after a report from Yale–New Haven Hospital confirmed that several fetuses in their nursery born with anencephaly died owing to withdrawal or withholding of treatment after discussions with parents given the poor prognosis of these children.[40] These fetuses are mostly present in anatomy labs in formaldehyde-filled jars, and sometimes make terrifying cameos in embryology textbooks. "If you put a flashlight to the back of the head the light comes out of the pupils. They have no brain," added Korein, to further spur one's imagination. Perhaps this only added fire to the public's curiosity, with the media realizing just how powerful an image can be to shape public discourse. Much of end-of-life discussions centers on pain and suffering. Descriptions that were vile, painting Karen in an inhuman fashion, were employed to amplify her suffering and to demonstrate how cruel it was to unnecessarily sustain her. It was no surprise that the Quinlans were offered $100,000 for a picture of Karen. Some reporters even tried to infiltrate her hospital disguised as nuns.

The rules of optics also applied to the Quinlans. Very soon, they were able to tell their story most clearly by just being who they were—ordinary, loving, God-fearing parents who had turned their world around in the hope of seeking respite for their daughter. Flanked by priests, friends, and their lawyer, Paul Armstrong, they commanded a great deal of respect from the media covering the suit, who would always put an end to their cacophonous jostling when the Quinlans would start speaking. The doctors, too, carried themselves with dignity and were clear about the patient being their first—and only—priority. What then was remarkable about this case was its complete lack of villains.

Everyone, it seemed, wanted what was best for Karen, which meant completely different things for those involved. In many ways, this resembled what so many complex ethical situations look like in modern medicine, where several well-meaning people see the same truth in very different lights.

The close attention to the Karen Quinlan case gave everyday people a transcendent experience of what it was like to have a loved one stuck somewhere between life and death, and between being a person and something else. Everyday people read the newspaper not knowing what they would find out. They followed the Quinlans as they avoided swarms of reporters, went to court, all to hasten the passing of the daughter they so dearly loved. As the ordeal went on, and Karen's condition remained unchanged, thus, too, set in the despair, the weight, and the numbing pain that surely the Quinlans themselves were experiencing.

For the media, the Karen Quinlan case demonstrated that readers and viewers were interested in death and that the appetite for this story had a human element of multiple, varying levels. From the smallest New Jersey newspaper to the cover of *Newsweek*,[41] Karen was a daily fixture in print and on television. The quality of the coverage also varied significantly.[42] The *New York Times* not only devoted its general-assignment writers out of New Jersey and New York to the case, it also had its legal and religious writers cover it. Perhaps the writer who had the most expertise in this area was Joan Kron, who wrote a lengthy story for *New York* magazine.

What made that story so special was Kron's personal experience with the issue: She had had to make the decision to withdraw care from her sixteen-year-old daughter in 1968. However, much of the other coverage of the Quinlan case was distorted, either owing to a lack of understanding of the issues at hand, or in an effort to drive up readership with controversy. From the start, the Quinlan case had been incorrectly labeled as a challenge to the legal definition of death. While certainly a hot button and relevant topic, in the Karen Quinlan case, this was perhaps the only thing that all parties agreed on: that Karen was not dead, not by any present-day definition. Perhaps one notable absence also was the lack of any physician-writers addressing the case in the mainstream media. According to a report by the Hastings Center, "No medical writer covered the case. If that had been the case, hard questions about the significance of Karen's EEG might have been asked earlier, because it is medical writers—rather than legal, religion or general science writers—who have to date been most interested in and alert to the ethical implications of their species."[43]

Some physicians did weigh in on Justice Muir's ruling. In a *Washington Post* story that ran on November 24, 1975, Jack E. Zimmerman, a critical-care doctor at George Washington University Medical Center, not only stated that if Karen were in his hospital the doctors would have already removed the respirator, but said that the physicians themselves would have initiated the discussion much earlier than the several months it took for Mr. Quinlan to decide to raise that subject. Also criticized was Justice Muir's physiciancentric view on medical decision making, which seemed to be at odds with a statement published by the American Medical Association in 1973, in which their delegates stated that the decision to prolong life when recovery to normal functionality is not likely ought to be made by "the patient and/or his immediate family."[44]

According to Justice Muir, physicians were supposed to be advocates for their patients yet they were duty-bound to protect and prolong life. Physicians, more than the patient's family and caregivers, were considered to be the most appropriate advocates for patients. What was not taken into account was that physicians themselves could have their own biases and vested interests that could be discordant with those of the patient. Therefore, unlike other cases—such as that of Kenneth Edelin,[45] whose initial conviction for manslaughter after he performed an elective abortion in the sixth month of pregnancy was unanimously overturned by the Supreme Court[46]—no official physician body ever backed the position of the physicians involved in the Karen Quinlan case. This was in spite of the fact that Justice Muir's opinion provided great autonomy to physicians to practice and enact life-altering decisions based on their personal codes.

BY JANUARY 26, 1976, two months after Justice Muir's decision in the New Jersey Superior Court, the appeal process began formally in the New Jersey Supreme Court. Another two months after the arguments began, Justice Richand Hughes delivered the judgment of the court in the landmark 7–0 decision *In the Matter of Karen Quinlan, an Alleged Incompetent.*[47] This court was cognizant of the matter placed in front of it and what the scope of its ruling might be:

The matter is of transcendent importance, involving questions related to the definition and existence of death; the prolongation of life through artificial means developed by medical technology undreamed of in past generations of the practice of the healing arts; the impact of such durationally indeterminate and artificial life prolongation on the rights of the incompetent, her family and society in general; the bearing of constitutional right and the scope of judicial responsibility, as to the appropriate response of an equity court of justice to the extraordinary prayer for relief of the plaintiff. Involved as well is the right of the plaintiff, Joseph Quinlan, to guardianship of the person of his daughter.

The facts had not changed much from when the case first went to the courts, but the climate was different. There was additional debate about what "extraordinary measures" entailed. Sidney Diamond, a neurologist and state witness, while noting that continuation of the respirator should be maintained unless the patient was brain dead, stated that it would be unreasonable to provide blood transfusions or perform surgical procedures in the present situation.

The ruling also noted that the end of life landed at the intersection of law, medicine, and religion. While the religious beliefs of the plaintiffs were acknowledged and respected, the definition of life and the definition of death were within the purview only of medicine. The ruling noted that in spite of this overlap, there was no conflict.

In their conclusion, the court agreed with the prior trial court's views that Karen's present state did not amount to cruel and unusual punishment in a purely constitutional fashion, as her current state was not the result of any penal punishment, but rather a tragic turn of events. The court also agreed that while the Constitution allowed for free exercise of religion, it was not immune from governmental oversight, particularly with regard to the preservation of life.

It was Karen's right of privacy, though, that the court interpreted in a manner much different from the trial court. The Supreme Court opined that, given her poor prognosis, "no external compelling interest could compel Karen to endure the unendurable, only to vegetate a few measurable months with no realistic possibility of returning to any semblance of cognitive or sapient life." This right or privacy had previously been cited in the landmark cases *Roe v. Wade* (1973) and *Griswold v. Connecticut* (1965). In *Griswold v. Connecticut,* the State of Connecticut, invoking an old state law prohibiting the use of contraceptives, arrested a Yale professor who had started a contraception clinic. The court adjudicated that the law violated the "right to marital privacy," with one judge calling it "an uncommonly silly law."

The Supreme Court also overturned the prior court's decision to bar Mr. Quinlan from being Karen's guardian. The decision to allow a parent to be the guardian was meant to use the family's best judgment of what option the patient would exercise were they competent and able to communicate their wishes. According to this judgment, the state's incentive for preserving life dwindled as the prognosis became poorer. One of the biggest differences between this opinion and the prior really lay in introducing the patient and the family member into medical decision making. The prior court had stated that the anguish Mr. Quinlan would face might make it difficult for him to concur (which he was obligated to do) with the treatment plan of his physicians, thus making him an unsuitable guardian.

Therefore, in sum, Justice Hughes affirmed in this 7–0 decision not only that patients have a right to withdraw or withhold life-sustaining treatments, but that that decision could be made by their guardians if they were not competent to make such a decision. The ruling also stated that no criminal liability lay on physicians for following such requests. Such was how the case that has had the most influence on end-of-life care was decided. And it was in the wake of this ruling that modern end-of-life care began its life outside the shadows and for the world to see.

Criticisms of the ruling were few and far between. In a commentary in the *Annals of Neurology,* H. Richard Beresford, a neurologist, pointed out that "by concentrating on the issue of the use of the respirator, the court dealt only obliquely with the more general question of whether there is a lower legal standard of care for non-cognitive patients than for cognitive patients."[48]

But this criticism was unjust, as the respirator was the only life-sustaining treatment presented to the court and addressing the overall level of care permissible under law for the care of these patients may have required a lot of hypothesis testing. Needless to say, the vast majority of physicians and all physician bodies welcomed the ruling. The New Jersey Supreme Court had made a brave foray into end-of-life care and presented to the world a template of what might be appropriate in these situations.

After the ruling, the Quinlans went back to the hospital and had the respirator removed. Karen Ann Quinlan, far from not being able to tolerate coming off the respirator, lived for another ten years in a nursing home, until she succumbed to pneumonia in June 1985. Her mother was at her bedside. While the Quinlans had instructed Karen's doctor to not give her antibiotics, they had her fed with a feeding tube throughout her coma. Joseph Quinlan, the man who had waged a national campaign to have his daughter removed from the respirator, drove several miles every day over the decade she spent in the nursing home to visit her before going to work.

The true legacy of the Karen Quinlan case is still being felt, as it is echoed in court rulings to this day on a daily basis. Terri Schiavo was thirty-seven years old when she had a cardiac arrest at home, which left her in a persistent vegetative state. In her case, which involved the highest echelons of government, including then president George W. Bush, Terri's husband and legal guardian wanted to remove her feeding tube, which he said was her wish, while her parents opposed that. The Quinlan ruling formed the basis of the courts eventually ruling in the husband's favor. But more than the courts, the case changed how care was delivered at the bedside and how physicians discussed grave matters with patients and their families. Finally, it started to become clear what the rights of the patient actually were.

BETH ISRAEL Hospital was built in 1916 by Boston's growing Jewish community, not only to provide care for the growing Jewish immigrant population, but also to provide employment to Jewish physicians who would have difficulty getting jobs at other area hospitals. After starting off as a storefront dispensary working out of a mansion in Roxbury, the hospital quickly grew on the back of donations by the local Jewish community, and it eventually moved to its present location in the heart of one of the most competitive health-care zip codes in the country, Longwood, shoulder-to-shoulder with hospitals such as the Brigham and Women's Hospital, the Deaconess Medical Center, Boston Children's Hospital, New England Baptist, and, a bit farther down, Massachusetts General Hospital.

Mitchell Rabkin was only thirty-five years old when a search committee nominated him to be the CEO of the Beth Israel Hospital, in 1966.[49] He had little to no experience in administrative matters, but brought a unique blend of humanity and intelligence to the hospital. Over his thirty years as hospital president, surrounded by local behemoths, Mitchell Rabkin did more to make the medical system patientcentric than most. One of his lasting legacies was the formulation, in 1972, of the first-ever patient bill of rights,[50] which went on to be incorporated into state law. Among other now seemingly obvious proclamations, the bill of rights guaranteed patients the highest level of medical care regardless of their "race, religion, national origin, any disability or handicap, gender, sexual orientation, age, military status or the source of payment."

In August 1976, in the aftermath of *In the Matter of Karen Quinlan,* Rabkin published a guideline in the *New England Journal of Medicine* formalizing the process of deciding not to resuscitate patients: "Notwithstanding the hospital's pro-life policy, the right of a patient to decline available medical procedures must be respected."[51] While taking care of an "irreversibly, irreparably ill patient whose death is imminent," the responsible primary physician might initiate a discussion with the patient and the family to withhold resuscitation after discussion with an ad hoc committee that comprised caregivers from other specialties as well as physicians not directly involved in taking care of the patient. The patient was required to be "competent," in that he or she must be able to understand the relevant risks and alternatives, and not hindered by any factors such as pain, medication, or metabolic abnormality. It was also clarified that an order not to resuscitate would not result in any "diminution of necessary and appropriate measures for the patient's care and comfort."

Before the Karen Quinlan case and the subsequent ruling, according to Rabkin, whom I met for coffee, individual physician decisions ran the entire gamut of intensity: "Not only were there variable decisions, there were non-decisions." When faced with a patient unlikely to benefit from resuscitation, a doctor might tell his colleague, "If the alarm rings, walk to the phone, don't run."

Rabkin has a deep voice but a soft touch. When I asked him how the doctors in his hospital reacted to this policy, he told me, "They found it relieving, because the decision was not going to be entirely theirs. Physicians would now have input from the patients, their surrogates, and their colleagues.... Senior physicians were relieved in part because the house officers were not making decisions on their own, and the house officers were relieved because these were burdens." But the most important effect of this policy was that it brought end-of-life care out of the shadows. "We put it on top of the table," said Rabkin, where it could no longer be ignored.

In the same issue of the *New England Journal of Medicine,* another set of recommendations were presented which were not widely adopted. It was suggested that patients admitted to the ICU be classified on a scale of the intensity of treatment they ought to receive.[52] The assessment of which classification to assign the patient remained a prerogative of the physicians and nurses, and the role of patients and their families in this was at a bare minimum in this document. If a patient or family member did have any questions regarding how they or their loved ones were classified, the responsible physician was advised to "explain the treatment rationale to the person who raised the question."

The Karen Quinlan case, therefore, had cleared the way for patients to officially consult with their physicians and institute "do not resuscitate" orders for themselves. In the event that patients were incapacitated and unable to participate meaningfully in this decision, their family members could make that decision for them. No longer would physicians speak down to patients from above the clouds as God himself might be imagined to, but would descend to the patient's side and actually reach an agreement after a conversation.

DEATH HAS ALWAYS been a wellspring for spiritual exploration and existential extrapolation. The unanswerable questions raised by our disanimation have found many takers among scholars, philosophers, theologians, and storytellers. Given that death is perhaps the most significant event that can occur in anyone's lifetime, all cultures have formed elaborate and complex rituals that center around the end of life, much like rituals centered around birth. Many rituals allow a time for reflection and healing for loved ones, allowing them to find support among each other as they mourn an irreversible loss.

Medicine, too, is very ceremonial. When people come to the hospital, they get asked the same questions by countless different people. Physicians examine patients on rounds every day, not because they expect to discover anything new, but because that is something they do which only sometimes will yield useful information. The medicalization of death has led to the development of many modern rituals of death.

When a patient dies in the hospital, the pronouncement itself is very ceremonial in nature. During my intern year, I was working overnight when a nurse paged me that one of her patients had stopped breathing. I asked her if she had called a code blue, but she told me the patient had not wished to be resuscitated. She asked me to come pronounce her as having died. Having never performed a pronouncement before, I asked my supervising resident, who gave me a checklist.

When I walked into the room, the stillness was eerie. I followed the steps as they had been described in the checklist. I lowered the sheet from her face to reveal an elderly woman, pale as chalk with her mouth wide open and her eyes shut tight. I had never met her before. I searched for a pulse, and found none. I put a stethoscope on her chest and found her heart to be completely silent. Finally, to check whether her brain was functioning, I had to assess whether she was retaining any basic brain reflexes. I pried her eye open with my fingers. I poked the corner of her eye with my gloved finger to see if she would blink. Nothing else I had touched felt like the moist, gelatinous, and perfectly still eyeball of a freshly deceased person. She didn't blink, and therefore the ritual, one repeated for anyone who dies in the hospital, was complete.

Much like the overarching experience of patienthood, the end of life has been sterilized. For most of human history, death has been an intensely spiritual experience. Frequently, some religious figure, a pastor or a shaman, would be at a patient's side at the end to help make it a deep and meaningful experience not only for the patient but for their family and friends. Studies show that most patients have great spiritual needs and many derive strength from their faith.[53] These days, instead of a shaman, patients are surrounded by strangers in scrubs. Death—one of the most complex events that can occur in a hospital—is usually handled by the youngest physicians.

The most enduring ritual through the history of mankind when we are faced with the end has been to ask for a miracle. In ancient times, such a request would be directed to a religious figure who would go ahead with whatever incantation they had on their speed dial. These days this ritual is staged by doctors.

For patients who desire "everything," their last moments usually include a physician or nurse performing CPR on them, with the base of their palms, elbows locked. Such a scene can be quite grotesque. I vividly remember performing chest compressions on a patient who had been getting dialysis through a tube in his abdomen. Every time I compressed the patient's chest, fluid from his belly sprayed out. Very soon, my shirt was drenched in abdominal fluid, and the floor was so slippery that I feared losing my balance and falling face-first on the ground. I had been performing CPR for way too long, and my shoulders, my back, and my wrists were about to give out. I looked across, and there were at least four or five interns standing in front of me, looking on as if they were watching Mufasa die in *The Lion King* for the first time. I tried to indicate to them that I needed one of them to take over, but none of them would, or could, oblige.

Any physician you talk to will have such a story that refuses to leave them. Performing CPR on an actual patient, I learned many years ago, is not the same as doing it on a plastic mannequin. In medical school, that was how I was first taught how to do CPR, and that is how most people learn. The vast majority witness CPR on television, where it is depicted as a wondrously effective mode of resurrection. In real life, particularly with patients in the hospital who are already very sick, it can look a lot different. Leslie Blackhall was a resident in internal medicine in 1987 when she wrote an article in the *New England Journal of Medicine* describing what she told me recently "seemed like human-rights abuse." When she wrote "Must We Always Use CPR?," the pendulum had swung fully away from the patriarchy of yore: "Everyone got CPR back then and we watched incredible suffering from this. . . . Doctors were afraid they would get sued, or arrested, and some of them were [if they refused to perform CPR]." Apologizing for the graphic nature of her description, she told me about a patient she had to perform CPR on who had a tumor in the esophagus that was eroding into his aorta. "His entire blood volume was pumping through his mouth." At other times, she described having to perform CPR on someone already in rigor mortis, the contractures a body undergoes long after it's been dead.

While CPR would traditionally occur behind closed drapes, increasingly it has become a performance for family members to witness. Contrary to what was previously thought, families actually appreciate being able to see CPR be performed on their family member. When the psychological effects of such a sight were studied, to many people's surprise it turned out that family members had lesser anxiety and depression if they had been around to see that final Hail Mary enacted.[54] Yet that study, published in the *New England Journal of Medicine,* had a secret weapon. After the patient expired, the researchers had a protocol that involved debriefing the family and helping them in their bereavement. Yet when a death occurs in the hospital, frequently the family is quickly forgotten.

Between the dawn of time and only a few decades ago, almost everything we could do for people who were knocking at death's door was probably futile. The concoctions conjured, prayers professed, and practices performed were likely highly placebogenic, providing a portrayal of an effort to undo the course of the cosmos. Physicians had as little control as their patients. Yet the advent of then-radical interventions such as anesthesia, surgery, antibiotics, and mechanical ventilation all appeared to provide doctors an unprecedented ability to alter a person's trajectory, akin to yanking around a comet hurtling toward the sun. CPR, though, was the most dramatic of these interventions, primarily because of how dramatic a turnaround it could achieve.

While CPR has now been established in the public imagination as a miraculous intervention that can pull people from the jaws of death, a different and troubling aspect has also emerged. CPR is increasingly performed in sicker patients, and as patients get sicker, the outcome of CPR gets worse. Patients who now get CPR are more likely to end up needing more mechanical ventilation and tube feeding and to experience more brain damage than ever before. More than four of five elderly Americans with a chronic disease who get CPR die before ever leaving the hospital again, and only 2 percent live for six months.[55] And despite seismic advances otherwise, the past few decades have not shown any improvement in the survival of patients undergoing CPR.[56]

The reason people increasingly don't want CPR is not that they are afraid it will fail but that they are afraid it will only partially work. Patients are afraid that if CPR makes their heart start beating again, their brain will have to pay a huge cost. I was taking a medical history from a patient, a salesman for a car dealership, who started telling me about what he wanted in life. "If my heart stops, Doctor, just let me go." I looked at him and he seemed to be very clear and unwavering about his stance. "There are worse states than death."

This to me was emblematic of how in many ways modern medicine has come full circle. We started out doing everything we could to avert death, knowing that death was the enemy. In every medical decision and every megatrial, the only outcome that ever mattered was mortality. Along the way, though, in our pursuit to at best delay death, we have seen outcomes emerge such as vegetative states which are in many ways more horrendous and unnatural than even death.

I remember I was working in the hospital when I overheard two nurses talking to each other. They had both been taking care of a patient who had been in the hospital for a while.

"What happened?" one of them asked.

"She died," the other nurse told her.

"Oh thank God."

How Death Was Redefined

Much of medicine is pattern recognition. Radiologists look at CAT scans and X-rays as if they were tea leaves, a truth foretold. Pathologists peer down microscopes into a festive gathering of cells and discern the normal ones from the too-tipsy, too-inappropriate ones. In medicine, the patient is the cipher doctors have to decode. We absorb information that we gather from labs, imaging, physical-exam findings, and most of all, the patient's story (which doctors call history), and come up with our best-guess diagnosis. A single diagnosis, though, is rarely a good place to start, as too frequently doctors can anchor on their initial hunch and are not persuaded by subsequent discordant data to think of an alternate ending. But it was hard not to anchor when all I knew from the text message the emergency department sent me on my pager was that the patient was a thirty-two-year-old man who had suffered a cardiac arrest. In these long, dark winter months, there was only one thing that would ever send a young man to a hospital with a cardiac arrest.

Heroin addicts give many different names to their destructive muse—"brown sugar," "hard candy," "tootsie roll"—but perhaps the most fitting name was "dead on arrival" that morning. It is always hard to tell how tall someone is when the only time you see them is when they're lying on a hospital bed. But this patient was tall, and lean, too. Looking is probably the most underappreciated aspect of the physical exam. He was tall but not tall enough to have a disorder like Marfan's syndrome—a condition where patients have dilated aortas that can easily rupture. I often start with touching someone's feet, a way to establish a relationship and also get priceless information about the health of an organ far away from them—the heart. Feet puffy with fluid are a frequent sign of heart failure, while cold feet can represent a sign of the heart not doing a good enough job of pumping blood to the tissues. His feet were cold, but that was likely because we had him hooked up to a device purposefully keeping him cool. I did not see any track marks along his arms or on his legs, giving some credence to him being clean. His hair was neatly cropped, he was freshly shaven, and all his tattoos were old.

I met the patient's girlfriend at the bedside. Her straw-blond hair was tousled. She was harried, and half the glittery lettering on her T-shirt had fallen off. When I looked at her, it was if she had already told me half the story. Their relationship had been through some amount of tumult. After they had a child together, things got rough. He was jobless and his heroin habit was sucking life right out of his eyes. She threw him out of the house, and perhaps that was the kick he needed, as he got a job and moved away from the drug. A year of abstinence allowed him to put his life back on track, and she took him back in. "He was clean for more than a year. He had a good job, a stable relationship," she told me as her voice became increasingly muffled and inaudible.

She had just had the most terrible morning of her life. She woke up to find her boyfriend, a man very much on the road to repairing his life, unconscious in the bathroom, not breathing, surrounded by the telltale paraphernalia of heroin delivery. She called 911, which immediately dispatched ambulances. In the meanwhile, she gave some ineffectual mouth-to-mouth breaths, and some earnest but ineffective chest compressions. When EMS arrived, they found him in ventricular fibrillation, and after a few shocks they were able to bring his heart back into a normal rhythm. They strapped a bag mask on his face and hurried him to the closest hospital they could drive to.

In the emergency room, he was intubated and hooked up to a breathing machine and was wrapped in an apparatus that served to cool the body far below normal temperatures. Research has shown that patients who suffer cardiac arrest have better brain recovery if they are cooled to very low temperatures.[1] It consists of pads filled with chilled water wrapped around the chest and extremities that can be used to regulate the temperature of the body. While our normal core body temperature is around thirty-seven degrees centigrade, some patients with cardiac arrest benefit from temperatures as low as thirty-three degrees centigrade. Reducing the metabolic demands of the body gives it time to recover some meaningful function. After he was cooled, he was transferred to the ICU, where I then met him.

His girlfriend asked me how he was going to do. I told her that I did not know, and it was true. The cooling protocol lasted for forty-eight hours; we planned for him to first be cooled for about twenty-four hours and then slowly rewarmed. During this whole time, probes placed on his scalp were recording his brain activity. During the first forty-eight hours, it was essential that he not feel, because a sensation of the degree of cold that he was placed under would be excruciating. Patients on cooling protocol are therefore frequently paralyzed with medications. This renders the neurologic exam—the key to really assessing whether a patient's brain will recover—useless, clouded by the paralytics.

This was what I told the girlfriend and the patient's father, the only family that came to see the patient. But I did caution them against optimism; he had been down for God knows how long, and brains love oxygen. It was going to be the longest forty-eight hours of their lives. For our part, we were investigating whether there was anything else that might have caused the arrest. An ultrasound revealed that, miraculously, his heart was in perfect condition, his kidneys and liver had not taken a big hit, and he had no sign of an infection anywhere.

The next morning, the neurology team dropped by during rounds. It was more of a duo than a team: a neurologist and a medical student.

The neurologist was one of our most experienced on staff; he had been practicing for three decades, and his old briefcase looked like it hadn't weathered the journey as well as he had. The medical student accompanying him was lanky and sharply dressed. We, the ICU team, were running rounds in our workroom when they poked their heads in. Not many were welcome to disturb us as we ran through the list of patients, but this neurologist was an exception. Cognizant of our time, he was concise in his description: "The man is dead."

"What do you mean?"

"He is brain dead."

In spite of what the neurologist had said, we were not yet able to diagnose brain death in this patient, but I was delegated to go the patient's bedside. I walked into the room, and he lay on the bed, chest rising rhythmically with the ventilator, heart beating regularly with a crisp rhythm on the monitor. His cheeks were flush with color. He looked like many other patients sedated on ventilators in the ICU—perhaps better, because he was younger and had not seen a day in the hospital prior to this. But there was one difference: Though he didn't look it, he was deader.

I had seen a lot of dead people. None of them looked anything like him. His girlfriend anxiously asked me, "Is he dead?"

Her question really came out of nowhere and caught me by surprise. In medical school, and during residency, we are taught to diagnose disease, but never to diagnose life, or the lack thereof. The last fifty or so years have seen the very fact of death being decoded, defined, and subsequently decried and perhaps debunked.

I was still processing all the information in front of me. During the course of my residency, I had pronounced the deaths of countless patients. I had been told that this man had died, but I had none of the tools I needed to confirm the fact. His heart was beating, his wrist pulsating; I looked at his girlfriend and said, "I don't know."

BEFORE THIRTEEN-YEAR-OLD JAHI MCMATH came to Children's Hospital Oakland on December 9, 2013, she was a regular kid. Classmates from the E. C. Reems Academy of Technology and Arts called her a "quiet leader."[2] Her favorite color was purple. She had sleep apnea, a condition somewhat rare for children her age but increasing in prevalence given the rise in childhood obesity.[3] She went to the hospital for an elective surgical procedure: she was to have several structures, such as her tonsils, uvula, turbinates, and adenoids, removed from her nose and throat to help her breathe better at night. It was by no means a simple procedure, even though it was portrayed in the media as a "routine tonsillectomy." What happened afterward is still not fully known, as the hospital has been restricted by the parents from sharing information. Her mother reported that Jahi felt fine and even wanted a popsicle after the surgery. Shortly after, though, Jahi started to bleed from where the surgery was performed in her throat and was transferred immediately to the intensive-care unit, where she suffered a cardiac arrest.

On December 12, just three days after she came to the hospital, Jahi was declared brain dead by the physicians taking care of her. She fulfilled all the criteria for brain death, verified by external state-appointed experts as well. Her parents, though, refused to accept this assessment and implored the doctors to place a feeding tube and to perform a tracheostomy. The hospital denied that request. Jahi's parents went to reporters and took over the airways. They acquired funding and support from groups around America campaigning against the modern legal and medical definitions of death. They also petitioned to have Paul Byrne, a neonatologist committed to opposing brain death and transplantation, to carry out his own investigation, but the court refused this.

As the court battle continued, Jahi's body kept degrading. Her intestines started sloughing off and the only bowel movement she had for weeks was in fact the lining of her intestines passing out. Her skin started to break down, and her blood pressure and body temperature swung wildly without any control from upstairs. The court finally delivered its verdict, agreeing that Jahi was in fact dead and that the hospital had the right to release her body to the coroner. After Jahi's body was released, she was transferred to a nursing facility in New Jersey, the only state to allow medical care for patients declared brain dead, which continues to provide her body "life support" to this day.[4]

If death has changed from being an indisputable binary fact to a contentious amorphous idea, life remains ever more complex and harder to discern. Physicians deal with life and death, but they rarely cross the chasm from the simple and concrete to the complex and abstract. We have enough difficulty differentiating sick from not-sick.

Life has always been seen as a privilege, and human beings are thought to embody the highest form of life. Despite our close relationship with life, we have had some degree of difficulty pinning down just what it is that makes things living and unliving. Life's complexity makes it possible for it to mean different things to a biologist, a theologian, an astrobiologist, a mathematician, a physicist, an ethicist, a judge, a philosopher, a physician, and, well, a person, and therefore, quite shockingly, there is not a single agreed-upon definition of life. But certainly the lack of a single definition has not been for lack of trying.

Long before we understood even the very basic concepts of biology, human beings came up with schema to differentiate living things from nonliving things. A rough estimation of our perception of life before the advent of science can perhaps be seen in children. The youngest children assign both life and consciousness to all objects around them. As they grow older, they evolve through stages of "animism," a term coined by child-behavior pioneer Jean Piaget.[5] A child at the first stage of animism sees life and consciousness in a glass pitcher, but not when it is broken (or killed, as they are likely to characterize its unmaking). As children progress through these stages, they associate life with dynamic movement.[6] A bicycle is alive when it moves and not when it is stationary. Similarly, children also identify the sun, the wind, clouds, and fire as living and being able to feel pain and have self-awareness. Furthermore, while children know that animals are living, up to a third of those between eight and eleven years do not think plants are living beings, even though they recognize that plants grow. Such associations are not only a relic of childhood; emotional attachment can cause us to find life in inanimate objects even at older ages.[7]

Modern curricula for fourth graders mirror ancient beliefs about what constitutes life: Living things have the ability to grow and change, react to their environment, need some form of energy source, and reproduce.[8] Such a definition of life was also once offered in the television series *Star*

Trek: The Next Generation to the android character named Data, who riposted that fire, too, consumed, excreted, moved, metabolized, and grew, therefore meeting all the above features of life.[9] Perhaps it is not surprising then that fire was so widely worshipped in ancient times.

Another characteristic that is often associated with a living organism is the ability to reproduce. Herman Muller, German Nobel Prize–winning scientist, at a conference in 1959, stated, "I think the most fundamental property distinguishing a living thing—and that can therefore be used to define life—is its ability to form copies of itself."[10] However, molecules such as crystals can also grow in size and can pass down characteristics, but are not considered living organisms. Even beyond these exceptions, the use of reproduction as a fundamental aspect of life is troublesome on other levels: If I am stranded on a deserted island, without a serviceable mate, and therefore unable to propagate the gene pool, am I *unliving*?

As science evolved, the focus of the definition of life shifted to metabolism. Metabolism is brought about by a series of chemical reactions that occur in a cell that allow it to maintain and regenerate itself. To scientists in the middle of the twentieth century, metabolism was the key feature of life, leading John Bernal, one of the most famous and controversial British scientists of his time, to pronounce that life was "the embodiment within a certain volume of self-maintaining chemical processes."[11] The definition of life is perhaps of greatest significance to astrobiologists as they strive to go the edges of space to look for the minutest evidence of life. The centrality of metabolism was reflected in the three experiments that were performed on Martian soil by landers launched by NASA's Viking mission in 1976.[12] The first experiment tested whether water would be broken down by life-forms hidden in the soil to form carbon dioxide, and the other two experiments sought to elicit whether a reaction similar to plant photosynthesis (the breakdown of water into oxygen and carbon dioxide) would be produced after exposure to water. Surprisingly, all three tests were positive, but more advanced subsequent testing revealed no evidence of living organisms. To me the falsely positive metabolic tests reveal a fatal flaw in using metabolism to define life, as our understanding of what constitutes metabolism is restricted to that demonstrated in life-forms on Earth. Such an observation ends up assuming the centrality of carbon in organic life, which may be limited by our observation of the universe.

While Charles Darwin never proposed a definition of life per se, most scientists agree that Darwinian evolution is perhaps the essential characteristic of life. Errors, manifest as mutations, are the centerpiece of replication in evolution. Errors lead to progeny of different levels of fitness—some that are better adapted and others that are maladapted to their environments. Enough errors will result in the continual production and improvement of life until it becomes supra-Darwinian, in that it can cure genetic diseases that would otherwise wipe it out, and overcome genetic deficiencies that would govern the fitness of a particular organism. Based on this principle, the closest we have gotten to a pithy all-encompassing description of life is a NASA working definition that describes life as a "self-sustaining chemical system capable of Darwinian evolution."[13]

But even this definition has been attacked. Take viruses, for example, which cannot sustain themselves on their own, and are constantly looking for hosts to take over in order to use their machinery to make more viruses. The inability to come up with a definition that would cover organisms as small as viruses to those as large as the blue whale has led some to conclude that life exists only in our heads and there is no such thing as life.[14] Life as a concept represents a convenient way to represent organized and complex machines that exist naturally. In fact, Gerald Joyce—the scientist some credit with coming up with the NASA definition of life—thinks of life more as a popular idea than as a scientific one, which precludes it from being defined in a scientifically rigorous fashion.[15]

Perhaps one reason a satisfactory definition of life doesn't exist is that we keep finding life in new places. As we have removed our focus from gross features of living beings, such as eating, breathing, moving, and defecating, we have started observing the processes common to all living things. We have discovered that life exists on a spectrum, with complex multicellular organisms, such as animals and plants, on one end and the simplest of organisms, such as viruses, which border on the inanimate, at the other. This variance represents the journey of life, which transitioned from mere chemical reactions to chemical reactions that sustained themselves indefinitely in self-contained machines with error-prone reproduction that would allow for evolution to occur. The desire to define all forms in one equation, an obsession of theoretical physicists and mathematicians, may not, however, be exportable to biology.

But our definitions are only as limited as our specimens. Self-reflection, a truly detached understanding of one's own self, still eludes us, and might represent a higher form of development and evolution that we are yet to reach. It is one thing to know how cells live or die, but another thing to realize life in its entirety. Perhaps one day we will learn to comprehend life as an intrinsic property of all things that surround us, much as children do.

Life, however, is not just a concept to me when I am at work. Nor is it merely a concept to family members as they wait in the family room, hoping to hear from their doctors whether their loved one is going to live or die. As my patient's girlfriend asked me whether he was going to live, she was certainly not asking me whether his cells were alive, whether they were hydrolyzing water or replicating and self-organizing. Yet what she was asking me was not simpler. If anything it was even more contentious: When was a human being *alive,* and by extension, when was someone irrevocably and *irreversibly* dead?

TECHNOLOGICAL ADVANCES DURING the twentieth century, such as ventilators and cardiac resuscitation, seriously challenged the definitions of death that had hitherto been developed. These technologies made previously developed signa of death quite obsolete. There were even reports of patients who were seen to have a flat heart rhythm having spontaneous return of circulation, if only briefly.

The heart had always retained monarchy over the other organs and was thought to possess the throne of life, and yet, increasingly, scientists began looking at the organ between our ears and behind our eyes in search of signs of life. But while the development, in the nineteenth century, of the stethoscope and the electrocardiogram (ECG), which could be obtained by simply placing a few wires on one's body, had opened up a special window into the heart, no such tool existed for the brain.

While for a long time the brain was thought to merely be a device to cool the body off from the heat produced in the heart, our understanding of brain function would change dramatically in more recent times.

The electroencephalogram (EEG), developed in the first half of the twentieth century, filled that void. EEGs are a series of waveforms generated by probes that are stuck to one's head, which capture the variations in electrical activity in the brain and graphically print them as waves. It was to the brain what the ECG was to the heart, a cipher that translated the complexities of the organ it studied into meaningful information. EEGs hold the key to the management of sleep and seizure disorders, and perhaps most importantly, the EEG was the first objective test to help differentiate whether someone's brain was dormant or dead.

The EEG provided another tool for the clinician to be more confident when declaring someone's demise, something that had become quite difficult in patients who were mechanically ventilated and who didn't experience the classic lurch as they gasped their last. However, the advent of technology served only to "maintain the look of life in the face of death," said neurologists writing in the *Journal of the American Medical Association*.[16] Instead of looking for flatlining of the ECG, indicating motionlessness of the heart, a sight still ever pervasive on television, physicians began looking at the EEG, looking for the rippling brain waves to fall silent,[17] and physicians started suggesting mechanisms to diagnose death using EEG.[18] The seminal contribution that connected what was seen on the EEG to what was going on at a tissue level in the brain came from two French physicians. In 1959, Pierre Mollaret and Maurice Goulon published a paper titled "Le coma dépassé," which means "the irreversible coma," and described the cases of twenty-three patients with silent EEGs and who were fully comatose, who on autopsy were found to have undergone extensive necrosis in the brain.[19] These findings formed the template upon which modern death would be established. Yet even this knowledge of irreversibility failed to convince the authors themselves to withdraw care from these patients who so ostensibly *looked* alive.

However, excitement about using EEGs to diagnose death with certainty was tempered by cases where patients recovered complete

function after brief silent periods on the EEG.[20] The EEG was also affected by conditions such as injuries, medications such as barbiturates,
and cold body temperatures, all of which could make the interpretation
of an EEG difficult. Yet there was immense pressure to use the EEG to
provide prognostic information to help physicians and family members
who looked on as patients continued to persist for long periods of time
on mechanical ventilators.

Several groups, to fill this void, came up with their own EEG-based
criteria for death. At Massachusetts General Hospital, neurologists came
up with their own criteria for death, based on the EEG as well as taking
into account other factors such as absent reflexes, absence of breathing
for sixty minutes, and laboratory results that ruled out any reversible
causes.[21] However, several aspects of this definition were unsatisfactory.
Having someone not breathe for sixty minutes was tantamount to killing
them if they were alive prior to the test. As a result, Richard Schwab,
who developed this criterion, gave a duration of twenty-four hours in an
interview he gave to *Time* magazine in 1966, demonstrating that even
he did not have a fixed rule about how long patients should be monitored
before they should be declared to have passed.

Around this same time, other tests were being developed to assess
brain damage. In 1956, a test was developed to assess the flow of blood
going to the brain using X-ray techniques. A paper describing six patients who were on mechanical ventilators, unable to breathe or demonstrate any brain reflexes, was published in an obscure Scandinavian
journal and wasn't recognized until fairly recently.[22]

Progress during the first half of the twentieth century had defini-
tively moved the chalice of life from the heart and lungs to the brain.
Nevertheless, death continued to be defined as the moment the heart
stopped beating. This continued to be the case even after the advent of
cardiopulmonary resuscitation, which showed that cardiac arrest was
not a terminal event, but something that could be intervened in, and reversed. Even Pierre Mollaret, the man whose work with EEGs would
influence how death would be redefined, did not yet "consider any proposed criterion as absolute."[23] This was in spite of the fact that the brains
of these patients were known to literally have turned to mush and were

seen at times to be "flowing like gruel through the burr holes." The first human EEG was recorded in the 1920s by Hans Berger,[24] but several decades passed and the EEG's insights into human life and death remained buried in medical journals without any scientific consensus on how to appropriately use it to diagnose death.

HENRY BEECHER NEVER received any formal training in anesthesiology, yet he held the first endowed professorship in anesthesiology in the United States in 1941. He had a PhD in chemistry, yet his research was in epidemiology. He never studied bioethics, yet he became perhaps the most influential bioethicist of the twentieth century. And most importantly, Beecher was not a neurologist, yet he would become the man responsible for defining death from a neurological perspective.

Born Harry Unangst in 1904 in Kansas, Beecher never got along with his father, a night watchman, and changed his name to Henry Knowles Beecher. After receiving his education and doctorate in chemistry, Beecher switched over to medicine and completed medical school and surgical training in Boston. While he did research initially in physiology, it was his experience as a military surgeon that started to pull him into previously unexplored areas within medicine. His experience with warriors who did not report pain in spite of being injured led him to make forays into the placebo effect, and he was one of the first people to introduce the concept of comparing medications with placebos rather than nothing at all in clinical trials.

It was Beecher's advocacy for the subjects of human experiments that cemented his place as one of the pioneers of bioethics. While he wrote about the general principles of human experimentation as early as 1959, it wasn't until the mid-1960s that he brought the horrors of human experimentation into direct focus for both the general public and the medical community.[25] In front of journalists at a conference in rural Michigan, he presented eighteen cases where an egregious breach of ethical standards had occurred.[26] His assertion that these practices were the norm in leading academic centers made for national news and made Beecher the target of a mountain of criticism from other physicians. When Beecher submitted a review of these cases to the *Journal of the American Medical Association,* the paper was rejected, but it was subsequently published in the *New England Journal of Medicine,* in 1966. The paper, "deemed the most influential single paper ever written about experimentation involving human subjects,"[27] detailed twenty-two cases in which patients had not adequately consented, were given inappropriate treatment, and were subjected to bizarre and harmful procedures.

Beecher was also attuned to the issues surrounding patients in irreversible comas. In a paper about the ethical problems surrounding the "hopelessly unconscious patient," he wrote of the need to define life and both what constituted death and when it was thought to occur in a world where the lungs and the heart had been superseded by the brain.[28] Beecher defined human life as "the ability to communicate with others," but he was wary of their right to be let alone, threatened as they were by "organ snatchers." He went on to recommend that the only means to overcome the impasse was to gather the "collaborative and precise thinking of physicians, lawyers, theologians and philosophers." Soon after the publication of this paper, in 1968, Henry Beecher would have his wish granted. And not only that; it would be he who got to lead the group that came to put together the modern definition of death, which holds to this date.

After Beecher wrote a letter to him in 1967, the dean of Harvard Medical School announced the creation of a committee that would address the question of when in fact someone was dead despite them having a heartbeat or being able to breathe on a mechanical ventilator. Beecher was appointed the chairman of this committee, and he put together a veritable "Ocean's Eleven" that included three neurologists, a neurosurgeon, a transplant surgeon, a law professor, and a medical historian, among others. Perhaps the committee understood that their findings had implications not just for medicine but for how death at large might come to be viewed by ordinary people. Their report was published in the *Journal of the American Medical Association* on August 5, 1968,[29] and not even its authors could have foreseen that it would come to influence the social, legal, medical, and philosophical facets of death in ways no single document had before it. Significantly, for better or for worse, it would introduce the term "brain death" into the common vernacular.

Before one can understand brain death, though, it's important to understand how the brain itself works and imparts our construct of life and consciousness. The brain and the spinal cord together form the central nervous system, and the brain can be divided largely into the brain stem and the "higher brain," which is made up of the two famous gnarly cerebral hemispheres that occupy our skull. The brain stem is the series of structures that emerge from the hemispheres and connect the brain to the spinal cord. The brain stem has several important functions: it carries all the nerve tracts coming from the spinal cord into the brain. These tracts are responsible for movement and sensation in all the structures below the face, such as the limbs, and the muscles that cause breathing to occur. The brain stem is also where the cranial nerves, those responsible for taste, smell, vision, and the movements and sensation of the face, connect to the brain. The brain stem also participates in the formulation of perhaps one of the most striking features of what we colloquially refer to as life—*consciousness*.

The Harvard committee spoke as much to the legal community as it did to the medical, keenly aware of just how far behind the courts had been left by advances in medical resuscitative science. The committee pointed out that "the law makes the assumption that the medical criteria for determining death are settled and not in doubt among physicians," noting that courts continued to rely on the antiquated use of vital signs to determine death.

The Harvard committee's primary purpose thus was to "define irreversible coma as a new criterion for death" and to "determine the characteristics of a *permanently* nonfunctioning brain." The committee focused on four major characteristics that constituted brain death. Firstly, unresponsiveness to any and all external stimuli, including severe pain and noise, was required. Secondly, a brain dead patient could not exhibit any movement or independent breathing. For patients who were on ventilators, directions were provided to perform an "apnea" test, which would allow doctors to test if a patient was truly not breathing without allowing non-brain-dead patients to be deprived of precious oxygen the ventilator was providing. Thirdly, none of the body's reflexes would be reproducible. There are several inbuilt and automatic reflexes that humans have evolved or failed to devolve over their evolution. A contraction of the thigh muscle in response to a sudden strike on the kneecap, causing the leg to jut forward, represents a spinal reflex; an automatic blink when the eye is touched and the constriction of pupils in reaction to light reflect cranial or brain reflexes. Absence of both spinal and cranial reflexes was considered necessary to define death. The fourth and final criterion required that the EEG remain flat for ten to twenty minutes, without any perceptible response to painful or noisy stimulus.

The committee recommended that physicians who were neither taking care of the patient directly nor involved in any subsequent transplantation perform these tests. The first three criteria are bedside tests that any physician can perform, but neurologists are best trained to do so. Notably, these three criteria would be present in anyone whose brain *stem* alone had suffered a massive and irreparable injury. The fourth criterion, the EEG, was reflective of electrical activity in the brain's cerebra, denoting purported higher brain function. It was required that these tests be performed twice, twenty-four hours apart, and in the absence of conditions such as hypothermia or an overdose with medication that would depress the nervous system. A patient who met all four of these criteria was not a person anymore. That patient was in fact a cadaver and was to be declared dead.

The Harvard committee propelled this new concept of brain death to an international audience in a way that had never been done in the past. The legacy of Henry Beecher, though, the man who chaired the formulation of these recommendations, is complicated. Beecher is considered by many to be the founder of modern bioethics. I, like countless others, was first exposed to Beecher's *New England Journal of Medicine* paper as part of bioethics classes. Yet recently declassified documents reveal a side of Beecher perhaps not even his staunchest opponents could have ever conjured.

Before Beecher was an ethicist, he was one of the top scientists working for the US military and the CIA in the development of drugs that could be used to enhance interrogation and torture.[30] According to reports declassified after Beecher's death, he was leading the CIA's program trying to use drugs such as mescaline and LSD to break down victims of torture. Not only was he conducting experiments on unwitting patients at Massachusetts General Hospital, which he described as "an almost ideal setup here in Boston for study of this problem," he also collaborated with physicians who had worked with the Nazi regime, including one Wehrmacht general who had performed lethal experiments on inmates in concentration camps. He even went on to recommend to the US Army's surgeon general to use drugs such as LSD "as tools of biological warfare." Ironically, it was the CIA's move away from using drugs to enhance torture and toward behavioral techniques that were pioneered by the psychologist Donald Hebb that dried up Beecher's funding, pushing him into making his mark as an ethicist.

Beecher was also principally responsible for popularizing the term "brain death." This was in spite of the fact that he was warned against using the term by fellow committee member and Nobel Prize winner Joseph Murray.[31] While the authors clearly imply that patients who are brain-dead are in fact *dead*, many in the public continue to be confused. What the committee sought to do was to define death in a way reflective of modern technological artifacts, yet because brain death is not merely called death, to many brain death is a different type of death—a softer death.

As THE MCMATH case played out in the background, our team went ahead with trying to understand whether our patient himself was in fact alive or dead. This was a delicate and meticulous process, and a part of me was nervous about whether the renewed attention to brain death on news networks would affect how this case would play out. We waited a few days until the heroin levels in his body became undetectable, which could be a potential confounder to the entire process. Even as we waited, the initial signs (or lack thereof) were ominous. The patient lacked all reflexes, and his blood pressure would sometimes go up to the 200s and then plummet to being almost undetectable. Sometimes he had a fever, and sometimes his body would need to be warmed with a heated blanket called a bear hugger.

Knowing that the end was near, the patient's father took me aside one day to the family room. It was a small windowless room, painted orange, with half a dozen chairs packed in and a stack of gossip magazines available just to distract from the pain. He sat next to his son's girl-friend, who was wearing a black T-shirt and jeans. I never saw him with-out his platoon hat. He was a proud veteran who had seen more than any single man's share of death, but never something like this.

"Is he going to make it?" he asked me. I was rehearsing in my mind the lines I had thought I would deliver. I hoped to be noncommittal, I hoped to buy time so that we could carry out the due process required, but I ended up doing none of that. I told him that while we couldn't be absolutely certain, there was almost no chance that his son would be able to recover brain function.

He lowered his head and took off his hat. His son's girlfriend was cry-ing. He looked at her and then turned to me. His gray eyes were weary, tired of weeping. He was a proud man, brought to his knees by senseless tragedy. He cleared his throat, hoping his voice wouldn't break. "He has suffered his whole life. . . ."

His words disappeared into the ether and hung around like ominous, heaving nimbus clouds. During medical training, countless hours are spent teaching medical students and trainees how to talk. They are taught how to take histories, how to elicit sensitive information, how to synthesize and present data, but mostly they are taught how to break bad news. After years of workshops and classes teaching communication skills, talking was perhaps the only thing I knew. Physicians are en-dowed with an immense and special knowledge that they mostly love spewing out for the common man. If you see a group of physicians, the one talking the most is usually also the most senior, with medical stu-dents usually the ones too timid to utter a word. Perhaps the reason phy-sicians talk, and overtalk, especially in meetings such as this, is to kill the silence. Silence, to the control-loving doctor, represents an uncer-tainty and chaos that physicians fear, that *I* feared.

At that moment, the air seemed to get heavier and the walls felt like they would cave in. My instinct was to comfort, to distract, to provide inert information, to say something—*any*thing—but I continued to hold my vigil. My pager rang, its shrill piercing tone interrupting my thoughts for a millisecond, throwing my discipline off balance. There were times when I found myself stuck in a meeting or a situation I didn't particularly enjoy, I would send a page to my own pager from my smartphone. When the pager rang after a ten-or-so-second lag, I would make a serious face, silently place it back, and move out with a sense of feigned purpose. Sometimes, the residents would exchange these "rescue" pages, allowing fatally bored friends an out. Was this my get-out-of-jail card?

I entertained the thought for the time it took me to mute it. I was curious to find out what the page was about but I fought that urge, too. I left my pager in its holster. For perhaps the only time during that day, I let the heavy quietness sink in. Words gave way to the sound of deep breathing. Instead of listening, I now found myself looking, intently.

The reason silence was so important for me to master was that I frequently found myself talking to people who were confused, overwhelmed, and alone. I would find patients and family members who seemed as if they were looking for subtitles to appear at the bottom of the screen as I continued harping on in what must have sounded like a foreign tongue. So many times, discussions at the end of life seemed more like a negotiation than a discussion. Silence allows emotions to equilibrate, and balance to be achieved between what the heart wants and what the mind knows. I imagined the father was thinking about his son, picturing all the memories he had accumulated of his only child, in one finite moment. When he spoke again, his voice was not tethered, and he appeared to finally understand what he really wanted to let me know about his son: "I don't want him to suffer any longer."

THE HARVARD CRITERIA came out at a time when death had experienced a resurgence in public life and popular culture. Driven by technology, spiced up by politics, and muddied by fear, death was a constant fixation, selling newspapers, books, movies, and music records starting in the 1960s. Starting in this decade, death experienced a "rediscovery," with interest from academics from all backgrounds including sociology, history, anthropology, law, ethics, and, of course, medicine.[32] At the same time, though, as death became more and more central to popular and academic discourse, fewer and fewer people actually witnessed death, as, increasingly, death and dying were shifted to the confines of hospitals.

After the Harvard criteria were published, the definition of death came into great focus. Previously, when decisions about the declaration of death were presented to courts, judges most frequently relied on *Black's Law Dictionary,* which defined death in unhelpful, inane ways as "the cessation of life; the ceasing to exist" but went on to be somewhat more specific in describing it as "a total stoppage of the circulation of the blood, and a cessation of the animal and vital functions consequent thereupon, such as respiration, pulsation, etc."[33] Prior to the Harvard criteria, courts took "judicial notice" of this definition, assuming falsely that it was an issue that enjoyed wide consensus within the medical community.

The Harvard criteria were instrumental in highlighting changes in the landscape of death, and their influence started to be felt in courtrooms fairly soon after the paper was published, in 1968. In fact, death was such a heated subject at that time that it took less than a year for this definition to be translated into a legal entity.

As recently as 1967, just a year before the Harvard criteria were published, in a case adjudicating the grisly murder of Della Pyke, who was seventy-nine years of age, by her husband, Isaac, eighty-five, who pumped five bullets into his wife's head before committing suicide with a single one to his own, the Supreme Court of Kansas defined death as the "complete cessation of all vital functions" even if these were maintained artificially.[34] Yet in 1970 the Kansas legislature became the first in US history to pass a statute that formally recognized the newly proposed definition of brain death in addition to the traditional vital-signs-based definition. This statute, although quickly adopted by several other states, including Maryland, New Mexico, Virginia, and Oklahoma, was plagued with wording that was both confusing and troubling. In the Kansas statute, vague colloquial language was used to define death after "attempts at resuscitation are considered hopeless" and it "appear[ed] that further attempts at resuscitation and supportive maintenance [would] not succeed." Furthermore, the Kansas statute used brain death as a means to define the demise of patients awaiting organ transplantation, further appearing to rouse suspicions that the only basis of redefining death was to facilitate organ harvest.

The Kansas statute was the recipient of both criticism and approbation, with one lawyer stating that the "statute was biased towards facilitating transplant surgery" and "could harm public respect for medicine"[35] and others calling it a "bold and innovative stand."[36] The Harvard criteria were not immune to criticism either, and several holes were poked during the 1970s in their edifice:[37] the use of the term "irreversible coma" to describe brain death was criticized for adding further confusion into what was already an esoteric milieu. The committee also incorrectly stated that spinal reflexes were absent in brain dead patients, which was subsequently known to be incorrect, as spinal reflexes (such as the jutting of the knee on tapping) can maintain an intact loop even with a totally destroyed brain and brain stem. While tests such as the apnea test were recommended to assess for the absence of breathing, and measures to rule out other sources of depressed brain function were recommended, no clear guidelines were then presented for clinicians about how best to reproduce these in their patients.

In 1978 the American Bar Association offered its own version of a "model" statute, which represented a step forward from the convoluted language of the Kansas statute.[38] This new statute stated quite simply, "For all legal purposes, a human body, with irreversible cessation of total brain function, according to usual and customary standards or medical practice, shall be considered dead." This model statute, adopted by several states, while recognizing brain death as a legal entity, had little to say about how the diagnosis of brain death would be made. The supposed link between the definition of brain death and transplantation was further strengthened by Illinois, which used the language provided by the American Bar Association but included it as an amendment to the Uniform Anatomical Gift Act, originally passed in 1968 to streamline organ donation. Increasingly, toward the end of 1970s, as more states adopted statutes accepting brain death as a legal entity, the language of these documents became increasingly problematic. Wyoming, for example, chose to define brain death by the loss of "purposeful activity of the brain as distinguished from random activity."[39] This opened another Pandora's box; the Harvard Criteria; required the absence of any and all brain activity, without any ascertainment for purposefulness. It was also not clear whether such an assessment could be made with available technologies.

It was at this time that President Jimmy Carter set up a panel to address ethical issues in medicine, and the first topic they chose was in fact to define death. The President's Commission for the Study of Ethical Problems in Medicine and Biomedical and Behavioral Research, set up in 1978, published its first report, "Defining Death," in 1981.[40] Headed by lawyer and ethicist Alexander Capron, the commission included individuals from a wide variety of backgrounds, including theologians. In this report, recognizing the state-by-state variation in the legal definition of death, the panel presented the Uniform Determination of Death Act (UDDA), and suggested all states enact it as their statute of death. The UDDA proposed both the continued use of the traditional circulatory definition of death to be used but also included "irreversible cessation of all functions of the entire brain, including the brain stem" as a definition of death.

The UDDA was quickly adopted by most states as their legal statute of death. While the UDDA legitimized brain death as a legal form of death, it did not dwell too long on how exactly to define brain death. However, an appendix was published in the report that talked briefly about the different tests that could be used to diagnose an absence of cerebral function and circulation as well as brain-stem reflexes.

To this day, the definition of brain death has not been changed after initially being devised in the 1960s. Yet it continues to be an increasingly controversial issue. If headlines on television and newspapers are to be believed, people who are declared brain dead recover all the time. Yet most of these patients have been declared dead without the full extent of testing being performed. If anything, it is a relief not only for physicians but for families when patients do meet the criteria for brain death. For as I was about to learn in my case, a vast gray expanse exists between when patients are in a coma and when they experience brain death.

AFTER THE MEETING with my patient's family, I went back to my work area in the ICU and told the rest of the team how the family was responding to unfolding events. News of the meeting had already reached my colleagues, and there was a new face sitting at the table. She was middle-aged, with spectacles dangling from her neck. She was a nurse working for the organ bank. Knowing where the situation was moving, the nursing staff had already called them. The nurse was overwhelmed, shuttling among hospitals from one brain dead patient to another. "There is an epidemic of heroin out there," she told us, with young men falling to the drug like moths around a fluorescent flame. The ever-elusive dragon was drawing people into its toxic cave by the hundreds, leaving them looking like hollow, threadbare frames.

We had yet to talk to the family directly about organ donation, and it was perhaps a bit early, given that we were still waiting for some of the confirmatory tests to be performed and interpreted. Yet the organ-bank people were here not to talk to the family, but to talk to us.

Organ donation has always been a very sensitive area. Tens of thousands of people around the world owe their lives to livers, kidneys, lungs, or hearts that they were not born with. In many diseases, transplant is the only "cure" that doctors can offer, and donor organs continue to remain perhaps the scarcest resource in the world. While people's knowledge about transplantation has been increasing, the rate of transplantation has actually remained largely unchanged for at least the past few decades.

Even the decision to initiate the discussion about organ transplantation is fraught with difficulties. Physicians who are treating the patients are wary of coming across as not being invested in the treatment and care of the patient and may have a conflict of interest. The last thing I would want is for my patients or their families to think that I have some sort of ulterior motive to acquire vital organs by withdrawing lifesaving treatment.

Physicians are also not always fully abreast of the criteria for declaring brain death. A study in 1989 showed that only about a third of physicians and providers who ought to have known about brain-death criteria actually did.[41] Despite its exposure, brain death is fairly uncommon outside of a neurosurgical or neurological ICU, where most patients with severe brain injury are admitted. Even among patients with traumatic brain injuries, the most common cause of brain death, the number of patients who develop brain death is going down, although a recent spike in brain deaths has occurred due to the opiate painkiller epidemic.[42] There are also minor variations between different hospitals about the exact procedure and the tests required for patients to meet brain-death criteria.[43] The organ-bank nurse actually told us very clearly that she wanted no one from the team to initiate the discussion before she and the social worker did.

That discussion, though, still seemed far away for my patient. Before we could do any testing, we waited for the opiates to disappear from his urine. When they did, in a few days, we performed EEGs that were completely flat, congruent with our clinical assessment that he was likely brain dead. When we performed the apnea test, the patient never started breathing while he was off the ventilator. By most standards, our patient was brain dead, but the specific hospital policy required another test to be performed—a CAT scan of the brain vessels to look for absence of blood flow to the brain. Yet, while the CAT scan can assess if blood is flowing to the brain, it does not say anything about the function of the brain.

As this process ensued, the family was practically living in the hospital. When I went to the cafeteria during my long night shifts, I would see them camped out in the family waiting room in their pajamas. I encouraged them to get some rest, to not forget to take care of themselves as they lived through this ordeal, but they wouldn't budge. While they were certainly hoping for a miracle, that somehow he would wake up and say hello, and that this would be some sort of twisted dream, it seemed more likely that they wanted to be around when the inevitable end occurred.

In spite of the fact that his brain had suffered a massive injury, my patient's organs were actually doing fairly well. His heart was pumping, his kidneys were filtering, his liver was synthesizing. Amid this tragedy, the fact that he might be able to provide a priceless gift to a few other human beings gave me some hope. But time was critical: his heart rate was very variable, his blood pressure labile, his temperature alternating between high fevers and shivering depths. We were desperate to move ahead with some definitive answers.

But we were only starting to realize that we were knee-deep in uncertainty, and the CAT scan only made things worse. The CAT scan showed that there was no blood flow in the arteries, but some movement was seen in the veins. What did this mean? Did the venous flow represent anything meaningful? Just the alternating compressions of the ventilator could cause enough of a change in chest pressure to account for some movement of blood in the veins. Also, blood flow to dead tissue should be of no consequence. The radiologists were initially uncertain but then came forward to declare that the findings met brain-death criteria. But my ICU attending was less certain. Anxious from previous murky situations, aware of the simultaneous national controversy hounding television screens, and perhaps sensitized by the radiologist's initial hesitancy, she decided that the patient did not fully meet brain-death criteria in spite of all testing and clinical-exam findings pointing toward it.

Perhaps this encapsulated the inherent tension that exists between physicians and their patients and their families. Behind the curtain of our doctorspeak, we were struggling with uncertainty. Even within our team, none of us was sure about what exactly was going on and what we could make of all the data we were dealing with on the back end. The family, too, was struggling with uncertainty. They saw their loved one in bed, looking seemingly alive, but without any of the features they had come to associate with him. Every time they spoke to one of us, they were hoping for some clarity. On our end, we understood the need to provide tangible and coherent information without falsely shrouding the inherent ambiguity that went into our assessment.

This new dash of uncertainty was like a stab in the dark for the family. In our team huddle, we also included the organ-bank nurse, who had sat in meetings such as this more than almost anyone else in the room. "Follow your protocol," she insisted—and not your gut, she implied. When we finally went up to the family again, as a team, we told them that while not quite there, their son was on the cusp of brain death, with no chance of meaningful neurological recovery. Having said that, however, he was not yet brain dead. . . .

The father, the patient's health-care proxy, did not dwell too long. He had certainly been waiting all these days to be given some tangible information about how his son was doing and seemed to have a clear idea about what his wishes would have been were he able to vocalize them himself. "He wouldn't want to go on like this," he told us. His son's girlfriend hugged him, burying her face in his jacket. It seemed to me like they hadn't really known each other too well before this. And now it seemed that the young man who had brought them together would not be around for much longer.

What I saw in his face was not pain, but relief, a sense that finally his son would stop suffering. He didn't know exactly what was coming, but he knew what would not be there anymore: the ventilator, the beepers, the EEG probes, and the procedures. In many ways, this was simpler, the way he had always perceived death to be. As we turned around to leave and let them have some time to themselves, we contemplated when to perform the so-called terminal extubation, the final disconnection of the patient from the ventilator. I was in the process of taking off my sanitary gown and gloves when the girlfriend surprised me with a question itself steeped in finality: "He always wanted to help others. Will he be able to donate his organs?"

I was wholly unprepared to answer this question. As he was not brain dead, I had thought it was futile to even talk about transplantation at this time. Unable to declare him brain dead, how could we fulfill this one final wish? I was relieved when my attending spoke up: "Yes, there is a way."

Indeed, there was a way. For, lest we forget, there was still another way people died: when their hearts stopped beating. Cardiac death, one would be safe to presume, was a death so simple a child with a finger on the wrist could pronounce it. And yet, I urge caution, for if preceding controversies are any indication, even cardiac death has not survived unscathed the heightened scrutiny placed on the end of life.

When the Heart Stops

None of our organs is as linked to life, both literally and symbolically, as is the heart. It has always had a special relationship with emotions and feelings, which are attributed to it to this day. Who knows when this first started—when a poet's heart raced as he stole glances at his lover, as a group of hunters ran away from a carnivorous beast to avoid being the hunted, or in moments of deep silence, when the rhythmic beat of the heart is the only thing that remains, like the ticking of a clock.

In ancient times, the heart was not only the center of emotions; it was also the thought to be the organ most central to life. Per the *Ebers Papyrus,* written in 1500 BC, not only did the heart cause the circulation of fluids such as blood, sweat, and semen throughout the body, it also doused the human body in the vital spirit, the essence of life. Contained within these texts was also perhaps the first clinical description of heart failure.[1] Knowledge gained in ancient Egypt spread throughout the world, and their baton was passed on to the ancient Greeks.[2]

Greek medicine is said to have started with Aesculapius.[3] His staff, entwined by serpents, remains a ubiquitous symbol of medicine and healthcare. The snakes, in fact, represent the nonvenomous snakes that would mill around in numbers in his temple, one of many purported cures that pilgrims from far and wide would travel to partake.

Chief among his mentors was Hippocrates, considered the father of medicine. Born on the island of Kos in 460 BC, Hippocrates was the first to separate medicine from its otherwise tightly bound cousins: magic, religion, and philosophy.[4] The heart was of particular interest to Hippocrates, yet even he couldn't fully pin down where human life resided, with some writings attributed to him pointing to consciousness being a construct of the brain and others suggesting that the spirit and emotions lay in the heart. Therefore, the cessation of blood circulation, up until the mid-eighteenth century, was considered the one true hallmark of death.[5]

As medicine became more objective during the seventeenth and eighteenth centuries, physical signa were used to diagnose the absence of life and included abortion of circulation and breathing, the development of rigor mortis, a drop in the temperature of the body and dilation of the pupils and the anus.[6] However, several of these were quite fallible. Low blood pressure and shock can frequently result in the pulse being very difficult to palpate. Several conditions, such as stroke, can cause the pupils to dilate. Spasm and catatonia can frequently mimic rigor mortis. Patients who nearly drowned or were left out in the cold would frequently have very slow heart rates, their body temperature would be very low, and they would be stiff from the cold, making them more likely than others to be "apparently dead." These loopholes led the *British Medical Journal* to posit, in 1885, "It is true that hardly any one sign of death, short of putrefaction, can be relied upon as infallible."[7] It was thus that putrefaction, the decomposition of the body after dying, became a "gold standard" to diagnose death with complete certainty in the seventeenth and eighteenth centuries, yet most deaths were pronounced prior to the commencement of that decay.

More than at any time before, during the nineteenth century people became obsessed with cases of so-called premature burial, where people

who were still alive were incorrectly ascertained to be dead and therefore buried alive. It was thus that the notion of "apparent death" became
extremely arresting to the public. Even Edgar Allan Poe found the topic
"too entirely horrible for the purposes of legitimate fiction." In his
story "The Premature Burial," written in 1844, he described this practice, which occurred "very frequently" and, even in Poe's macabre universe, represented "the most terrible of these extremes which has ever
fallen to the lot of mortality."[8] He told several tales of mostly beautiful
young women who underwent surreptitious sepulture after entering a
state of suspended animation wherein the usual mechanisms characteristic of life stopped.

The leading medical journals of the time, the *Lancet* and the *British
Medical Journal,* frequently carried reports of patients who had been declared dead only for that diagnosis to be refuted. These mostly occurred
in patients who entered states of "hysterical trance" or "lethargic stupor."[9] In a letter to *Scientific American* in 1896, a Mr. Williamson from
London offered his experience with "several authenticated cases" of apparent death, "a state that resembles real death so closely that even the
most experienced persons believe such a person to be really dead."[10] Such
was the depth of this state that "not even the most experienced physician,
coroner, or undertaker can distinguish a case of apparent death from
real death, neither by external examination nor by means of the stethoscope, nor by any of the various tests which have been proposed."

Elaborate tests with almost no scientific basis were developed and
publicized to confirm whether someone was in fact dead.[11] It was hy-
pothesized that those in a state of apparent death had entered a state
called anabiosis, where "life exists only as a possibility of revival."
Most reports of those who endured a premature diagnosis were contentious, and their subjects were never documented to have been examined by an experienced physician. In fact, one physician in 1896
investigated the resurrection of a local boy and found out that the whole
story—about the boy first being chronically ill, then being declared
dead, and then waking up prior to being placed in his coffin—was
made up.[12]

Bills were passed to observe corpses for longer in mortuaries;[13] also developed were escapable "safety coffins" and crypts. Tests to confirm death were developed to be employed above and beyond the signa that had been used since the time of Hippocrates. These tests were much more invasive and quite grotesque: bodies were scalded with hot water or had sharp instruments or stimulants such as mustard probed down their noses to elicit a response. They were submerged under water to look for bubbles representing respiration.[14] Ammonia was injected under the skin to look for signs of inflammation. Some advocated inserting pins into a body through to the heart with a flag at the external end; if the flag waved, it was taken to indicate that the heart was still beating. "Foubert's test" actually involved the chest being cut open with a scalpel and a finger inserted to feel whether the heart was still beating.

Even though death has been our constant companion, the battle to diagnose death, even with the advent of advanced diagnostic technologies, has not died down. If the Jahi McMath case is any indicator, the diagnosis of death—or life, depending on your perspective—remains as harrowing as it was in the stories of Edgar Allan Poe.

The advent of stethoscopes and ECGs made monitoring of cardiac activity much easier. However, the reliance on using the cessation of heart activity to declare death ended in the 1960s after the Harvard criteria were published, when another advance in medicine would finally spur physicians to take adjudicating the moment of death seriously. Many in history, such as Aristotle, had held that the passage from life to death was a blurry and gradual one; this view was shared by contemporary leaders such as Thomas Starzl, the first man to perform human liver transplantation, in 1963, who described life as a "declining curve,"[15] slowly leaving the individual as they approached death. Organ transplantation proved to be a game changer not only in discarding antiquated ideas about death but forcing physicians to face head-on the ethical and legal ramifications of defining objectively when an individual was in fact not an individual anymore. A year after Christiaan Barnard transplanted the first human heart, in 1967, the editors of the *Journal of the American Medical Association* editorialized that "physicians rather than barristers must be the ones to establish the rules."[16]

BEFORE THE TWENTIETH century, a surgeon was only as good as how fast his hands were. Anesthesia and hygiene gave surgeons the one thing they had always been short of—time. And with time, the horizons of surgery spread to include transplanting organs from one human being into another, but it was a process of trial and fatal error. Mathieu Jaboulay, a French surgeon who along with Alexis Carrel helped develop the science of stitching blood vessels together, was the first to attempt organ transplantation in human beings.[17] In 1906, he transplanted two patients with a kidney each from a goat and a pig, but made the ruinous flaw of connecting the wrong vessels. Both of Jaboulay's patients, of course, died shortly thereafter. In Kiev, a surgeon named Yu Yu Voronay attempted to reverse the suicide attempts of six patients who had ingested mercury, which causes severe kidney failure. However, all six patients' wish to end their lives overpowered Voronay's endeavors, and they all died regardless.

After some of the early deficiencies in transplant surgery were overcome, surgeons began realizing that the immune system of patients who received kidneys from donors would put up a massive fight against this unknown invader. The human immune system trains its entire life to detect cells and materials that lack the signature of the host system, and therefore are considered foreign. The immune system's xenophobia would reject the palpably foreign organ, unleashing a Death Star–esque response that would almost certainly result in the host dying. While this immune response was averted successfully by Joseph Murray, who transplanted kidneys between identical twins in 1956,[18] there was as yet no durable way of transplanting organs between most of the world's populations, who did not have a conveniently identical twin. While some ambitiously tried whole-body radiation to suppress the host's immune system, it was the advent of immunosuppressant medications such as azathioprine that helped dampen the immune system and allowed for long-term acceptance of donor organs.

During the development of transplantation, surgeons realized that the success of transplantation, especially when taking from a dead donor, was how quickly the organ was harvested after the demise of the donor. Some surgeons, such as Guy Alexandre, in Belgium, did not wait for consensus and created their own criteria to decide whether someone was dead.[19] While some organs such as kidneys could be extracted from living donors, there were many organs that couldn't be taken without killing whomever the organ belonged to. Even kidneys were more frequently taken from the recently dead, owing to the dearth of living donors.

People have been dying since the dawn of time, but never before could someone's death be a source of actual life. In death, by donating one's organs, people could bequeath hope and life where there would have been none. Perhaps this drove people to define death in a way that was not merely philosophical but could be empirical, reproducible, and infallible. Even a single man wrongly declared dead could jeopardize the otherwise benevolent mission of organ transplantation. However, the absence of a true definition didn't stop many surgeons from testing the frontiers of surgery at the end of life.

Christiaan Barnard didn't take the traditional road to surgery stardom, which usually led through the operating rooms of one of the preeminent academic medical centers in either the United States or Europe. But this didn't stop him from dreaming of conquering the greatest of all challenges—the transplantation of the human heart. Growing up and studying in South Africa, the Afrikaner didn't have the pedigree that other surgeons of his time had, nor did he have the extensive research experience of surgeons such as Adrian Kantrowitz, who worked in Maimonides Hospital, in Brooklyn, and had perfected his technique of heart transplantation on hundreds of dogs in the lab. Kantrowitz perhaps came closest to crossing the chasm in 1966, when he got a call in the middle of the night. He was to transplant a heart from a child with a flat EEG into another child with multiple congenital heart defects. But his scalpel was tempered by colleagues who implored that he wait until the donor child was *dead-dead,* by which they meant that his heart stopped beating. After the child's heart eventually stopped, an hour later, Kantrowitz opened his chest only to find the heart to have already started degrading. It was unsuitable for transplant.

However, Barnard was serious about wanting to be the first man to perform heart transplantation, and when he received the "perfect" donor heart, it was under the most tragic of circumstances. Denise Darvall was twenty-five and was driving home after watching the film *Doctor Zhivago* on December 2, 1967, along with her parents and brother. Their journey was interrupted when they decided to get a caramel cake from a local bakery. Denise and her mother were crossing the road when they were run over by a drunk driver. Denise's mother died on the spot, while Denise herself was knocked into the gutter, fracturing her skull. She was taken to the hospital emergently and hooked up to a mechanical ventilator, but her chance of neurological recovery was deemed to be nil.

Physicians at the hospital told Edward Darvall, Denise's father, that there was no chance his daughter would recover neurologically. As he digested the fact of losing both his wife and daughter on the same day, doctors also informed Edward about Louis Washkansky. Louis was fifty-four, a Jewish man from Lithuania, who was dying of congestive heart failure from diabetes. Edward consented to having his daughter's heart donated, and the very next day, Denise and Louis were in operating rooms, side by side. Barnard led the surgery, with twenty other surgeons, and after five hours of operating, zapped electricity into Louis's newly transplanted heart to make it start beating in its new home. Louis Washkansky became the first man to live with someone else's heart beating in his body, but not for long. Just eighteen days after the surgery, he succumbed to pneumonia. Barnard wasn't even in the country when Louis died, as he had started his ascension to international superstardom. Three days after Barnard's surgery, Kantrowitz in Brooklyn became the first person to transplant a child's heart, but this child lived for only another six hours. Nevertheless, Barnard had won the race. However, his subsequent contributions were negligible, as it was other surgeons who continued to improve heart transplantation, transforming it from a curiosity to a reality for thousands of patients.

There was, however, one big difference between how Barnard

acquired his heart and what Kantrowitz had tried previously. Unlike Kantrowitz, Barnard didn't wait for the donor's heart to stop beating on its own, and on his brother and fellow surgeon Marius Barnard's urging, he injected Denise's heart full of potassium chloride, a powerful toxin that paralyzed her heart, effectively "killing" her. While this dark secret was revealed only in 2006, decades after the momentous surgery, it perhaps reflected the sort of tension that existed at that time.

Transplantation had already destroyed the previously held "decentralist" theory of life, which posited that the soul permeated not one but all of the organs, cells, and humors that made up the human body.[20] In fact, the inability to transplant the brain is perhaps the biggest factor in making it clear that life truly is a central process that resides within the confines of the brain and its nervous extensions that permeate the entire body. As surgeons battled their dual instincts of protecting dying patients from harm and trying to help those who would benefit from fresh organs, the need to be precise about the moment of death became more pressing than ever before.

BY ITS VERY nature, brain death is messy, amorphous territory. As our struggle with my heroin-overdose patient in the ICU revealed, there are many patients who do not fully meet brain-death criteria yet are almost certain to have no recovery of their vital functions. Confirming with stethoscopes and heart monitors that the heart had stopped beating almost harked back to a romantic time where death was simple and uncomplicated.

As the concept of brain death grew and spread around the world, it became abundantly clear that there were many patients who did not fit neatly into the prepackaged criteria that had been devised by the Harvard committee and refined by the president's commission. ICUs were chockablock with patients who were otherwise healthy but had experienced a terrible injury that had left them on the verge of death—but were not quite there.

To shield these patients from ravenous surgeons and prevent death from becoming a twisted free-for-all, the Uniform Anatomical Gift Act, passed in 1968, proposed what is now known as the dead-donor rule.[21] The act and its subsequent revisions have declared quite simply that an organ can be procured only from someone who is already dead. Furthermore, the act of the donation should not result in death (i.e., the procurement of an organ should not kill the person donating it). The dead-donor rule was put in place to protect patients, and it was promulgated even before the modern definition of death came to be.

The dead-donor rule comes into play mostly for patients who are not dead enough to be quite brain dead, such as my patient. There was also a series of cases in the 1990s that involved patients or families who wanted to donate organs in spite of the donor not being brain dead. Recognizing that there was a large group of patients who were going to the grave with perfectly healthy organs and who had consented to transplantation, the University of Pittsburgh devised a protocol for organ donation from patients who weren't brain dead.[22] Their protocol stated that if a patient were to remain breathless and pulseless for two minutes after being taken off the ventilator, the patient could be declared dead, and therefore could become a legitimate donor. It wasn't clear how they had come up with the magic number of "two." Others, such as the Institute of Medicine, expanded the requirement to five minutes.[23] The tension at the heart of these arbitrary durations was the onset of "warm ischemia,"[24] a process of decay that starts as soon as the organs of the body become devoid of meaningful blood circulation.

My patient was taken to the operating room the next day. Transplant teams from three hospitals had flown in. After conditions were optimized, his breathing tube was taken out. It emerged covered with viscous mucus and was thrown into the waste bin. And now the surgeons, the residents, the anesthesiologist, and the technicians held a vigil. After a little over two minutes, scalpels were drawn. After his chest was cut open, the heart was found to already be undergoing the initial changes associated with irreversible decay. The surgeons looked on to the lungs and found them unsalvageable. The liver, too, seemed to be beyond repair. They were left only with a pair of kidneys.

When I heard the news, I was both heartbroken and angry. After seeing his son go through so much, his father had only wanted him to have a peaceful death. Yet he "died" on the operating-room table with not a single familiar face near him. And I was frustrated that while he could have had his wish to donate his organs and give others a renewed shot at life, the strange twisted logic of the brain-death criteria disallowed us from being able to do that either.

The average American lives for 2,481,883,200 seconds.[25] But it is the handful of seconds after one dies that might be perhaps the most important and hotly contested ones in our lives. As we learn more about the final few seconds of our lives, and the first few of our death, we are finding things that nothing in the past could have ever prepared us for.

I NEVER KNEW Charlie well. The first time I had met him was when he was rolled up to the ICU in a gurney. In addition to him, the bed was laden with monitors, with medical charts, with IV fluids and medications hung on poles waving around like flags in a gale as the rickety apparatus moved on through the hospital corridors. There was one man pushing the bed forward, and another desperately holding on to the mask on Charlie's face, bagging oxygen as he ran along. The entire contraption looked like a hastily put-together flotilla ricocheting through cascading rapids.

Charlie and his sister never got along. They lived close to each other, both single, both in their sixties, yet the only times they met were when one or the other was in the hospital and they got a call from a doctor or nurse. Charlie had Chronic Obstructive Pulmonary Disease (COPD) from years and years of smoking cigarettes. Even as his COPD continued to get worse, even when he couldn't get up from his couch to go to the bathroom without getting short of breath, even when he became permanently dependent on an oxygen tank, a fire hazard itself that he lugged around, he never stopped smoking.

I read through his chart; this was perhaps his fourth admission for pneumonia in the past few months. Patients with COPD tend more than others to have infections in their lungs, but this seemed suspicious. The mystery did not persist for long: a high-resolution CAT scan of his chest revealed a cancerous mass eroding into his airways right where he had been having these recurrent infections.

When I first called Charlie's sister, I actually had to convince her to come to the hospital. Even when she did, she preferred to stay outside in the waiting area and had me come outside to talk to her. She asked me how Charlie was doing, and I told her we thought he had lung cancer. She took a deep breath. I asked her how that made her feel, and she let out a deep sigh. "I want you guys to give him a shot . . . a real shot," she told me.

We did. We splayed his veins with broad-spectrum antibiotics. We put in a chest tube to drain the cancerous fluid accumulating in his lungs. We kept trying to optimize his ventilator settings. His blood vessels became increasingly leaky, and fluid filled his legs and his lungs. Everything came to a head one day: His blood pressure inexplicably spiked. His heart was weak, and was unable to push blood through the impossibly high blood pressure in his vessels. Before we could meaningfully bring his blood pressure down, his heart went into cardiac arrest.

A code blue was called, and we pumped him full of drugs to kickstart his heart. The nurses pounded his chest as I arranged a rotating queue of CPR performers. Fifteen minutes into the code, I paused to check his rhythm. He had a feeble pulse, and the heart monitor was registering a normal "sinus" rhythm. One of my colleagues called Charlie's sister, who never even bothered to show up.

Days went by and we just couldn't get him off the ventilator. I called his sister every day and she never picked up her phone. One day, the nurse told me that a woman was waiting outside and wanted to speak to me. I walked outside to find Charlie's sister. She told me she had gotten my voice mails. She told me she just didn't have the courage to reply or come over. Who knows what had gone on between the two siblings, but it was not enough to diminish the sense of loss she felt now as she found herself staring at the inevitable. I told her we were still struggling. We had confirmed the cancer diagnosis and that it had spread throughout his body.

She stared at the ground in silence. "You gave him a chance, Doc. He hated his oxygen pump. I doubt he would want to be hooked up to machines the way he is now."

"I understand. . . . We can disconnect him from the ventilator if you feel that is what he would have wanted. We will make sure he is comfortable and pain-free."

She looked on in silence. "Do you think he will last long without the ventilator?"

"Not too long," I told her.

"Then I will come see him when he has passed. Give me a call, Doc."

She turned and left. I don't think she wanted me to say good-bye.

I went back inside and told the nurses about what had transpired. Everyone felt relieved. The last thing anyone wanted was to be doing CPR on Charlie's bony, flailing chest again. I put in the "DNR/DNI" order in the computer. We cranked up the morphine to keep him comfortable and pain-free and took out the tube. Surprisingly, he continued to breathe on his own, though his brain never really woke up otherwise. I was working on a computer just outside his room when I heard an alarm go off, an unswerving monotone that usually occurred after an ECG lead came off by mistake, but in this case did so because the heart had actually come to a standstill. Perhaps an hour ago, this would have been the spur to mobilize the unit to perform CPR, but now that he was DNR/DNI, we all just stood there from behind the glass door, looking at the final few wayward crests and artifacts on his ECG as it petered to a standstill.

After a few long minutes, I stepped inside his room, and silenced the alarm. I placed a stethoscope on his chest and heard nothing. I heard no air pursing through his decrepit, tar-filled airways. I pressed on his eyeball but did not elicit a blink reflex. My pager went off, and it seemed like we were getting a new patient from the emergency room. I pulled the white sheet up to his face, but it exposed his feet. The sheet was only long enough to cover either his face or his feet. I chose to cover his feet, leaving his face exposed. I lathered my hands with hand sanitizer and made my way out. I went for the nearest telephone and called Charlie's sister. I told her that Charlie had died. Her voice was shaky, and for once she sounded unsure about what she ought to do. I convinced her to come in.

After I hung up and was poring over the computer, I noticed something out of the corner of my eye. In the top right corner of Charlie's

ECG monitor, a green light was blinking. His nurse was standing in his room, staring into the monitor, transfixed. He turned around and saw me looking right at him. I walked up to the glass door and saw, unmistakably, a rhythm on the heart monitor.

I had never seen anything like it. Neither had the nurse, an ICU nurse who had been working in the trenches for at least ten years. I went into his room and checked for a pulse, and for sure he had a thready, faint pulse. His blood pressure, though, was almost undetectable, and I could not elicit any brain-stem reflexes; his eyes were still closed and his lungs were barely moving. A part of me was thrilled—I had seen something I had never imagined was possible. And yet I was also mortified: I had told Charlie's sister that he had died and I had no idea how she would react when she found out that her brother was in fact not dead.

Before I could resolve my turmoil, it was resolved for me. His ECG went flat again, this time for good. Moments after we had Charlie moved to the morgue, I did what every physician desperate for answers, awash in incredulity, would do: I searched for it in the internet's repository of medical research—PubMed. And it was only then that I first learned about the Lazarus phenomenon and how it has complicated the age-old declaration of death by cessation of heartbeat.

LITTLE IS KNOWN about Eleazer's life, but much is known about his premature death. Known today by his Latinized name, Lazarus was a follower of Jesus and had demonstrated a special devotion to his cause. In the Gospel of John,[26] when Lazarus fell ill, his two sisters had a message delivered to Jesus to come see him. By the time Jesus came to Lazarus's hometown of Bethany, near Jerusalem, Lazarus had been dead for several days. Undeterred, Jesus went up to his freshly put-together tomb and told his sister, "He that believeth in me, though he were dead, yet shall he live." Jesus proceeded to have the stone covering the mouth of Lazarus's tomb removed, and said a prayer. Moments after, "the dead man" emerged from the tomb, "his hands and feet bound in bandages, and his face wrapped with a cloth."

The advent of continuous monitoring of heart activity at the time of death has revealed the exceedingly rare but mind-boggling phenomenon of autoresuscitation, called the Lazarus phenomenon, wherein patients who have lost their pulse mysteriously regain either a palpable pulse or some electrical activity on the ECG monitor. Usually this phenomenon occurs within a few minutes after a pulse is lost, and most of these folks die in any case soon thereafter.[27]

The Lazarus phenomenon, however, may be more common than we think. It is well known that autoresuscitation is widely underreported in the scientific literature, and the reasons doctors don't want to talk about it are many:[28] Physicians and responders feel terrible and incompetent if they declare someone dead or stop resuscitative efforts only to find that patients spontaneously recover some function. Providers may also be wary of medicolegal consequences of such an episode, as well as the emotional effects such an event might have on family members.

The Lazarus effect reflects how death is observed differently in modern society. Because death is occurring away from homes and away from communities, it is shrouded from view. At the same time, death is being increasingly detected with electrodes, whether they be stuck to the scalp or the chest. Physicians are now looking at waveforms as the representation of life. These waveforms represent the transmission of electrical impulses through human tissue. The significance of these waveforms as it relates to human life and not just cellular life remains badly characterized. The president's commission made it clear that they were less concerned "if life continues in individual cells or organs" but were focused on the "integrated whole" that comes to be when the complex multilevel machinery functions in unison to animate the organism.

Another way to think about death might be through the act of killing. The act of killing is the most heinous of crimes, and has been considered the most abominable of acts through all time and among all societies. What is it about murder that makes it wrong, one might ask? Is it the seizure of personhood, the erasure of consciousness, or the annulment of activities that we associate with life? If a deranged psychopath shoots an innocent bystander right at the top of the spinal cord, leaving them paraplegic or in such a deep coma that they retain all consciousness but are unable to even move an eyebrow, is that murder? Or if someone hurts another individual in a way that they retain their ability to breathe on their own, feel pain, and partake in the regulatory functions of a living organism without retaining any vestige of the person they were before their injury—is that murder? If both are on the spectrum of killing, which one is worse?

Perhaps the "cleanest" and most visibly unambiguous death is one via decapitation. Throughout history, decapitation has been the purveyor of a death so certain, so absolute, that I daresay no one has ever bothered to check a pulse on a body without a head, or poked the eyes of a head without a body. More so than perhaps any other form of death, decapitation enacts the sharpest distinction between an organism that is living and one that is dead.

Knowing academics, I am not wholly surprised that there is no consensus among bioethicists, philosophers, and neurologists as to whether even a decapitated organism is in fact necessarily dead. To explain it in a way that people can actually understand what it means, brain death has frequently been called "physiological decapitation."[29] But those pesky scientists have even taken the previously self-evident truthiness of death out of decapitation. In an experiment that might even put some of the egregiously morbid experiments of yore to shame, monkeys were decapitated and their decapitated heads were transplanted onto the previously decapitated bodies of other monkeys that had been artificially maintained.[30] The investigators showed that the transplanted heads maintained consciousness for up to thirty-six hours.

Watching the television show *Game of Thrones*, one would never realize the philosophical questions raised by the heads that are frequently scythed off from the bodies that sustain them. Yet decapitation has digestible parables that shed light on personal identity and life. Dwell briefly on the monkeys whose heads were detached from their bodies and then artificially sustained. It is natural to feel that those heads, especially if they are conscious, carry on the life and identity of the original organism. What then of the bodies they leave behind? Are they not alive, too, given that they can be brought to breathe and pump? If so, instead of killing, decapitation resulted in the multiplication of life, not its subtraction.[31]

What then of my patient, the one who overdosed on heroin? When exactly did he die? According to our present medicolegal system, my patient went from being alive to being dead within the sixty or so seconds after his ventilator was taken out. Yet I would argue that he died almost a week before, in the early morning when he stopped breathing in his girlfriend's bathroom after overdosing on heroin. Legally, though, he was alive, even though his brain stem exhibited no responses and he wasn't able to take a single breath of his own.

The present paradigm of brain death is perched on a precipice. While errant journalists have proclaimed the collapse of its foundation, what has kept the modern definition of brain death steady has been the complete and utter absence of any single episode of a reversal of brain death. Imagine then my surprise when I received an e-mail from a neurologist, part of a large research consortium, who claimed to have demonstrated the first-ever reversal of brain death. Not only that, he had presented these results at a leading neurology conference. As I clicked on the attachment, it was knowing that a single reliable observation could turn around everything we have learned about death over the past century.

JONATHAN FELLUS IS a neurologist who, per his account, first became interested in studying patients who were brain dead after he and some of his colleagues were contacted to see a young woman from a prominent family from overseas. "We quickly realized none of us had ever seen what brain death could look like five months after the event," he told me. At the behest of the family, his team started treating this patient with "nutraceuticals and electric stimulation," and he reports that her EEG went from "essentially flat-line to a robust and differentiated pattern." He seemed to be much vaguer about whether there was any actual clinical change in her condition, writing to me that the patient began to "apparently follow commands by turning her head" and "seemed to raise her thumb." Throughout her "treatment," though, the woman remained dependent on a ventilator and never opened her eyes.

The unnamed patient described in Fellus's case report was a twenty-eight-year-old female who was brought to the hospital after a cardiac arrest. She overdosed on antipsychotic and antianxiety medications and after thirty minutes of CPR was able to regain a pulse but none of her brain function. She was declared brain dead, but her family wished to continue treatment given religious convictions. New Jersey is the only state in the United States that allows for brain-dead patients to continue to receive medical care if the patient's family wishes it on religious grounds. In any other state, there is no such thing as a brain-dead person, for they are considered to be deceased corpses.

I first heard of Fellus when I was talking about brain death with one of my colleagues, who told me about how Fellus, a cousin of his, was working on research that showed that brain death was not in fact *irreversible*. The poster that Fellus's group presented at the neurology conference described the group meeting the girl a month after the cardiac arrest. It was an unusual poster: there were several typos and words were capitalized and bolded for emphasis, something almost blasphemous in academic publications.[32] The EEG was actually not flat; it demonstrated some activity, though of unclear significance and thought to be artifact. The group treated the patient with a combination of electrical therapy, multivitamins, and psychotropic medications for six months.

The group reports that after six months of treatment, they were able to reverse brain death, claiming boldly how "one counterexample may destroy a theory." But what exactly were they able to reverse? The patient had an increase in activity on the EEG, though certainly not representing any meaningful activity, and had a "slight pupillary response to light." That's it. I reread the poorly written and comically inept report a few times, as I could hardly believe this was all there was. Months after my conversation with Fellus, when I was doing some follow-up research, I found that he had been found guilty of having inappropriate sexual relations with a patient and was forced to pay millions in damages and hand over his medical license.[33]

EEGs and ECGs don't give us any information about the life of the organism. A blip on an ECG may mean that there are some cells in the heart that stubbornly continue to contract despite the annihilation of most of their brothers and sisters. Such is true also of the EEG, which could demonstrate deflections even if a few errant neurons continue to emit signals.

Even as there has been such an emphasis on drawing an absolute line between life and death, the struggle to do so on a granular and individual level continues to this date. The president's commission perhaps inadvertently acknowledged this even as they sought to rigorously delineate life: "The dead do not think, interact, auto regulate or maintain organic activity. . . . What is missing in the dead is a cluster of attributes, all of which form part of an organism's responsiveness to its internal and external environment."[34] What exactly is the threshold for the cluster to become significant was not so well detailed.

We live in a world where our knowledge of biology has expanded exponentially what we understand about life. Human life, however, is not a merely biological construct. Just because a few neurons continue to fire, or a few cardiac muscle fibers continue to contract, doesn't mean that someone is alive. Perhaps this has been one of the darkest legacies of the last century. Instead of redefining death, we have redefined life. Life, a word which is used frequently to describe a flourish of activity, an explosion of vitality, is now being conferred on bodies permanently intubated with not a flicker on an EEG strip.

When Death Transcends

Perhaps no son had ever tested the love of his mother the way David had. Well into middle age, he never married, had several children, never had a job, spent a few years in jail, and continued to live with his mom. He had been addicted to heroin since he was in his early twenties and was consuming around a bag a day before he came to the hospital. When social workers and physicians inquired about why he continued to use heroin, he told them, "I feel like me when I use heroin." One of his daughters once told of when she had found him at home after an overdose and thought he had died. She loved him more than anything else in the world.

The years of heroin abuse had taken a great toll on David's body. He had HIV and hepatitis C, both from using intravenous drugs. His kidneys had broken down a long time ago and he was on dialysis thrice a week. His heart was also bearing the brunt, dilated and ballooned, too weak to keep blood moving in the right direction. His blood pressure was so poorly controlled that even though he was on six medications, it still remained out of whack. Some would say things couldn't possibly get any worse for him, but my years in medicine have convinced me that there is no such thing. Things can always get worse.

He came to the hospital with abdominal pain, something he had experienced dozens of times without any discernible cause being found, but this time things would take a different turn. By the time David made it from the emergency room to the medical floor, he was short of breath, huffing and puffing, and his blood pressure was twice that of normal. His already weak heart could not pump against such high pressures, and fluid started to accumulate in his lungs. The team rushed to his aid, obtained an urgent X-ray, and pushed medications to help lower his blood pressure as fast as they could, but they were not able to keep pace with his deterioration. Sensing impending doom, they called a code blue to rush the anesthesiologists to his room to emergently connect him to the ventilator. Of course, their worst fear also was soon realized—David lost his pulse. CPR was initiated.

The next five minutes, probably the most crucial minutes of his entire life thus far, saw doctors and nurses giving him critical drugs and pounding on his chest. Miraculously, given how bad his overall state of health had been, the team was able to recover his pulse. As soon as they did, they rushed him to the ICU. He was seizing before they paralyzed him with medications and hooked him to a cooling apparatus. David was cooled for the standard forty-eight hours before the neurologists came in. When weaned off the paralytics and the sedatives, David had only some basic reflexes left, such as his eyes constricting in response to light, indicating brain-stem activity. But he presented no other responses, which meant that he had likely lost all higher brain function. Just based on this information, he had a nine out of ten chance of continuing to be in a vegetative state or to maintain severe disability.[1] However, when the neurologists factored in the seizure activity he experienced immediately after his cardiac arrest, and which he kept having even when he was being cooled, they wrote in their note that the likelihood of a poor outcome was 100 percent.[2] Witness to this revelation were several of the patient's immediate family members, and other relatives who had flown in.

The patient's mother and the rest of the family were devout Christians, and David's room was decorated with religious mementos. They were clutching onto their faith for strength both figuratively and literally, in the shape of crosses and small figurines. With an ICU social worker and the hospital chaplain by her side, the mother had simple questions about her son's condition that none of us had answers to. Does he feel? Does he hear? Does he know? Does he sense us around him?

The team met with the family and expressed how they felt that another cardiac arrest in David's present state would almost certainly be a terminal event and CPR under those circumstances would be completely futile and potentially harmful. The family agreed that CPR should not be done. In their view, another cardiac arrest would represent an act of God that would help transition David from this world to the next.

Short of CPR, though, the family wanted everything done. Even without any hope of him recovering at this point, David's family wanted to do whatever was available to sustain him. They had the team make a hole in his neck and place a breathing tube down to his lungs and a feeding tube through his stomach.

Given that David obviously couldn't communicate, we relied on his family to transmit his wishes, but at many times, they had difficulty separating their story from his. His mother told us that he didn't even like getting dialysis and would be very upset about being hooked up to a ventilator. Yet she didn't find it in herself to withdraw any of the care he was getting, as it would amount to "killing" him. The weight of the ordeal was dawning on his family, who talked of him in the past tense. His mother would often express to God a wish to exchange places with her son. Yet in one instance she told the social worker that the miracle she was waiting for was for him to die, so that his suffering would end.

By the time he was transferred to the medical wards and I took over his care, his family had settled into a set ritual, with waves of family members taking shifts, sitting by his side, moistening his lips with sponge lollipops, reading him the Bible, as his eyes looked eerily into nothing, completely unaware. He had slipped into a persistent vegetative state, and as the weeks passed by, complications piled on. He developed a huge, gaping ulcer in his back, the size of a football, that tracked all the way to his hipbone. His bone marrow completely lost the ability to form blood, and he needed transfusions almost every other day.

As the weeks went by, every day my intern would go up to him in the morning, stick a stethoscope on his chest, press on his belly, shine a light into his eyes, yell out his name, grind on his sternum, without any hope of any of this being actually useful or any different from the innumerable times he had examined him before. He would write a note in the chart, update the labs, replete his electrolytes.

The next steps to be taken in David's case were eventually discussed in our weekly Morbidity and Mortality meeting, a venue for only the most tragic of stories, the most horrifying of ends. Our efforts to transfer him to a rehabilitation facility were met with much resistance. For one, facilities wanted him to have a legal guardian. While in this case there was no dispute regarding the mother being the legal guardian, it meant another mountain of paperwork, innumerable e-mails, and waiting for court dates. Eventually, though, the court decided to appoint the mother as the guardian, and we moved toward transferring him to a rehabilitation facility, where he would likely spend the rest of his life.

Later that day, as we were wrapping up our work and hoping to sign off, my intern came up to me, looking rather disheveled, and said, "You won't believe what just happened."

"What?" I asked him.

"David just said, 'Hello, Doctor!'"

I looked at my intern dismissingly, but his expression told me that this was no joke. Within moments I found myself standing at the door of David's room, slipping on the yellow gown. David was surrounded by his family, who were chanting prayers aloud; his face was turned over to the side, and he was looking toward the door with a blank glaze in his eyes as he said again, "Hello, Doctor."

His condition wasn't entirely normal: His responses were unpredictable and only sporadic. At times he would say the same thing over and over again, and could follow only the simplest commands. He had little in common with the person who had come to the hospital many weeks ago.

To the family, though, this was just the result of the weeks of prayer they had accumulated. To them his burden of sin had tipped over, resulting in a turnaround that would come to shape all those who witnessed it. Their faith had given them the strength to go through this ordeal as if it were a rite of passage, and now it was clear that every decision they made would be vetted by the unseen eye that watched over them.

Religion and spirituality can offer an alternate prism that paints reality in a way that only the devoutly religious can see. To David's mother, his seizures, which he continued to have, were like the shaking sobs he would have as a child after he had cried a lot. After initially thinking of CPR as denying David a natural death, she now felt that CPR was part of God's plan: CPR doesn't always work, and its failure would represent God's will. She understood that he would likely be bedridden for the rest of his life, but was certain that he was enjoying his present state. God will "take him when it is his time," she insisted.

While religion does not pervade every aspect of life in the United States, religion remains inseparable from death and the end of life. As medicine has become increasingly secularized, patients are increasingly looking beyond the manifest for support, especially in the throes of sickness.

The demise of religion has been announced prematurely many a time. While religion has seen an unprecedented revival in the past fifty-odd years, the medical world is only now recognizing the increasing role played by religion and spirituality in shaping fundamentally how people come to view life, aging, and death.

DISCOUNTING SOME MODERN Scandinavian societies, there has been no human society that did not incorporate religion into their worldview.[3] Religion is a large part of what we consider human culture, and in many ways might be considered the most human of traits. While many animals have complex societies, to date none demonstrate the development of an organized spirituality or the expression of metaphysical investigation unique to us. That being said, a recent paper published in *Scientific Reports* by anthropologist Hjalmar Kuehl and others showed chimpanzees practicing rituals such as throwing rocks at trees, which could represent a spiritual exercise.

Scientists have gone in two broad directions looking for how religion came to be part of our lives. While anthropologists have flown around the world digging up ancient artifacts, and exploring bygone civilizations for the first signs of transcendent thought, cognitive psychologists are prying into the deepest recesses of the mind, looking for the biochemical machinery within us that led to the formulation of a theological frame of mind in human beings.

Symbolism is at the heart of religion. Even the newest religions use intermediaries to denote the divine. Only recently were the ancient roots of symbolism discovered in a remote cave on the southern tip of Africa. While it was initially thought that the first attempts by ancient humans to imbue objects in their vicinity with higher meaning occurred about forty thousand years ago, the Blombos Cave in South Africa revealed what is now considered the earliest manifestation of symbolic intent.[4] Archaeologists found geometrical shapes carved on ocher stones a hundred thousand years ago, representing the earliest efforts of *Homo sapiens* to construct a narrative in the world around them. These stones "functioned as artifacts within a society where behavior was mediated by symbols."

Many philosophers hold that the cessation of our individual existence—death—was the inspiration behind religion and supernatural belief. Certainly, it didn't take long for rituals to be formed that centered on death. The first ritualized burial dates around 95,000 years ago was found in Qafzeh, in Israel.[5] There, archaeologists discovered the remains of a nine-year-old girl, buried with her arms and legs bent cradling a pair of deer antlers. While it is difficult to attribute meaning to these rituals, it is clear that death bore a special place in the most ancient of societies, worthy of ceremony and decorum.

It is the now-famous Grotte Chauvet–Pont d'Arc, in France, where humanity's aspirations for an otherworld became apparent.[6] In that cave, beyond the human and animal figures painted on the walls, were supernatural beings that were at once human and animal and neither. The humanoid figures with lion heads, drawn by people more than thirty thousand years ago, represent not only those people's creative talents but also our enduring ability to see the unseeable and know the unknowable. Soon societies were erecting temples and building the social constructs that now form the spine of organized religions around the world. The arrival of the written word has since allowed us to better chart the progress of these societies as each found its own way of making a connection with the divine.

While modern societies have progressed to a point where we can imagine a culture that can exist independent of religion, for much of history it has been impossible to extricate one from the other. The innateness of the spiritual experience to human life has made many believe that our brains are hardwired to lean toward a spiritual mind-set.[7] The origins of these protoreligious thoughts are best studied in children, who are thought to be somewhat purified of sociocultural confounders.

Children, as discussed previously, have evolving concepts of life and death, and they associate consciousness with nonliving things. Children, however, are not the only ones capable of associating higher thoughts with objects around them. The theory of mind posits that human beings are especially vulnerable to assigning purposeful thoughts, hopes, and desires to "agents" around them.[8] The theory of mind allows us to function as a society; it allows us to believe that others around us have independent minds similar to our own. It allows us to behave as a cohesive society, which involves respecting the rights of others, and allows us to follow the rules society has set for us even when no one is watching. The theory of mind also allows us to attribute meaningful thoughts to inanimate and nonliving objects, such as religious artifacts and books. It is also what allows us to imagine a supernatural god, whose thoughts are independent of our own.

This desire for agency begins in early childhood. In an experiment in which children were asked about how various rocks acquired their shapes, they chose to think it was so as to acquire some protective mechanism rather than as an almost random act of geology.[9] Such teleological thinking is also apparent in adults, particularly under duress.[10] In fact, religious ideas such as gods and spirits and figures such as Santa Claus are much easily understood by children than more rigorous natural concepts.[11] In many ways, supernatural beings are much simpler to understand. An individual we meet may or may not know about a certain thing, or may or may not be lying, leaving us with the task of fishing out what the individual's level of awareness is. As opposed to that, a supernatural being, especially an omnipresent god, knows everything, and because of his or her strict moral standing is much more unambiguous and simple to gather than the individuals we interact with otherwise.

The most intriguing theory for the origin of religion emerges from sociologists. As human society grew in size, human beings had to devise means to increase intergroup reciprocity, to include commitment signals that would alert members of how far someone would go to retain membership, and to optimize coalition psychology to help manage increasingly large units of men and women. In many ways, this is seen most clearly at a smaller scale in frat houses, which establish unique codes of conduct and require some form of hazing prior to entry in exchange for community.

By having strict inclusion criteria, and by requiring both material inputs such as donations and recurring activities such as rituals, prayers, abstinence, etc., religion institutes rules that can be used to vet an individual's commitment to the common purpose of the group.[12] The idea of being watched by a supernatural being also helps to optimize positive behaviors, and the fear of his or her wrath prevents ill-advised acts and prevents desertion. Perhaps it is because of these characteristics that religious groups appear to be far more robust and long-lasting than nonreligious ones.[13]

While all of these theories have merits, it is probable that there would likely be no religion if there were no death. In many ways the raison d'être of religion stems from the existential curve ball imbued so deep within us. As beings capable of an imagination that can span the universe, we to date remain incapable of imagining nothingness. Thinking about nothing is to watch a cat catch its tail. This dilemma was implanted into our subconscious at inception, since even children are prone to think of the soul as being transcendent even after the body perishes.[14] Therefore, the greatest fear that most people have is not even that of being sentenced to eternal damnation. It is the thought of not existing, of *actually* dying.

THE JOB OF a physician is challenging on many levels. One of the most unusual aspects is that a significantly large proportion of people we interact with on a daily basis are scared stiff. Scared of needles. Scared of white coats. Scared of scalpels. But most of all, scared of that lump in the armpit, that funky-looking mole on the chest, and that nagging ache in the back of the head, scared that any symptom might be a harbinger of death.

Of course, this is not surprising: the fear of death is one of the most primal fears that we harbor, one we share with every other species that actively tries to prevent death to whatever degree it can. But the extent of this fear is only now being realized. It is increasingly believed now that the fear of death shapes every aspect of our lives and each one of our daily decisions. Religion has a particularly important role in modulating this fear of death.

In modern discourse, the fear of death is often painted as a weakness, as a failure on one's part, with those unafraid of death thought to be chivalrous and selfless. Yet the fear of death is as important to us and as natural as our immune system. Just as on a cellular level our white blood cells are always waging battle against the known unknowns and the unknown unknowns within our bodies, at a greater level the fear of death is perhaps what allows us to continue surviving in an environment full of dangers. The human body has well-developed mechanisms that allow us to act quickly when we are suddenly filled with mortal terror (when being chased down by a rabid animal or when trapped in a fire). Death anxiety, therefore, among all our phobias, is perhaps the most natural and necessary of fears.

The fear of death is very much physiological, but the extent to which it dictates our lives has only recently been realized. While philosophers and psychologists have always noted the role of death in our daily actions, no one did this with greater detail than the anthropologist Ernest Becker in his Pulitzer Prize–winning book, *The Denial of Death,* published in 1973.[15] Becker's ideas were picked up by psychologists Jeff Greenberg, Sheldon Solomon, and Tome Pyszczynski, who formalized them in the shape of the terror management theory (TMT).[16] According to the TMT, human beings have a burning desire to live and to keep living, but, unlike most other organisms, because of their hypertrophied self-awareness, simultaneously remain keenly aware of their own mortality. While our initial instinct is to deny this inevitable outcome, we overcome the horror that this duality creates by forming social institutions and ideas that imbue our existence with meaning. These social institutions include morality, culture, nationality, and ethnic groups. To enhance our self-worth, we indulge in activities that we hope will outlive us in the shape of art, literature, charitable donations, unassailable feats, and inexhaustible resources. We invest in our children, who we hope will carry on our legacy and keep us alive in their memories.

Reminders of our mortality also make individuals become more protective of their cultural beliefs and worldview and much less likely to view favorably those who seem to differ from them in any way. In one experiment, judges reminded of death set an average bond for alleged prostitutes at $455, compared with just $50 by those not reminded of death.[17] Simply flashing the word "death" to an American audience for twenty-eight milliseconds significantly increased their negative emotions toward an author criticizing the United States.[18] Subtle reminders of death even make people more likely to advocate for war.[19] Yet even after hundreds of studies were published supporting this theory, American academics (unlike Europeans) remained skeptical. This changed after the most potent death reminder in recent American history, 9/11, following which the theory became much more widely accepted.[20]

Religion, in many ways, is the most potent by-product of terror management. Unlike other constructs, such as culture and morality, religion helps to allay the fear of death not only by increasing self-worth through investments such as prayer, pilgrimage, and congregation but by being the most direct denial of death at our disposal. With the promise of an afterlife offered by almost all religions, death is reduced to a mere inflection point rather than a full stop—a transition from one life to another. Unsurprisingly, rumination on death spurs religious thoughts, even among atheists.[21]

Whether religion truly reduces the fear of death has still not been fully fleshed out, with research finding contradictory results. Studies have run the gamut, showing a negative, a neutral, and a positive relationship between religiosity and death anxiety.[22] These results likely are a marker of the great degree of heterogeneity present between religions and their followers. Yet the most plausible relationship between the fear of death and religiosity was put together in a paper by Derek Pyne, an economist based in Ontario.[23] On a spectrum with strict atheists on one end and the very religious at the other, it seems that the fear of death is felt most strongly by the moderately religious. The finding, based on mathematical modeling, makes intuitive sense: A staunch atheist invests nothing to prepare for the afterlife and faces no uncertainty about the future. Very religious people make a relatively large investment in the afterlife in the shape of beliefs, prayers, and other religious activities and feel a high probability of going to heaven compared with their chances of going to hell. Moderately religious people, however, find themselves in a bind. They are firstly not sure about the presence or absence of an afterlife, and in the event that there is an afterlife, don't like their chances of going to heaven given less generous ritualistic investments. This nonlinear relationship has been noted by some other studies as well and probably explains why most people, who likely fit into the moderately religious group, the vast majority of common folk, continue to feel a tremendous amount of insecurity and distress at the end of life.

Modern medicine has done much to stave off death but little to ameliorate people's fear of dying. If anything, people appear to fear death more today than at any time in the past. Some of that has to do with medicine's great success in prolonging people's life spans. Now that the vast majority of people in developed economies live to what was previously considered to be an elderly age, people plan a life that fits modern estimates of longevity. Even though none of us can predict when we will die, the choices we make reflect that we are adapting to the incredible degree of life extension achieved over the past century.

For one, people would not train until they are in their mid-thirties to be physicians or lawyers if their life spans were constrained to nineteenth-century limits. Furthermore, people stave off milestones such as marriage and childbirth, expecting to live many years longer than their ancestors did. People also have fewer children now than they did in the past because of the predictably higher survival rates of offspring these days than in the past. In fact, when I asked my *nano* why she had eight children, she gave me two reasons: first, that she had to have six daughters before her first son, a prized possession in rural Pakistan, and second, that she just wasn't sure how many of them would grow to adulthood. Because people truly expected death to be around the corner at all times, facing it became a familiar experience. While no one will admit these days that death is much more predictable, how we live our lives proves that all of us, unconsciously, have accepted that a longer life awaits us compared with our ancestors. No wonder people are willing to delay until they are in their mid-thirties life events such as starting a family and being financially independent. As mentioned previously, only 12 percent of deaths in the United States occur in people younger than fifty, and that number is bound to go further down. Almost counterintuitively, therefore, death's past unpredictability made it much less fearful.

The changing ecology of death, brought about by medicine, is another reason people fear death more now than they have in the past. In the words of Elisabeth Kübler-Ross, the Swiss American psychiatrist who pioneered the hospice movement in the United States, "I think there are many reasons for this flight away from facing death calmly. One of the most important facts is that dying nowadays is more gruesome in many ways, namely, more lonely, mechanical and dehumanized; at times it is even difficult to determine technically when the time of death has occurred."[24] These observations are probably as prescient today as they were back in 1969, if not more so.

Another important reason death has become so fearful is the sanitization and secularization of medicine that has taken place over the past few decades.[25] Since ancient times, death has been a passage enshrined in tradition, customs, and ritual and chaperoned by those specializing in the spiritual needs of the dying and their families, such as priests, shamans, rabbis, and maulvies. As this protective layer is removed, patients and their families are increasingly exposed to ambiguity and terror at the end of life. But contrary to previously held opinion, religion and spirituality continue to be highly important to patients at the end of life and have an increasingly important role as one approaches the inevitable final countdown.

AMERICA REMAINS A deeply religious country, and Americans only get more religious as they get older and approach death. Around 85 percent of Americans consider themselves religious, with more than half of Americans saying religion continues to be "very important" in their own lives. These poll figures, collected by Gallup over decades, indicate the stability of these beliefs, even as a large number of people perhaps incorrectly believe that religion is losing its influence in American life.[26]

This is also true of patients in the hospital: One study showed that over 85 percent of patients held intrinsic religious beliefs, with more than half attending religious services, praying, and reading the Bible regularly.[27] For 40 percent of the patients in this study, faith was the most important factor helping them cope with their illness. Having a serious illness only strengthens people's faith: Of women diagnosed with cancer, three-fourths stated that religion had an important role in their lives, with half saying that their faith had become stronger since they were diagnosed. Not a single woman said that she had become less religious since her cancer diagnosis.[28]

However, religion is just one manifestation of the larger but elusive phenomenon of spirituality. While religion can perhaps be adequately defined as "an organized faith system, beliefs, worship, religious rituals, and relationship with a divine being," the definition of spirituality is a bit more difficult to pin down.[29] In fact, this difficulty is cited as being one of the reasons spirituality remains understudied. One group came up with a definition using refined academic crowdsourcing: They looked at around a thousand articles studying spirituality and synthesized a list of articles from different authors who provided a definition of what they thought spirituality was.[30] From among these papers, they picked out the main features used and conceptualized spirituality as a "developmental and conscious process, characterized by two movements of transcendence; either deep within the self or beyond the self." While organized religion is the means through which the vast majority of people express their spirituality, an increasing number of people identify themselves as spiritual but not religious.[31] Both religion and spirituality greatly modulate the experience of death and the choices patients make at the end of life.

At the end of life, religion and spirituality may be the only means that patients have of finding comfort. More than physical comfort, patients are frequently looking for meaning. Patients ask, "Why am I suffering?," and frequently medicine does not provide any neat answers. Frequently, thus, patients look to religion and spirituality for comfort,[32] and the dependence on religious coping increases as illness worsens and treatment options dwindle.[33] Current evidence suggests that spirituality may have some benefit in the throes of disease: one analysis that pooled data from several studies showed a minuscule trend toward less depression with increasing religiousness.[34] Interestingly, though, *extrinsically* religious persons—those who adhere to religion for social gains associated with attachment to religion rather than sincerely believing in the tenets of the faith—and those with a conflicted relationship with religion demonstrate higher rates of depression. One study published in the *Lancet* showed spiritual well-being as the strongest protector from hopelessness, thoughts of suicide, and a desire to hasten death among patients at the end of life.[35]

It is easy to see why a religious outlook and belief in an omnipresent all-controlling deity would bring comfort to someone surrounded by dread. When asked by an interviewer about whether his suffering from cancer was the will of God, Jack, an elderly cancer patient, told him, "Yes. Well it's all the suffering, the will of God . . . and I just have to accept it with joy."[36] Feeling that he had a personal angel who was helping to heal him, Jack dreamed that he went to heaven and saw himself recovering from his disease.

Religious belief also provides patients with the feeling that they are never alone, that God is always by their side. Women with breast cancer have described feeling that God walks with them through their journey with cancer and that they find him by their sides at all times.[37] But perhaps the most important means by which religion provides comfort to patients and helps them cope with illness is by giving their life, their very existence and the perils it faces, a context. Patients ask, "What was the meaning of my life?" and "What will happen after I die?," and frequently physicians can offer little useful in response.[38] Religious patients look to God to provide a narrative for their suffering, while the spiritual look toward art, science, and the self to find the answers to some of life's most difficult questions.

While age, gender, underlying disease, race, and socioeconomics all factor into patients' decision making, religiosity guides decisions independent of everything else. While religion and spirituality certainly help people cope better with terminal illness, in many cases they lead them down a more painful and violent path. Study after study has shown that people who rate higher on scales of religiosity tend to want more aggressive care, more invasive procedures, and more time in the intensive-care unit at the end of life and are less likely to want to withhold or withdraw care.[39] One multicenter study that followed terminally ill patients in sites across the United States found that more-religious patients were more likely to be on a ventilator and receive intensive life-prolonging care at the end of life.[40] Furthermore, they were more likely to want "heroic measures" at the end of life and much less likely to have a do-not-resuscitate order or to have a health-care proxy or a living will. While more-religious patients in this study were more likely to be black or Hispanic, were less educated, and were less likely to have health insurance or be married, religious coping remained positively associated with desiring more aggressive treatment even after accounting for these other factors.

For all this data showing that more-religious people want more treatment close to death, the question is whether this care is even beneficial or not. Given that it has now become clear that being more religious does not confer a longer life, it is quite likely that the additional care that they desire and consequently receive is futile and possibly harmful.[41]

Why do religious people desire more aggressive treatments at the end of life? Partly because other socioeconomic factors, such as income and levels of education, overlap with increased religiosity.[42] These factors are associated with wanting more aggressive care at the end of life, which sounds counterintuitive, as one would think that people who are religious would want to be closer to their creator than those who aren't.[43] Yet religion has effects far beyond these factors.

Religion emphasizes the sanctity of life; on the whole this is a positive sentiment, making religion pro-social, but there are times when the sanctity of life is equated with prolonging life at any cost. A large proportion of religious people retain hope of a magical turnaround, even when chances of one are minuscule. One study of critically ill patients showed that a majority of religious patients and family members believed that a cure could occur even after physicians had declared medical futility.[44] While religious patients do look to their doctors for advice and direction, they always seek a second opinion from God. One national survey found that while both lung cancer patients and their caregivers value their oncologist's opinion the most, the second most important factor determining their decisions regarding treatment was faith in God. Patients with less formal education placed an even greater value on their faith. Faith in God was more important even than the ability of the treatment to cure the disease, while it was the least important factor for physicians.[45]

Religion can also shape treatment decisions in other ways. One day I was working in the emergency room when we received a patient who had been transferred from another hospital. His arms were laced in tattoos, his skin was golden like egg yolk, his eyes looked like they were floating in amber. From years of drinking, he had cirrhosis of the liver and was now bleeding profusely from his stomach and esophagus. His blood level was less than half of the minimum acceptable value. Up until then, he had nothing we could not fix: patients with alcoholic liver disease, who are bleeding from enlarged veins in their esophagus, come to the hospital frequently, and we have become increasingly good at treating these patients. The only complicating factor, and it was a big one, was that the patient was a Jehovah's Witness, a sect of Christianity who believed that blood transfusions were sinful even as a matter of life and death. I had taken care of such patients in the past, so it was not an entirely unusual situation for me. Yet the patient was the single parent of young children, and I was worried what would become of them if something awful were to happen and who would care for them. The patient himself seemed to be completely calm, almost aloof from what was at stake, and dutifully produced a form that stated that his sister would take care of his children in the event of his death. This form—a state requirement—was developed from cases around the world in which Jehovah's Witnesses died, some at childbirth, after refusing to receive blood products.[46]

My patient was transferred to the ICU, where all physicians could practically do was watch on and come up with ways to control the bleeding without being able to give him blood. He made it through this episode, but given that his liver was unlikely to get better, he would have to go through this cycle countless more times.

Physicians very frequently find themselves in difficult situations with patients who have a strong faith, but rarely do they talk about religion and spirituality. One study of residents who had conducted discussions with patients regarding their code status showed that only 10 percent of them had talked about religion or spirituality with those patients.[47] One important reason physicians are not comfortable talking with their patients about these issues, which hold such an important place in their patients' lives, is that patients come from diverse backgrounds and different religious denominations. Much like all else, all the major religions converge and differ on answers to some of the most crucial questions of life and, of course, death.

The United States has long attracted people from around the world, from different cultures, and importantly from many different religions. I, like most if not all of my colleagues, have been involved with patients and families from countless religious backgrounds at the most difficult time in their lives. While we perhaps don't take this into consideration as much as we should as health-care providers, differences do exist among religions with regard to care at the end of life.

Traditional Christian belief places a lot of importance on the concept of repentance. Christianity does not condone intentionally cutting a life short, and this was reaffirmed in the US Supreme Court's decision prohibiting physician-assisted suicide. Yet Christianity "prohibits using medicine in an all-consuming pursuit of health and postponing death."[48] This was stated most clearly by Pope Pius XII in 1957 in his address to an international congress of anesthesiologists.[49] This statement was ahead of its time and provided guidance to both medicine and the judiciary as it grappled with the challenges brought about by medical technology. The allowance to limit or withdraw care when recovery is unlikely was reaffirmed again in 1995 by Pope John Paul II.[50] This address also formed the basis of the Karen Ann Quinlan judgment, which cited it repeatedly. Yet because of the central role of repentance, Christian belief cautions against obtunding patients with medications at the end of life, so as to not "take away a final opportunity for repentance."

Given the great diversity of those who identify themselves as Christian but who may be Mormon, Unitarian, Roman Catholic, Protestant, or Orthodox, there can be important differences, precluding a cookie-cutter approach from physicians. Even within groups, consensus about all aspects of treatment close to death hasn't been fully reached, such as acceptability of euthanasia. Unitarians, for example, in advocating patients' right to self-determination, support physician-assisted suicide, and in a statement passed in 1988 stated their desire to "support legislation that will create legal protection for the right to die with dignity, in accordance with one's own choice."[51] On the other end of the spectrum is the Greek Orthodox Church, which prohibits any down-titration of care regardless of medical futility, stating that "there is always the possibility of an erroneous medical appraisal or of an unforeseen outcome of the disease, or even a miracle."[52]

Jewish law, halacha, emphasizes that the human body is the property of God and that humans should not do anything that would actively harm their bodies. This is reflected in opposition in Judaism to suicide and euthanasia. Yet in certain grim situations, passive euthanasia, either through withdrawal of treatment or by giving pain medications that may hasten death, is allowed.[53] While traditionally the spirit has been thought to reside in one's breath—*ruach*—Jewish authorities have evolved to incorporate modern definitions of death, including brain death, outlined first in the Harvard criteria.[54] Lesser consensus has been established about when it is permissible to withhold or withdraw care. Controversy revolves around the definition of *goses,* a dying person perched between life and death. While some sources identify *goses* as someone unable to swallow and expected to die within four days, others define it as someone who has been inflicted with an incurable injury or disease.[55] Further divergent opinions exist with regard to artificial nutrition, through feeding tubes or intravenously.[56]

Jewish people, like people in all other religions, are encouraged to participate fully in their well-being. Interestingly, though, according to Rabbi Elliott Dorff, a professor of ethics, "patient autonomy has a smaller role in Jewish sources than in American secular ethics; in Jewish sources, the doctor has much more authority to determine the appropriate course of treatment. . . . Doctors just as much as patients are full partners in medical care."[57] While Orthodox and Conservative Jews follow Judaic law to the letter and frequently consult with their rabbi, Reform Jews tend to make more autonomous decisions.

Islam, the world's fastest-growing religion, continues to remain a mystery, particularly to Americans. Islam sees itself as the continuation of the monotheistic religions that flourished in the Middle East, and is the last great religion that emerged from that region.[58] The central pillar of Islam lies in its very name, which means "submission." Human beings have been sent to the world to prove their fealty and obedience to the will of God, which according to Islam has been broadcast to humans by way of thousands of prophets, including Moses, Noah, and Jesus, culminating with Muhammad.

The modern Islamic world remains highly observant. Seven of the ten most religious countries in the world have a Muslim majority.[59] Yet Muslims are a very diverse group, and the lack of a central theological leader or institution helps maintain a high degree of plurality. To a great degree, Muslim religious figures defer end-of-life decisions to the physicians taking care of the patient, reflective of the paternalistic attitude prevalent in most Muslim-majority countries. This is perhaps shaped by the fact that a large proportion of Muslim countries are developing countries. To cross the void created by the lack of a central directive, the Organization of Islamic Countries created several councils, which have affirmed most modern positions taken toward end-of-life care, such as the prohibition of euthanasia and the acceptance of the definition of brain death, as other major religions have.[60]

Muslims, like people from some other religions, have a complicated relationship with pain and suffering. Suffering in Muslim tradition is considered a test, part of the trial that defines life.[61] Muslims believe that all things happen by God's will, even pain, and that God delivers physical pain and mental anguish to assess the resolve of the afflicted.[62] In fact, it has been suggested that in Islam suffering is part of a believer's journey to be able to achieve self-realization and to appreciate contact with the divine.[63] Some religious experts state that "end-of-life suffering may be a way to purify previous sins so that by the time you meet God, you do so in a [more pure] state."[64] Many Muslims also believe that those who suffer in this life will be free from any suffering in the afterlife. These sets of beliefs are said to represent theodicy—a defense of God's goodness and justice in the face of evil and suffering. While present to a degree in all the major monotheistic religions, theodicy is especially prominent in Islamic tradition. However, Islam allows for pain medications to be given close to death even if it hastens death, as long as that is not the intention of the physician.[65]

Hinduism, too, houses a diversity of opinions within its fold. In Hinduism, the finality of death is also denied, and is viewed more as a transition, either to another life, to heaven, or to an immersion into Brahma, the ubiquitous and absolute reality.[66] The emphasis therefore is on the nature of death, binarized as either good or bad. A good death is defined as one that occurs either at home or, ideally, at the banks of the Ganges River. A good death entails the dying person having fulfilled all of his worldly duties; positive karma leads to reincarnation into a better life, and bad karma is realized as a demotion.[67] A good death is also considered to be a nontraumatic death, devoid of bodily waste. There-fore there is frequently little push from patients to prolong resuscitation and artificial support, given that it portends a bad death. Withdrawal and withholding of care is well accepted by Hindus, particularly since some sects are known to fast to their own deaths. Euthanasia, however, particularly if due to pain and intolerance of suffering, is not allowed.[68]

While broadly knowing where major religions stand with regard to how best to manage dying patients is vital for physicians, additional layers complicate matters. The degree of an individual's observance and knowledge of religious rites changes how they foresee the end of life playing out. Adherents may not literally believe in the metaphysi-cal aspects of their respective religions, such as the existence of an af-terlife or the presence or absence of a heaven and hell.[69] The degree of acculturation can also affect the extent to which believers follow the rules of their religion as opposed to the prevalent ideals of their natu-ralized homeland.[70] All adherents also do not have a positive relation-ship with God; many patients feel angry with God, as if they are being cynically punished, or feel like God has abandoned them. Negative religious coping can in fact increase anguish and hopelessness in the terminally ill.[71]

Modern bioethics remains a purely Western concept that devel-oped in the wake of technological advances and has since been widely exported to cultures and traditions still struggling to get around to understanding what it all means. Importantly, though, physicians have critical conversations with individuals without any knowledge of their spiritual fingerprints.

It is easy to forget that patients and their families are not the only ones involved in furnishing the landscape at the end of life. Physi-cians, owing to their traditional role as well as their experience in these settings, are naturally an integral part of this dialogue. In many instances, physicians are driving the conversation and ultimately have to make life-or-death calls. It is being increasingly realized that the religious and spiritual views of those at the bedside are as likely to affect outcomes as those of the ones on the beds.

IN SPITE OF the fact that the entire face of medicine has changed, as it has gone from being a cottage industry of suggestion to being a full-fledged scientific behemoth that publishes half a million research papers annually, the practice of medicine still remains an art. Every day doctors make hundreds if not thousands of microdecisions as well as several major decisions with absolutely no data to guide them. It is here that medical training really comes to the fore. When data is present, as it is for how frequently to get colonoscopies or who should get a cholesterol-lowering medication, medicine can be very algorithmic. It is in the data-free zone that doctors can use their judgment, carved out of years of training, and truly contemplate the bigger picture.

A physician's training certainly shapes his or her decision making. Increasingly, however, it is being noted that physicians' personalities, too, shape important medical decisions. Physicians who are more risk-averse are more likely to admit to the hospital patients with chest pain who are not in fact having a heart attack,[72] and are more likely to order imaging tests.[73] Physicians who are more empathic are less likely to prescribe medications or interventions but actually provide better quality care.[74] Other factors, such as the experience of the physician, their gender, and their workload, all contribute to the medical decisions they make.[75] While these factors are certainly nowhere as important as patient-specific factors, they do count in the greater calculus.

It is only natural to assume that physicians' religion, too, would come into play, especially when they are making life-or-death decisions for their patients. But what is the religious makeup of physicians in the United States? A study published in 2005 sought to answer that very question.[76] Investigators sent out a survey to two thousand randomly selected physicians around the United States, two-thirds of whom responded. Turns out that the proportion of physicians who are religious is similar to that of the US population; 90 percent of physicians compared to 87 percent of the general US populace considered themselves affiliated with a religion. Beyond this overt similarity there were many differences: Physicians were much more likely than the average American to be Jewish, Hindu, or Muslim and were also much more likely to consider themselves spiritual but not religious, as opposed to the general American population, for whom religion and spirituality (or the lack thereof) appeared to stick together (they are either both religious and spiritual or neither). Physicians were also much less likely to believe in God or in an afterlife and more likely to make decisions "without relying on God."

Physicians, therefore, while ostensibly similar to the average American with regard to religious affiliation, are quite different in how they incorporate religion into their thought processes. Minority physicians were also much less likely to say that they carried over their religion into other walks of life, compared with Christian physicians. This number may be even lower in reality given that a third of all physicians, and half of all physicians who graduated from a foreign medical school, did not even respond to the survey.

Nevertheless, most physicians believe that religion is a force of good, especially for their patients. Three out of four physicians believe that religion helps their patients cope and provides them a positive state of mind.[77] Yet more-religious physicians tend to have a somewhat different worldview. Physicians who are more religious tend to report patients bringing up religious and spiritual issues thrice more than less-religious ones and are five times more likely to feel that spirituality strongly influences health. More-religious physicians are in fact three times more likely to feel that they spend too little time discussing their patients' spiritual beliefs.[78] Religious physicians are therefore much more likely to bring up religion and spirituality with their patients and might also appear more accessible in these matters to their patients.

While only 6 percent of physicians believe that religion affects "hard" outcomes,[79] innumerable studies have now shown that physicians' religious affiliation and extent of belief affect their decisions regarding treatments (or the lack thereof) at the end of life. Analyses of physicians from Israel,[80] the United States,[81] and across Europe[82] have shown that more-religious physicians are more likely to oppose euthanasia and the withdrawal of treatment in terminally ill patients. Similar patterns have been shown for nurses as well.[83] One European study showed that patients of physicians with no religious affiliation lived the longest after they withdrew life-prolonging treatment, suggesting that more-religious physicians were more likely to delay the decision close to the point of death.[84]

Physicians' beliefs, however, are flexible and usually follow the cultural norms of the country of practice.[85] For example, while there are some Muslim countries where DNR orders aren't even present and physicians feel compelled to continue resuscitation indefinitely,[86] Muslim physicians practicing in the United States seem to reflect the views of other American physicians.[87]

Every now and then, I get asked about where I am from by my patients. People are interested in knowing their doctors better. At times they are playing a guessing game in their heads and want to know if they won. The idea, though, is to add context to the very serious conversations they anticipate having with me. As soon as they hear "Pakistan," the conversation can go a few different ways. They will remember the only other Pakistani they know and ask if I know them (I never do). Infrequently, they will surprise me with intimate and nuanced knowledge of Pakistan, its brief history, and its major cities. Occasionally, though, the conversation enters political waters better left untouched, and I have to find a good way to extricate myself. I guess once people know I am from Pakistan, asking about my religious belief becomes a mere formality. One very sweet lady, when I went to see her in the ward, smiled when she saw me and joined her palms. "*Namaste*," she said. I smiled and told her, "I am from Pakistan, but a *namaste* was much appreciated." She smiled and gave her best rendition of an *assalam-u-alaikum*.

I was recently taking care of an elderly black gentleman battling infection after infection. He was in serious trouble: an encroaching infection in his belly was threatening his life, and was becoming impossible to treat, especially in someone who was already terminally ill. He himself was very stoic—would hardly say more than was needed and was certainly not one to indulge in prolonged conversation. Some of his brevity was also due to his liver disease, which kept his thinking cloudy most of the time. At an impasse, unable to explain to him the gravity of the infection, we called his family in to meet with them.

His wife was a vivacious and dynamic woman, instantly raising the energy level in the room. My patient was now chirping away, making jokes, bantering with his brother—he felt like he was home. When she looked at my name tag, she seemed to have a eureka moment, and she quickly asked me, "Are you Muslim?"

I have been asked this question only a handful of times. When I was growing up in Pakistan, a country that despite great ethnic diversity is about as religiously homogeneous as it gets, no one had ever asked me what my religion was. There was almost no need to have a religious identity, given that there was never any need to establish it.

Before I could answer, she spoke again: "So is he."

At a macrocosmic level, religion is frequently used to wedge people away from each other, to draw lines in the sand and on maps, but physicians need to use it as a weight that will help lower them to the ground and make them more human for their patients. As physicians, we already have a lot of otherness stuffed in our lab-coat pockets, and anything that helps patients feel like their physician is more than that, a human being, helps.

What the best way is of introducing religion and spirituality into a medical conversation remains controversial. In many societies and cultures, physicians invoke religion frequently and do not feel the need to confer with others about their decisions, but is that even possible in the multiethnic and multireligious America of today?

FOR MOST PEOPLE there is no fine distinction between where their religious or spiritual lives end and the rest begins. If anything, when people become sick, that distinction becomes even blurrier. And as they get sicker and approach the end of life, the desire to think about life and the world in more abstract terms increases. While about a third of clinic patients want their physicians to ask them about their faith, the number rises to 70 percent among those who are seriously ill in the hospital.[88] Why is it then that so few physicians ever initiate a discussion about beliefs held dear by a patient?[89]

If you aren't well acquainted with doctors by now, the one thing you may want to know is that they are extremely stretched. Physicians talk fast, walk fast, eat fast, and think fast. And when they're asked about why they don't talk about patients' spiritual lives, a lack of time frequently comes up. While most patients prefer their physicians to talk about their medical issues, some, particularly African Americans, would rather talk about their spiritual issues even if it encroaches on time spent discussing their health.[90]

Physicians also worry about projecting their own beliefs onto patients or uncovering differences in belief that might adversely affect the patient-doctor relationship.[91] Physicians also may not have adequate training to be able to have these conversations.[92] This is certainly a valid concern. Early during my internship, it was past midnight in the intensive-care unit when I received news that a patient was being admitted, bleeding excessively from his esophagus. He had received no prior care in my hospital and I had no idea what his past medical history was. He had two large tubes going down his throat, draining blood, filling container after container. We initiated a "massive transfusion protocol," trying desperately to keep pace with his bleeding. In one of the most impressive sequences of care that I have ever witnessed, the nursing team transfused around sixty units of blood and blood products within a few hours, heroically trying to save the man's life in a moment of operatic beauty and gruesome efficiency. By the time the family came in with some records, I found myself getting to know a young man with a liver cirrhotic from years of drinking and with cancer that had spread to the brain. A recent note from a palliative care visit had given him less than a month to live.

This information flipped the entire scenario: Instead of fighting to save a young man's life, we were now fighting uphill, delaying the inevitable for someone who was already terminally ill. While I was trying to talk to the surgeons and the interventional radiologists about whether we still had any other options left, I realized that no one had spoken to the family yet. I walked down the hall from the ICU to the family room, where around a dozen family members of all ages were waiting. I wasn't even done introducing myself when his mother quietly asked me, "Is he dying?"

"He is."

I explained to them the situation, and, knowing there was little we could do this time around, they agreed that it was perhaps time to let go and allow him to pass. I looked around the room; there were some elderly relatives listening intently, some sobbing, and a few children running around obliviously. After the conversation ended, I went back to the ICU and told the nurses about my meeting with the family and told them to start cleaning up the room, as the mother wanted to come see her son one last time. One of the more experienced nurses, though, asked me whether I had asked them whether they needed a pastor. I paced back down the hallway and asked them whether they would like to have a pastor, and they immediately felt relieved and replied in the affirmative. I went back to the unit but then figured out that I had forgotten to ask what denomination they belonged to. After I did, though, following another walk down the hallway that connected the chaos in the unit to the somber waiting area, the Catholic pastor was paged, and he showed up fairly soon, at about dawn. He stood solemnly next to the bed as the mother came in to say good-bye to her son. The patient died an hour later.

Such spiritual interventions, not only at the time of death but during the journey leading up to it, do matter. One study that prospectively followed 343 cancer patients until they died showed that the patients provided with spiritual care had a better quality of life prior to their deaths, were more likely to pass in hospice, and were less likely to receive aggressive and unnecessary care close to death than the patients who weren't provided the spiritual intervention. This effect was fivefold in patients who used religion to cope to a higher degree but was also noted in patients who were not that religious.[93] Furthermore, this effect was similar whether spiritual guidance was provided by the physician or a pastor.

The role of spiritual intervention is perhaps even more important in patients who rely a lot on religious support in the community. Further analysis of the previous patients showed that patients who reported greater spiritual support from religious communities died more frequently in the ICU, were more likely to get aggressive care, and had poorer quality of life close to death.[94] These patients were also more likely to belong to an ethnic minority who were less likely to have a high school education or health insurance, but the differences in end-of-life experience were noted even when these socioeconomic factors were equalized. Yet when the medical team provided spiritual assistance, a reversal was noted, and patients were more amenable to having a more comfortable death.

This paradox reveals the gap that exists between religious culture outside of a medical context and one within. Religious communities often anchor on aspects of hope and fighting disease. Thus patients who derived more support from religious communities started off with more awareness of the terminal nature of their disease yet had higher quality of life. Yet as their disease progressed, the same concepts that provided them strength became incongruent with the facts of the illness, leading to a lower quality of life at the end of life. By providing spiritual support, physicians and the medical staff can help fill this gap and provide spiritual guidance and comfort within the context of the disease state. This makes a strong case for physicians proactively providing spiritual and religious coping resources, whether through themselves or through pastoral services.

The greatest barrier for physicians in discussing spirituality with patients is the initiation. The medical history remains the most sacred of medical traditions. Almost from their first day in medical school, students are taught to be sleuths, digging for every detail that might uncover the cause of the cough, the fever, the pain. Did you go spelunking in a cave? Did you have reheated fried rice? Does your urine turn black after a while? Answers to these questions trigger specific neural connections in anyone who has been to medical school. Residents are taught how to gather sensitive information from patients, such as eliciting history from a rape victim. Yet I have rarely if ever been taught how to take a spiritual history.

One way to start might be to simply ask, "Do you consider yourself spiritual or religious?" A question as open-ended and nonjudgmental as this is a gentle way of wading into possibly stormy waters.[95] Usually just the initiation will lead the patient to provide whatever information he or she may be interested in providing. Patients will usually tell what significance their beliefs have to them and how they intertwine with their medical care. A closing question can always be "How would you like me as your provider to address these issues in your care?"

Another dilemma that physicians face after asking such a question is a request to join in a prayer.[96] Physicians I have talked to about this provide a spectrum of responses. Some avidly join patients and their families in their traditions and customs even when those traditions and customs are discordant with their own. Some physicians, though, are cautious, particularly if what they're being asked to do conflicts with their own belief system. Sometimes patients will pray for something, such as a "miracle," that the physician might believe to be a harmful expectation.

Patients' relationship with God can also be fraught. Many patients feel they have been singled out to suffer. Physicians can provide comfort in those situations, but it is hard to do so without providing any reassurance, which might in fact be misleading, or by talking about a subject one is not an expert in. At times like these, simply lending an attentive ear and letting patients vent is the most therapeutic thing a physician can do.

Stark silence is perhaps even more comforting than what most physicians can offer patients who consider themselves atheist or agnostic. Nonbelievers make up an increasingly large proportion of hospitalized patients, and their spiritual needs at the end of life differ from those of religious patients. Many physicians, too, do not consider themselves religious. Even as the medical literature becomes inundated with studies on spirituality in medicine, with scientific papers skyrocketing from 24 in the 1960s to 2,271 between 2000 and 2005, nonbelievers remain woefully underexamined and understudied, particularly as they approach the end of their material existence.[97]

WHEN A MATHEMATICIAN professor was admitted to my hospital with terminal cancer and wanted physicians to help him end his life, it was one of the most difficult cases any of the oncologists and palliative care specialists had ever dealt with. While up to one in five Americans asked to list a religious affiliation check "none," these nones rarely present as dying patients.[98] Palliative care specialists, so experienced in the transcendent, were speechless in the face of his straight and rational talk.

If the origin of belief in supernatural agents and deities is shrouded in mystery (and layer upon layer of archaeological rubble), that of disbelief remains even more elusive. Nonbelievers see their roots in the traditions of the Enlightenment and the Renaissance and in the writings of philosophers such as Hume, Nietzsche, Kant, and Russell. For all the arguments made by cognitive psychologists, archaeologists, sociologists, and evolutionary philosophers, the persistence of disbelief and its spread in affluent societies points away from human beings being hardwired for religious belief.[99] Disbelief can take root in ways similar to religion: It can be passed down from mother or society to child, particularly in Scandinavian countries and other developed societies where modern disbelief has become increasingly pervasive.[100] Just as religion requires the mind to possess characteristics of animism, those lacking in these tools can fail to conjure a sentient overlord. Atheistic beliefs are therefore found in autistic children who are unable to fathom a divine lord.[101] Irreligion is also strongly linked to affluence.[102] Daily struggles over finances and a lack of prosperity attract people to a righteous and just force in the universe who will make their worries worthwhile. For many people, though, breaking from religion means fighting all the instincts and traditions instilled in them since birth, all in a search for narrative context. A journey to a lack of religion therefore can mirror how many people find religion and spirituality in their lives.

No one really knows too well how many people consider themselves nonbelievers, and surveys have traditionally been challenging in this regard. Many people who consider themselves as affiliated with a religion do not possess any intrinsic religiosity. For example, in one study in Europe, of physicians who identified themselves as Jewish, only 33 percent actually believed in the metaphysics of their religious teachings.[103] This is similar to studies done in America, in which only 34 percent of Jewish physicians exhibited innate religiosity.[104] Similar data is present for believers of other religions.

Terminology is also problematic. Unlike religious groups, nonbelievers are fairly heterogeneous, and don't necessarily have a common identity. The term "atheist" is used frequently to describe those who do not believe in a higher force, lumping them into one group. This term, though, not only fails to encompass the wide variety of nones but is disapproved by many who would traditionally be considered to be atheists. In one survey sent out to members of atheist organizations, respondents preferred the terms "skeptics," "free thinkers," and "secular humanists."[105] Some prefer the term "secular" or "naturalist," while some have coined the term "bright" to refer to themselves.[106]

The greatest reason nonbelievers dislike the term "atheist" is the stigma that it carries. A recent Pew survey showed that atheists remain (along with Muslims) the least liked theological demographic in the United States.[107] Americans do not approve electing atheists[108] or marrying atheists.[109] One startling study showed that to the average American an untrustworthy and criminally inclined person was considered to be on a par with an atheist or a rapist, but not someone affiliated with a religion.[110]

Discrimination against atheists, though, is not simply driven by the moniker. In one study, people were as likely to discriminate against someone labeled an atheist as against someone with "no belief in God."[111] This distrust is primarily driven by an association between immorality and irreligion.[112] This widespread wariness of atheists means that atheists and nonbelievers are likely to keep their identity hidden.[113]

Nonbelievers, though, even as they hide in plain sight from each other, make up an increasingly large proportion of the population, with one survey estimating half a billion nonbelievers worldwide.[114] This also includes agnostics, who are unsure about the presence or absence of a deity, and feel they may be unequipped to detect or reject a supernatural being's presence. One recent survey of Americans demonstrated that while 14 percent do not consider themselves affiliated with a religion, 26 percent were found to be neither spiritual nor religious.[115]

Studies have shown that patients tend to be somewhat more religious than the general population. In one study of women with cancer, overwhelmingly participants reported being very religious and getting more religious as the end approached.[116] When patients are close to dying, they find themselves vacillating between the conflicting yet mutually stimulating emotions of fear and hope. In this state, spirituality is entertained even by those without any prior religious belief. One Scottish study recruited six patients close to death who were not previously religious but had developed spiritual thoughts and existential questions over the course of their disease.[117] A patient described taking things for granted when she was healthy but expressed, "It's when your back is to the corner that you're needing a wee bit [of] extra help." Some patients expressed anger at God ("God looks after his own people"), while others expressed more basic questions ("What form will my body take?" and "How will I recognize others?").

Contrary to the maxim, there are in fact atheists in foxholes, and how they view their lives is diametrically opposed to how those who are religious view theirs. One atheist patient described his view of life and death as "We live, we improve and renew, and then we make room," with another saying that "I simply believe that we are born, live, and die in a largely random manner."[118]

Some atheists do not respond as well to spiritual talk close to death, with one saying, "The single most important thing I would want is protection from those who might use my health situation as a lever to extort some kind of conversion to a belief in a magical being and the ultimate product of everlasting life."[119] Priests are frequently referred to nonbelievers, sometimes by concerned members of the hospital staff and sometimes by family who do not share the patient's lack of belief.[120] While some patients are receptive to such an intervention, others feel greatly disrespected. An analogy is that if one had a Hindu patient, would one ever knowingly send a rabbi to them. When options are limited, some nonbelievers prefer nothing to be said rather than have that space filled with supernaturalism.

Nonbelievers' quest for rational understanding extends to the very final moment of life. Given their lack of belief in an afterlife, nones usually place all value in the tangible life they live. They focus on minimizing suffering and on doing their duties pertaining to those they love. Their desire for autonomy extends to them wanting to control even when they take their last breath. This is one reason 95 percent of atheists, a larger percentage than in any other denomination, support euthanasia and assisted suicide.[121] A similar trend is even noted in non-religious physicians, who are more likely than their religious counter-parts to support euthanasia.[122]

Just as in any other belief system, though, the strength of these beliefs and views varies from one individual to another. Because of a complete lack of structure, and because nonbelievers really serve as a convenient category for a diverse group of people who do not associ-ate with any major religion, they represent a smorgasbord of ideals about dying. Thoughts of death can strengthen religious beliefs in reli-gious people, and they can also shift agnostics, oscillating with doubt, toward faith. Reminders of mortality, however, tend to have no effect on atheists.[123]

In many ways, atheists are like people who adhere to the supernatu-ral: They look around and deep within to find meaning in their lives and the world they inhabit. Some find beauty in God, while others can find beauty only in the magical concoction of neurotransmitters and electrical impulses that makes up our conscious experience. Some see design, while others witness chaos. Death, however, is feared by the most passionate of believers and the fiercest of heretics. A doctor's duty is to guide his or her patient through these most troubling of times. Death visits everyone just once, yet physicians witness more death than anyone else does, and they witness all phases of it. One of our duties, whether we accept it or not, is to speak a language that is most cognizant of our pa-tient's beliefs. Irreligion is not just a negative worldview; there is more to nonbelievers than the absence of religion. Even as physicians try and fail to develop competence as spiritual guides for the faithful, they have even more catching up to do with those for whom death does not transcend.

FOR MUCH OF history, religion and spirituality were deeply intertwined with medical care. Physicians doubled as shamans, and religious hymns doubled as prescriptions. In some societies, that distinction continues to be absent. I remember I was in a community clinic back in Pakistan and a young man came to a family physician for erectile dysfunction. The physician, a devout Muslim with a bushy beard, wrote a small prayer in Arabic on prescription paper and handed it to the patient. When the patient struggled to recite it, he stopped him abruptly: "Say it from your throat, not your mouth. If you don't say it right, it won't work." The patient felt disappointed with his enunciation.

Religion, like politics, while a force for good, also evokes impassioned beliefs. In many places in the world, religious differences drive massacres and genocide. While not all people talk about their faith, it remains important for many. Appropriately, perhaps, talk of religion has been taken out of the modern workplace. This is particularly true in the Northeast, where I trained.

The distinction between their faith and everything else does not exist for patients the way it does for their doctors, particularly when patients are approaching the end of their mortal lives. The experience is akin to being trapped in a falling building: One reaches out for whatever can be held on to no matter how frail or slippery. For people, death is as much about control as life is. Much as in life, sometimes we present ourselves with illusions of influence. Yet people find different ways to exert control: some by control itself and some by consciously letting go. Patients defer decision making to their doctors, to their loved ones, or to their god.

The mathematician who wanted the physicians to end his life didn't get his wish. Short of that, though, the team offered him everything, yet he remained dissatisfied. Just a short time after he went home, he died under mysterious circumstances. Unable to author his life with someone else's hand, perhaps he took matters into his own.

The cross section between religion, spirituality, and death is anathema to most physicians. Most think of it as a Pandora's box, the opening of which might cause irreparable harm. Yet not talking about a patient's faith is tantamount to not treating them as a person. In fact, according to the Joint Commission on Accreditation of Healthcare Organizations and the World Health Organization, physicians are required to provide care that is in accordance with the spiritual views and needs of their patients.[124] Palliative care guidelines mandate a spiritual history that elicits patients' faith and what their needs in that regard might be.

The key to helping patients is helping them find what gives them comfort at a time when their world is falling apart. Julie Knopp, one of the most experienced palliative care specialists in my hospital, told me on a rainy day, "For some patients, it is their family system or a dear friend, who helps them during challenging times. Some people walk in the woods and commune with nature." It is only natural that faith is important to those with strong beliefs. "For someone who has deep faith, they have something they can fall back on, which is so comforting, and which they have had for a long time. They have always relied on it when things are difficult."

With this in mind, I found myself at the side of an elderly lady who had been dealt an awful hand. After years of struggle with debilitating rheumatoid arthritis, she developed difficulty breathing. She went to the hospital, where a CAT scan showed that she had lung cancer. A biopsy showed that it was the most aggressive type: small-cell lung cancer. Her disease progressed until she had to be connected to a breathing machine. High-dose chemotherapy was started emergently, and it took multiple failed attempts at taking her off the ventilator before finally she was successfully disconnected.

From underneath the fog of anesthesia rose a woman full of humor, full of wit, and full of warmth. She asked the ICU team, "So what happens if I decide I don't want all this anymore?" She wanted to give intubation a chance but was definitely against CPR. A week later, though, she was going downhill again. It took every muscle in her body for her to take even a single breath. After I had exhausted all means, I paged the ICU resident that I would be sending her back to the unit. When I went up to tell her that she was going back, to my surprise, she refused. She had had enough.

I didn't know what to make of what she was telling me. She was huffing and puffing, heaving until her nostrils fluttered; this was definitely not when I liked to talk about such decisions, but she surprised me with her lucidity. She had given chemotherapy a chance and she knew it hadn't worked. She was tired of her trips in and out of the hospital. She told me and the rest of the team at her bedside that she wanted to be comfortable and wanted to be left alone. When we asked her whether she wanted some medications that might make her breathing more comfortable but might make her drowsy, she was fine with that. When asked if she knew there was a chance she would not make it back home, she was completely unfazed.

I stood next to her bed as she continued to attend to the show she was watching on the Food Network playing on the television behind my back. She was a frail woman, with her hands turned in knots from her arthritis, wearing oversized glasses. She had a stylish haircut. If anything, she seemed too well composed, and it was a situation none of us were used to.

"Do you want us to call anyone?"

"No."

"Do you have any affairs you need to tend to?"

"No."

"Does religion or spirituality hold any significance in your life?" I asked, and she looked at me with an almost incredulous look and replied, "No."

"Do you want to talk to a pastor or priest?"

"No."

She was in no rush as she saw the blond Food Network chef sip on her cocktail and sway as she savored the afternoon delight. Some people need all the help we can give them. They need us to hold their hand, to say a prayer, to talk about their dreams, to go through their pictures, to share their food, to walk with them in the hallways and yearn for pain to go away, far, far away. But there are some who don't need us at all, who are prepared to die as if it were the only thing they knew. So much of humanity's greatest endeavors were forged in the fires of fear—religion, medicine, and humor, to name a few. Yet to have someone look death in the face, stare it down with unflinching nonchalance, is still a sight that lifts the heart and testifies to the limitless strength all of us have within.

When Guardians Are Burdened

Death has always been a family affair. But the metamorphosis of death has changed the role family plays as patients undergo a protracted dying. People these days, as they prepare for their retirements, frequently become the primary caregivers of their parents, given how much longer people live. In spite of great changes, few deaths occur in isolation, and in that, death affects many who surround the dying.

Ostensibly, all hospital rooms look the same. Same white sheets and towels, stock photos and soft boards on the walls, bags of saline and IV tubing hanging by the side. Patients, too, end up looking identical, with their light blue johnnies, slip-resistant slippers, and hospitalization hair—when patients' hair starts to stand up straight after they've remained chronically bedridden. Their doctors, too, look the same, with their lab coats with pockets stuffed with pens and papers, scrubs with pagers at their waists, leaving patients confused about who their doctors actually are as people. But when I look hard enough, and pay enough attention, there is much I learn about my patients just by what their rooms look like.

There are some patients who bring barely anything with them but their own person. This usually means two things: Either the patient came to the hospital emergently or the patient is not used to being admitted to the hospital. The only reason I know this is that I have witnessed how well prepared patients who frequent the hospital are. Just looking around their room, looking at the spare pajamas, the snacks and the shampoos, one can tell that their pathologies have transformed them into "professional patients." Some of them keep diaries that detail every aspect of their health, charting how much urine they made every day, how many bowel movements they had, what their blood pressure or blood glucose level was, among other vitals and variables.

One recurring item that always caught my eye was grown-up patients bringing large stuffed animals with them when they presented to the hospital. The patients most likely to have stuffed animals also frequently had furry blankets with unicorns or the like printed on them. These toys, though, always tended to be juxtaposed with some sort of terrible condition. Frequently, these patients would have intractable addictions to narcotic pain medications and display marked features of mental and psychological instability. Turns out that my observation was not isolated; the presence of teddy bears at the bedside had been recognized as a telltale sign of borderline personality disorder in a study conducted at Walter Reed Army Medical Center in the nineties.[1] Another study showed that adults with the "teddy bear sign" were three times more likely to have psychiatrically mediated seizures rather than true epileptic seizures.[2] One case told the story of a thirty-year-old-female who came to the hospital with seventeen stuffed koala bears, each of whom represented a prior therapist.[3]

On the bedside tables, clues are frequently strewn. Religious totes such as little baby Jesus figurines or menorahs give insight into patients' spiritual lives. The choice of books people bring with them can also be illuminating; many cancer patients read books written by survivors. If it is a book I am familiar with, I frequently talk about it. On the walls, or on the soft board, other clues can be found. Cards from friends and family members can key one into a patient's social network. Pictures present a window into a day in the life of the diseased—

usually happy, smiling, and surrounded by those who are important to them.

When I walked into Christina's room, my eyes first darted to the framed picture of her wedding that sat next to her bed. Having worked all her life in the government as a clerk, she was in her late thirties when she met and fell in love with her now husband. They had known each other for years before tying the knot. Shortly after the wedding, though, Christina had started to lose a lot of weight. An MRI revealed a tumor in her ovaries; she had her uterus, fallopian tubes, and ovaries removed surgically, but remnants of the tumor remained and kept growing. After her first chemotherapy treatment failed, the tumor started to block her intestines. She was now in the hospital on second-line treatment—a newlywed fighting for her life.

Looking at her, though, you wouldn't be able to tell what she had been through. She was the brightest person in the room, always optimistic and never complaining. The physicians and nurses actually had to coax her to let us know when she was in pain. She didn't want to be a bother, she told us. Her smile in the room was no different from that in the wedding picture from less than a year ago. But she was just half the wedding picture. The other and increasingly important half was sitting in the bedside chair, sometimes waiting in the family room or anxiously walking the lengths of the hallways, fighting to get answers. That other half was the patient's spouse, the primary voice of extended family and loved ones. More than through anything else in a patient's room, one learns most about patients through the brave guardians at their side.

While Christina, through perhaps the strength of her goodness, managed to remain cheerful through this ordeal, even as her hair fell like flakes and she suffered from ever-worsening blockages in her gut, her husband was less unshaken. He had the look of someone weathered with fear and anxiety, but at the same time trying his best to be there for his wife, willing her along this painful and ultimately doomed journey.

So if you just look hard enough around a patient's room, you get to learn by seeing, but if you also attend to the relatives and friends in a patient's room, every patient starts telling a different story. At the same time as Christina, I was also taking care of an old gentleman

with Alzheimer's dementia, who the night before had fled his retirement home on a motorized scooter, and was found on the freeway after
his fuel ran out. When I met him in the morning he was very solemn, to
the extent of almost being mute. Yet when his grandkids came to the
room, in their colorful clothes and accompanied by their parents, his
face lit up. It turned out that the night before, he had missed them so
much that, in a bit of dementia-induced delirium, he had embarked on
his scooter hoping to reach them.

Since primordial times, family has served as the purveyor of care and
comfort for the sick and debilitated. Modern caregiving, though, has
little if anything in common with the care families have provided their
sick loved ones in the past. Caregiving these days has become increasingly demanding and has resulted in the emergence of the second
victim—the family member spending long days and nights giving intravenous antibiotics, filling bags of tube feedings, changing diapers, buy-
ing medical equipment, at times with no end in sight. Few deaths in
history ever occurred in isolation, but more than ever before, today
death touches all those around it.

WHEN I WAS growing up in Pakistan, it was always rare to see someone
who wasn't married or didn't have children. In spite of its ubiquity, marriage seemed like an unnecessary nuisance to my uninitiated mind. A
part of me thought that the prospect of living one's life as a veritable
"dude" was quite promising. When I asked my parents why it was necessary to get married and have children, they didn't give me the talk;
instead they (and everyone else I asked) told me that children were
necessary to help when one is old and sick.

This made sense to me. My grandfather died when I was very young,
but my paternal grandmother, my *daadi,* lived with us. Caregiving was
another reason sons were and continue to be so deeply desired in our
part of the world: the vast majority of elderly parents live with their sons.
It remains rare for parents to live with their daughters, although that is
largely changing, as women increasingly make an important economic
contribution in the family unit.

Taking care of *daadi* was never really hard. She had only ever been to the hospital a handful of times. Other than antidepressants, she took no medications. She lived to her nineties with little evidence of dementia. She once fell down a few stairs and had a large cut on her leg that healed remarkably well. When she fractured her femur, my father took her back to the village after her surgery and did whatever ad hoc physical therapy he could come up with. Then one day in the village she developed some chest pain and passed away.

Looking after *daadi* was very easy for us: My parents were young and we had tons of help. There was a lot of family around, but additional help could be hired for next to nothing. In many ways, this is what taking care of the elderly and dying entailed in the United States a few decades back. A lack of chronic disease and an overabundance of acute causes of death from the three big "I"s—injury, infection, and ischemia (heart disease)—meant that years lived with disability were very few. However, the increase in longevity has also greatly changed the nature of modern caregiving.

In previous times the only people who would survive to their nineties were people who truly enjoyed the best of health, such as my *daadi*. People like her, though, are as rare in the United States as they are back in Pakistan. Most people in Pakistan don't live to be that old and therefore their children are fairly young, too. Modern medicine, however, has allowed us to extend the lives of many people who would otherwise have succumbed to an early death. Great advances in everything from heart and lung disease to cancer now allow a lot of people to live on despite their illnesses.

Our efforts to delay death have come at a price. A price paid by many, including Mrs. Douglas (not her real name), who at the age of eighty-four shot herself three times the day she had planned a family picnic.[4] When she woke up in the hospital, having miraculously survived her attempted suicide, she was relieved, because for once she did not have to take care of her eighty-six-year-old husband. Mrs. Douglas's husband had become weak and dependent on her, and she was his sole caregiver even though she had two daughters who lived close by. This was not the first time she had thought about committing suicide, stuck in an endless and unrecognized cycle of caring for a debilitated loved one. She confessed later that she had been thinking about suicide for two years and just the thought of having that option gave her respite.

Informal caregivers, while ubiquitous, become almost invisible. Mrs. Douglas's daughters offered help but could never really understand the extent to which she was overstretched. Mrs. Douglas went to the doctor with her husband but had no doctor of her own despite her old age. Even the individual receiving care can be blind to the weight they place on the shoulders of those taking care of them. The main reason Mrs. Douglas didn't have any help was that her husband didn't want anyone else in the house and wouldn't accept home care. "I could not stand another twenty-four hours," she told the doctors in the hospital. "I asked my husband more than once, wouldn't he like some of those people to come in and help? At least bathe and things like that . . . he said no." When he did die, two months after she had attempted to take her own life, Mrs. Douglas, who had loved him and served him all her life, felt relieved.

Another time, I was in the geriatric clinic when I met an elderly man who had moved from out of state a few months before to spend his retirement in the Boston area. He had given up a successful law practice and was accompanied by a younger woman. Turns out his last wife had died, and now that he was getting older he had married someone younger who could help through his twilight years. His illnesses, though, were catching up to him, and he was becoming increasingly difficult to manage at home. As I sat across from him and his wife in clinic asking them questions, it was becoming clear that he was getting increasingly confused. He was having difficulty remembering his medications and had little idea about what was going on in general. At the same time, though, he aggressively cut off his wife when she started to say anything. Outbursts of anger are a common manifestation of dementia.[5]

After the visit ended and the retired lawyer left, the wife returned to talk to me in the clinic as I was finishing up my notes. Her eyes were teary and her hands were shaking: she had been diagnosed with a very aggressive form of thyroid cancer. Instead of being able to take care of herself as she was coming to grips with a diagnosis that almost certainly represented a death sentence, she had been struggling just to carry on taking care of her husband. At the same time, though, even as she was trying her best to take care of her elderly husband, the terrible guilt of perhaps not doing a good enough job was taking a toll on her. She told me that he married her so that she could care for him and not the other way around.

In spite of her severe rheumatoid arthritis, Mrs. Roberts took care of her husband long before he was seventy years old and got diagnosed with incurable pancreatic cancer.[6] "I knew I would take care of him myself because we had always done things together," she said. "We worked together for thirty years. We played together, we did everything together since I was eighteen years old." Because Mr. Roberts had been legally blind since the early 1970s, his wife had always been by his side. "There was never a question whether I would continue to be [with him] during this period or not," she added. Yet even she became overwhelmed with the escalating demands accompanying an impending death from cancer. Between several hospital admissions for infections, diarrhea, vomiting, and dehydration, she took care of him at home as he became bedbound owing to severe weakness. She had two children who were only rarely around and was spending about ten hours tending to him every day. "To me, it just never stopped. It wasn't the care, it was the whole commitment," she said. As patients grow sicker, the fear of being unable to provide one's loved one with adequate care escalates: "I realized that if anything untoward occurred, I wouldn't be able to do anything for him," she said.

These stories are but a tip of the iceberg: One in four American adults provides informal caregiving at any given moment.[7] With the process of death becoming increasingly prolonged, the number of people slated to participate in carrying loved ones through the end of life and into the awaiting arms of death is only slated to increase. The toll of modern death on caregivers is only now being unearthed.

WHEN I SPOKE to Meryl Comer, she told me that it had been twelve years since her husband, who developed early-onset dementia, had last recognized who she was, "but I know he recognizes my touch." Harvey Gralnick was the head of hematology and oncology at the National Institutes of Health, and had lived life well, before he developed early-onset dementia, in his fifties, more than twenty years ago. Meryl Comer had a successful career as a business journalist, but that now seems like another life, as she has been spending twelve hours a day and more as a full-time caregiver for almost two decades now. Her story encapsulates everything that has become routine for caregivers in America.

Providing care to dying friends and relatives is increasingly becoming a rite of passage for all Americans. In 2014, 43.5 million Americans served as the caregiver for a family member struggling with illness.[8] Of these, about 40 percent demonstrate a high degree of caregiver burden.[9] As in most of the stories I have described here, the overwhelming majority of caregivers are female, and 85 percent of them are related to the patient.[10]

The time investment that caregivers make is also quite substantial: On average, caregivers spend twenty-one hours a week helping their loved ones eat, bathe, shop, take medications, manage finances, make appointments, drive around, and change diapers, and become proficient with medical equipment such as catheters, feeding tubes, and IVs. A fifth of caregivers spend more than forty hours a week providing this pro bono help.[11] Meryl, too, works long hours: "I lead the team, I do twelve-hour shifts, but I am also the case manager."

Informal caregivers account for 90 percent of all home care delivered to dying patients. In doing so, they save the health-care system an enormous amount of money. According to estimates, informal caregivers provided up to $450 billion in unpaid voluntary services in 2009, and this number is likely to be higher now.[12] Another study estimates that friends and relatives taking care of dementia patients provide an average of $56,290 per year in services.[13] And as finances dwindle, it stretches families in all other areas. Resources that would otherwise go toward food, housing, travel, education, or downtime are funneled toward the care of the ailing. The care itself suffers, too: "When caregivers are squeezed financially, they go for the cheapest quality: the catheters leak, the diapers shred and you end up changing the sheets several times a night." Up to a fifth of caregivers end up having to quit their day jobs, and a third lose most or all of their life savings during the course of their voluntary duties.[14]

Caregivers suffer not only in resources but also in health: one study showed that people actively taking care of a loved one are at 63 percent higher risk of dying than those who are not involved in caregiving.[15] Furthermore, if someone had a disabled spouse but was not involved in their care, they did not accrue any increase in mortality. Even more interesting was the finding that there was no increase in the risk of death among caregivers who were taking care of loved ones but not experiencing strain doing so. Caregivers perhaps understandably experience increased rates of depression,[16] anxiety,[17] and insomnia and an increased risk of suicide.[18] As a result of these comorbidities, as well as the responsibilities of being so focused on the well-being of family or friends, caregivers routinely ignore their own health.

What is surprising about this is that caregivers understand the healthcare system better than most people. As a physician, I see caregivers sometimes more often than I do patients. They are the people waiting in hospital lobbies and hallways, getting coffee at odd hours and sleeping in recliners at the patient's bedside. They are holding hands in waiting areas outside operating theaters and emergency rooms. Very frequently, they accompany my patients when they come to the clinic, diary in hand, medications in a Ziploc bag, and questions scribbled on a folded piece of paper. More so than even many patients, they are the ones calling to have disability paperwork signed, following up on lab results and setting up appointments. Yet despite being so intimately plugged into the system, too many times they are so invested in the well-being of another that they forget about themselves.

But perhaps the greater problem is not that caregivers are ignoring their healthcare but that healthcare ignores caregivers. Caregivers have no recognized role in medicine, and their needs remain largely unaddressed. "It's a lonely space," Meryl told me. When I see a caregiver with a patient, I have no legal role in being able to address their health needs unless they also happen to be a patient of mine, which is extremely rare. It is because of this lack of recognition that the system at large does not cater to the well-being of those voluntarily doing their bit to take care of patients in their homes. And as caregivers fall ill, the care they provide their loved ones suffers, which in turn further strains the caregiver, who is already starved for motivation. Caregivers who are spouses tend to be far more burdened than those who are children, because frequently they have no choice but to assume that role.[19]

Speaking of caregivers who fare worse than others, females, who constitute the vast majority of caregivers,[20] suffer twice the burden men do in a similar role.[21] Low levels of education and high levels of poverty, too, are associated with increased burden, as are other factors, such as loss of employment, lack of choice, and increased time spent in caregiving.[22] The relationship that caregivers have with the patient prior to their illness is also an important determinant of how much of a burden they will feel when they take on the added responsibility.[23] Interestingly, neither the nature of the patient's illness (whether cancer, lung disease, or heart failure) nor the severity of the illness had an effect on the degree of caregiver burden, as social support does. Caregivers, whose cries for help frequently go unheeded, desire more help from family and friends, and this support can offset the weight any severe illness places on them.[24]

It is not difficult to see why taking care of someone trapped in a prolonged phase of dying is deeply depressing. Caregivers come to define themselves through the people they are shepherding. In most cases, the recipients of this care carry a grim prognosis, fighting diseases that they cannot defeat. As the end approaches, the feedback and response they receive from the patient starts to dwindle as well. Over this arduous process, caregivers assume the role of the "invisible patient," always present, but never really there, consumed by the needs of the patient.[25]

Caregivers, to date, haven't been formally integrated in healthcare, and while their help remains appreciated by health-care providers, physicians haven't figured out how to either provide care for them or leverage their services to improve care for patients. Meryl told me that over the course of twenty years, only one physician asked her how she was doing. "When you have a disease that always wins no matter what one does, you need someone to make you feel what you are doing matters."

As WEIGHTY AS the duties of caregiving might be, when the end approaches, another challenge arises for guardians. Ours is a culture obsessed with death and dying. Open a book, watch a television show, read a newspaper, browse a Web site and you will find evidence of Americans' appetite for death in all its forms. In fact, since you are reading this book right now, I guess I need not make any further arguments. Yet despite this pervasive cultural preoccupation, actual conversations about death occur far too infrequently. In fact, many patients I have taken care of, even when moments away from death, have never had a serious conversation about the end of life. Increasingly, though, that conversation, about what one would want at the end of life, is turning out to be the most important conversation most of us will ever have in our lifetimes.

Ellen Goodman, a Pulitzer Prize–winning columnist for the *Boston Globe,* was the primary caregiver of her elderly mother. This was not too surprising given that she had already assumed that role during the latter half of her career without fully realizing all the trappings it came with. One story she told me was about a day when she was at work with a deadline hanging over her head and she got a call from her mother's care facility. There was a doctor on the other end of the line who told her that her mother had gotten pneumonia again. "He was asking me whether I wanted to have her get antibiotics or not." This was just one of countless microdecisions that Ellen and other caregivers have to make on a regular basis when taking care of an elderly loved one. "I was faced with this cascading number of decisions for which I was really not prepared."

Ellen was very close to her mother, and as with many daughters and mothers, no topic was off-limits, and they shared everything "except of course, this one thing." This one thing that they didn't talk about was how her mother would want to die. By the time Ellen realized how important this conversation was, her mother's dementia had progressed to the extent that she couldn't even talk about something as simple as food, let alone grasp the complexities of end-of-life care in the era of modern medicine.

Ellen's situation, however, is not unique. If anything, it is the norm. A national survey demonstrated that only 30 percent of patients share their preference regarding what sort of treatment they would like to receive around the time of death.[26] Only 7 percent of patients report having a conversation about their preferences with their doctors. This dismal rate is not from people not realizing the significance of this topic; between 82 and 90 percent of people believe it is important to talk about what sort of treatment one should receive at the end of life.

Despite our never-dissipating fascination with death, actually talking about death remains very much a fringe pastime. Even when we do talk about death, it is rarely a discussion with a personal bent. Throughout history, talking about death has remained taboo. In many cultures even these days, people don't talk about dying, even with death knocking at the door. A middle-aged Asian man who spoke only Japanese and had recently been diagnosed with liver failure was admitted to the ICU after his blood pressure plummeted. He got better quite quickly after receiving some intravenous fluids, but we sent him downstairs to receive an MRI scan of his abdomen to make sure everything was stable. As he was being rolled downstairs, his wife and son walked up to us and told us that whatever the results were, we should first run them by the family. The patient had already indicated that he was fine with that.

When he returned to the ICU and we were preparing to transfer him to a lower-acuity ward, the MRI images were uploaded. Curious to get a head start on the radiologist's reading, I pulled up the scan. I wasn't confident I would discern anything: as a physician trained in internal medicine, I would be able to pick something up only if it was gargantuan in size. So when my amateur eyes detected said gargantuan tumor eroding through his liver and his gallbladder and matted onto his stomach, I knew this was something terribly serious. Sure enough, the radiologist diagnosed him with metastatic cancer that had left little of his belly unscathed. I immediately called his liver doctor, who left whatever he was in the middle of and arrived in the ICU. I told him that the family wanted to shield the patient, so we took the son and the mother to a vacant office filled with beige file cabinets and excess printers and monitors.

The mother spoke only Japanese, but the son spoke fully acculturated American English. He was awfully young but was eager to be the representative for his family. With many senior physicians, I am wary about how they will share information with the patient or whether they will water down the situation. This particular physician, though, was from Ireland, and had a reputation of laying things out as simply and honestly as possible. He told the son, quite cleanly, that his father had untreatable cancer with no treatment options, which would lead to him dying anytime within the next few weeks or months. My eyes were transfixed on the son as he absorbed all this information. He seemed to take in the information really gracefully, but as he turned toward his anxious mother and started translating for her, it was then that he started to realize exactly what had just been said to him.

As he translated, I could see his face melt with every word, and by the time he was done talking, he and his mother were wrapped in each other's arms, crying. They didn't want us in the room and asked us to let them be. When they returned to the ICU, they had dried their eyes and muffled the shakes, and they came back to the patient's side acting as if nothing had happened. As I saw them through the glass door, it seemed like some sort of macabre performance, with the family forcing smiles, striking conversation. The patient later left the ICU with no idea that his life had been cut in half.

Some cultures are extremely averse to discussing death. In Navajo culture, merely talking about death is said to bring it about, and therefore talking about end-of-life care with elderly Navajo is particularly challenging.[27] Our present culture, too, has been particularly creative in avoiding not only talk about death and dying in general, but the words "death" and "dying" specifically. A survey conducted in the United Kingdom found that while a third of people think about dying on a weekly basis, two-thirds of people were not comfortable talking about the end.[28] And while people generally think that a more open conversation about death would improve end-of-life care, less than a third of the general public reported having talked to a family member about death or discussing their own preferences for end-of-life care. Physicians, too, are squeamish about having discussions about dying; in this survey, 35 percent (a surprisingly large number) of general practitioners had not had a discussion about death with *any* of their patients.

While to me it is unacceptable for physicians to not discuss dying with their patients, I can see why some physicians might be reluctant to do so with patients. Most people think about death as an abstract and hypothetical event, one that can always be pushed forward into the future. Once people are put on the spot to talk about death—not just death as a general concept, but their own personal inevitable culmination—the cosmic schism between our mortality and our consciousness's inability to absorb that concept comes to a head.

Every time a patient gets admitted to the hospital and I take their history, I am checking off a few boxes. What brought them in? What medical conditions do they have? What medications do they take? Do they smoke, drink, or use any recreational substances? Practice allows me to get through this rather exhaustive list fairly quickly, but I always pause before one final box: *What type of treatment would you want close to death?*

Early in my intern year, naively, I would assume that if people were sick enough to come to the emergency room and then be admitted, especially since for the vast majority of the people I saw this was not their first trip to the hospital, they would have given this issue a thought. To my surprise, most people, some even on the verge of death, some who had been battling life-threatening diseases for decades, some who had still not recovered from high-risk surgery, had never thought about what they would consider a good death for themselves.

Many times when I ask patients if they have thought about what they would want us to do if something catastrophic were to happen, it stops them in their tracks. Providing details about the heart attack that started off as a tingling in the chest and landed the historian anesthetized on an operating room table getting heart surgery slips as easily as a rap sheet off the tongue, but as soon as the "d" word comes up, the first thought that occurs is "Not me, not now." And these words consume every other sentient thought in most patients' heads.

People like Ellen Goodman, however, don't think that a conversation as important as that pertaining to how one would want to die should be had in a hospital; they think it should be had much sooner and in the comfort of one's home and with people one loves and trusts. "You should have these conversations at the kitchen table, rather than in a crisis," she tells me. Ellen is not the only one who wants to raise the decibels on the conversation, but she and others face an uphill task. Caregivers and loved ones now face another burden—to talk about the one thing absolutely no one ever wants to talk about.

ROZ CHAST, THE longtime cartoonist for the *New Yorker,* recently published a memoir describing her parents' aging and her attempts to talk to them about how they would like to die. Tellingly, the book is titled *Can't We Talk About Something More Pleasant?* In her graphic memoir, she draws a scene where she shares that she discussed everything with her parents except for death. When she does try to bring up the subject, her parents first feign ignorance, then progress through confusion, hysterical laughter, and convulsive anxiety until she says dejectedly, "You know what? Forget it. Never mind. *Qué será será.*" (Bloomsbury, 2014) In the next panel, both Roz and her parents appear to be separately relieved that the conversation ended where it did, going nowhere.

Ellen Goodman chalks up the difficulty faced in initiating a discussion about the end of life to a "conspiracy of silence." "Parents don't want to worry their children. Children are reluctant to bring up a subject so intimate and fraught; some worry their parents will think they're expecting or waiting for them to die."

The inability to have this conversation has real consequences. Whether anyone consciously or formally voices their wishes to another or has it put down in writing, everyone has their own individual idea about what would constitute a good death for them. Some people want to feel nothing and some want to feel everything until they can't feel anymore. Some people want to die in their own bed while others want to leave their home untainted from loss and tragedy. Some want to rest, others want to fight.

In life, we don't always get what we want. To me that's okay: if you don't ace the SATs on your first attempt you still have a few more shots at redemption. Death, though, given that it has a 100 percent historical success rate in curtailing any attempts at second chances, is much more high-stakes. Death usually means the end of wishes, and as a physician, death means there is nothing more one can do for a patient. Allowing a final wish to be fulfilled is sometimes the most meaningful thing a doctor can do. Lachlan Forrow, a palliative care specialist in Boston goes a step further—considering unwanted interventions to be preventable harm.[29]

To help others not miss the opportunity to have this conversation, various groups have come up with forms and Web sites to walk people through having this conversation with both family and friends. One such endeavor was put together by Ellen Goodman and is called The Conversation Project. "We need to change the cultural norm from not talking about the end of life," she told me. The Conversation Project is one of many ambitious initiatives that seek to make the "How would you like to die?" conversation as routine as the "Where do babies come from?" one.

As uncomfortable as parents probably find talking to their children about sex, talking about death is an entirely different beast because of the complexity of modern medicine, and the myriad permutations that might represent what a patient considers to be a suitable end.

The precursor to modern advance care planning were living wills, also called advance directives. The term "living will" was coined by Luis Kutner, a lawyer, a human-rights activist, and a cofounder of Amnesty International, who expressed his views in the *Indiana Law Journal* in 1969.[30] Kutner describes the state of affairs: in the late 1960s, patients could refuse treatment, but if they were incapacitated and unable to express their views, physicians were liable to treat them to the nth extent. "Therefore, the suggested solution is that the individual, while fully in control of his faculties and his ability to express himself, would indicate to what extent he would consent to treatment," he summed up. This proposal did have one limitation: It was reserved for patients who become "completely vegetative" and who "cannot regain [their] mental and physical capacities." While this final clause limited the catchment of this document, it was widely adopted, especially after the Karen Ann Quinlan case. The first time a living will was incorporated into law was in 1976 in California's Natural Death Act; however, this statute was even more limited.[31] The act allowed patients to withdraw life-sustaining treatment only if they had a "terminal illness," one that would cause death imminently. Furthermore, the directive to withdraw or withhold such care could not be signed in the first two weeks after the patient had been diagnosed. However, living wills spread through the United States and were adopted by most states into law. The surge in adoption of living wills was formally endorsed by the US Congress who declared in the Patient Self-Determination Act in 1990 that hospitals are required to provide Medicare beneficiaries materials to educate them about their right to formulate an advance directive.[32] Living wills now do not require a terminal illness and can be filled out by people in any state of health.

Advance directives have been around for decades and have since evolved into comprehensive advance care planning. Instruments have now been developed that seek to take patients through thinking about these difficult questions rather than just have them check boxes and sign. These decision aids variably inquire about patients' preferences with regard to life-sustaining treatment, organ and tissue donation, kidney dialysis, pain management, artificial nutrition and hydration, life support and CPR, and location of treatment.[33] They provide computer programs, Web sites, booklets, videos, and DVDs and CDs to help patients make decisions and spell out choices. While most aids have been developed for individuals, others have been developed for medical organizations to record these preferences in their electronic medical-record system.

Despite these advances, living wills and their more advanced cousins remain deeply flawed, and while they represent a stopgap measure, they do not represent a long-term solution. Despite the coverage these forms have received in the mainstream, and their endorsement by the federal government, by the US Supreme Court,[34] and by the medical complex, the vast majority of people do not fill them out. One survey conducted in Boston showed that only about 18 percent of the general public and 15 percent of patients in clinics had filled out these forms, as opposed to 74 percent and 57 percent respectively who had filled out

estate wills.[35] Among patients who are much sicker, and therefore should
be thinking about these issues—such as, say, those on dialysis—that
number increases only to about 35 percent.[36] Even when patients have
filled out these forms, the information contained within the forms does
not reach the medical chart 74 percent of the time, with only 16 percent
of charts actually containing the form itself.[37]

When a form is signed or a preference declared is also very crucial to
what type of decision is reached. Patients who have just left the hospital
are much more likely to not want aggressive care, but within six months
that attitude is reversed.[38] How well one knows their disease and its
prognosis is also very important. A disease such as cancer is more predictable, since the prognosis is mostly linear with some room for variation. A patient therefore who has lung cancer that has metastasized
knows that he or she has months at best, and this information is crucial
to what route of treatment they take. As opposed to that, patients who
have end-stage kidney disease, any form of heart or lung disease, and
most noncancer illnesses have little predictable information about how
their disease will progress and what sort of time they may have left.

How information is framed is also crucial to how choices are made.
Physicians are usually the source of information that patients use to make
these decisions, and how a physician frames the conversation actually
changes what decision the patient makes. When physicians call ductal
carcinoma in situ (a precursor of breast cancer) a noninvasive cancer as
opposed to a breast lesion, patients are much more likely to opt for surgery.[39] How physicians quote statistics—whether they use success rates or
failure rates, whether they describe short-term effects or long-term effects,
and what amount of detail they use—can have an additional effect on
which way patients lean. Up to four of five patients will actually change
their minds when information is phrased in a different manner.[40]

Physicians don't always do a great job of talking to patients about these
tough situations. There are many times when I am cringing in a patient's
room at how one of my colleagues is phrasing a delicate situation. Truth is,
doctors are great at describing both really catastrophic situations and
really benign ones. Certainty, though, is rare in medicine, and therefore
may not apply to most scenarios that we encounter. It is nuance where we

struggle, and perhaps that is understandable. But nuance and subtlety are hard to convey, especially when one is dabbling in hypotheticals.

To me, perhaps the most important factor in determining the outcome of a conversation between a doctor and his patient is how the patient is feeling. Healthy people are much less likely to take such conversations seriously as opposed to those who consider death a tangible possibility. When I ask young healthy patients if they have ever thought about the end of life, I do so knowing that most people who have never experienced modern mortality in a significant way have little idea of what it entails. I also know that any verdict patients reach is labile and subject to change. In one study of patients who had signed living wills and wanted maximal treatment, only 43 percent wanted similar treatment when asked the same question after two years.[41]

Of course, I don't need a study to tell me that. Many things make people think twice about how they would like to die. A new diagnosis, a new hospitalization, a successful cycle of chemotherapy are certainly things that can shift gears in patient's minds, but there are other factors, too, that are less tangible but that I see all the time. Seeing a loved one sick and suffering, waiting for an important wedding or birth, achieving an important milestone are all things that can affect preferences. So much so that one of the the hospital where I used to work did not even log advance directives in its electronic medical record: What if someone wanted no heroic measures on a previous admission but has since changed his mind? It is possible that the patient may not get the care he or she wants because a physician may erroneously assume something based on a prior preference a patient expressed under different circumstances.

Living wills are also plagued by being either too vague or too specific. The New York Bar Association, to illustrate this point, published a living will, which stated, "If I am: a) in a terminal condition; b) permanently unconscious; or c) if I am conscious but have irreversible brain damage . . . I do not want cardiac resuscitation . . . mechanical respiration . . . tube feeding . . . antibiotics."[42] Now, while this living will is fairly concrete, it doesn't help me understand what this patient would want if he were to develop dementia or heart failure (both terminal conditions) and then develop pneumonia, which is not terminal and can frequently be reversible just with oral antibiotics or perhaps may require a few days of mechanical ventilation to give lungs the time to heal. Many living wills may also present internally inconsistent instructions that just don't make sense: one physician described a patient of his who would want blood transfusions if he were bleeding but not an endoscopic procedure that would be able to treat the cause of his bleeding and prevent him from hemorrhaging any further.[43] This is similar to the case I described earlier in which a patient wanted to be ventilated with a breathing machine but was opposed to cardiac resuscitation.

One place living wills *have* worked is the quaint and beautiful town of La Crosse in western Wisconsin. Nestled in a valley next to the Mississippi River, surrounded by hills, La Crosse is now considered by many people one of the best places in the United States to die. I didn't know this when I was there having salmon at a restaurant by the Mississippi or driving around in the overlying bluffs, enjoying gorgeous views of the valley. When I was there, I could never have guessed that 95 percent of the residents in La Crosse, from teenagers to octogenarians, had filled out advance directives.[44] While it is difficult to ascertain causality, La Crosse also has one of the lowest per-capita health expenditures in the country, at around $18,000 per resident. Perhaps that is because 98 percent of all residents who die in La Crosse do not desire life-prolonging treatment. Tellingly, all the patients who had previously undergone CPR before this drive to increase advance-directive documentation decided not to have CPR reinitiated if the need arose.[45]

La Crosse, though, is an outlier, and by quite a bit. It is geographically and demographically homogeneous (92 percent white) in a way that continues to reflect an America of the past.[46] Truth is, Americans in general have rejected advance directives, and this is reflected by the continued low rates of people filling these out despite them being around for decades. The problem with a living will is that it is a static directive that hopes to address a very dynamic and complex situation. Research has shown that between 71 percent and 78 percent of people would rather have a loved one or caregiver make a treatment decision, even if it supersedes their own preference.[47] Caregivers are making the most difficult decisions for patients, and of all the burdens guardians carry, this is the most crushing.

How Death Is Negotiated

Sven was a medical student from Germany who had come to my hospital to do an elective rotation. He had a tall and thin frame, would wear checked shirts and suede shoes without fail, and was never seen with a belt. In addition to the usual stuff medical students carry (stethoscope, pocket textbook, reflex hammer, tuning fork, etc.), he carried a small stout book that he would consult very frequently. It was an English-to-German medical dictionary.

Sven had come all the way from Frankfurt, and I really wanted to show him something unique about American medicine. Germany, of course, has all the shiny toys we have—the most advanced cardiac catheters and devices, the most fancy robotic surgeries, shiny hospitals, crisp lab coats, and whatnot. If anything, German medicine is way ahead of the United States' in having far superior medical outcomes on a population-based level. After much thought, I figured out that there was one thing I could not deprive him of which was quintessentially American: I took him to a family meeting.

The patient was an elderly lady who had come in from New

Hampshire. Everything started after she had a heart attack. She came to the hospital but was found to be in multiorgan failure. Too sick to get a cardiac catheterization, she was stabilized in the ICU. Her heart was so weak it wasn't really beating; it was quivering just enough to get a fraction of the required amount of blood pumping. Her kidneys, too, were barely functioning at this point, and were unable to filter the body's toxins. The ICU team had emergently started dialysis at the bedside, to help lend a hand to her dying kidneys. The hope was that whatever had caused her kidneys to come to a standstill would dissipate and that she would not require dialysis long-term. Days became weeks, and it seemed that her kidneys were done for. Dialysis was a bridge to nowhere.

Increasingly, her clinical state became an untenable Band-Aid at best. Because her heart was so weak, every time she was on dialysis her blood pressure would drop to dangerous levels. Things had reached a point where the dialysis-unit staff felt uncomfortable even trying dialysis, given how she was not tolerating it at all. The status quo had become very tenuous, and I felt that it was time to meet the family and discuss what the course going forward ought to be.

Back when the patient was first admitted, her husband had brought in a wrinkled piece of paper; it was her living will. On that piece of paper, she had blackened out the square next to the option indicating that she would not want CPR or mechanical ventilation. To me, the form was not very useful. It didn't tell me what circumstance she had signed the form in, what she knew about these procedures, or what she considered a good death. As we were weighing the competing risks of depriving her brain of oxygen by performing dialysis or letting unfiltered toxins accumulate in her system, I learned nothing about what she would want at that very moment.

It was for just this type of a moment that society, judiciary, and medicine came up with a solution. A patient, in addition to having a document that would carry forward their wishes should they become incapacitated, would appoint a person who would serve as their voice should they be unable to fully comprehend the prevailing clinical situation or participate in any meaningful way. That person, also referred to as a health-care proxy, would be someone who not only would have the patient's best interest front and center, but also would be able to relay what the patient would say or decide in any situation. Thankfully, my patient had already designated her husband as her health-care proxy, so I called him on the phone and let him know that the team wanted to meet him. He told us that his two daughters would also be at the meeting.

I asked Sven to page all the people who needed to be at the meeting: the cardiologist, who could talk about the heart failure; the nephrologist, to discuss the dialysis; the social worker, who knew the family very well; and of course the other members of our medical team, who were primarily taking care of her on a day-to-day basis. When we entered the room, the patient was looking at the ceiling, mouth open, saying nothing. I surveyed the room to find one daughter, the younger, leaning over her mother and crying, while the older sister was looking out the window, and the father was sitting on a chair clutching his hat.

After the customary introductions, I tried to orchestrate a digestible update of the situation for the family, starting with the cardiologist, who told them that her heart was still as weak as ever and there was little we could do for it, and ending with the nephrologist, who told the family that at this point continuing with dialysis would do more harm than good. He concluded by saying that he would recommend withdrawing dialysis.

The older daughter, who referred to herself frequently as "the meanie," was the pessimist who seemed to agree with our recommendation. She kept saying how she also believed that at this time, doing more was in fact going to only bring more harm upon her. But she was struggling: "Sometimes I wake up at night thinking that not doing more would be like killing her." The younger one, though, rarely left her mother's side, and she was decidedly stricken by the situation. She was crying, laughing, trying to talk to her mother, and from time to time would interrupt the conversation, after prematurely and incorrectly discovering that her mother was alert and oriented. She wasn't really listening to anyone, but would frequently let us know how we all hated her mother, how we were tired of taking care of her and just wanted "to get rid of her." She was her mother's favorite, she told us, and even though she knew she wasn't the health-care proxy, she knew it was she who loved her most.

Outside the room, from nowhere, a blizzard had taken hold. I vividly remember the wind blowing snow in all directions other than down. I could see swirls of snow climb the maroon walls against a gray desaturated background. The father was the proxy, and he was almost shaking. Not only was he burdened by being the tiebreaker, but the entire situation was just overwhelming for him. "I feel like my heart and my mind are at war," he told us. "My mind knows it is futile but my heart wants her to not die and leave us."

I looked around the room, and tension was hanging in the air like industrial-grade smog. I looked at Sven, and he was red as a beet; I could tell that this was not something he was used to back in Germany. Any more stress and I thought he would start bleeding out of his eyes. What we felt was of course nothing compared with what the family members were feeling. They had taken care of their mother for many years as her body grew weaker, but this was not only a different ball game, it was a completely different sport. "I just don't have it in me to pull the plug," the father told us.

Being a health-care proxy is one of the hardest things one can be nominated to be. In caregiving, no matter what one does, the disease wins, and such is the proxy's paradox as well. At best, a health-care proxy can ensure that his or her loved one is able to achieve a reasonable death, for it is only then that the proxy can graduate. A proxy never faces any easy questions: When doctors have a good solution, a proxy's role is straightforward and superficial; it is only when we are stuck with two bad options that we really need a proxy's deciding vote. Knowing what I know now, I can say that almost no one who signs up to be a health-care proxy for a friend or family member has any idea what he or she is getting into.

THE ROLE OF a health-care proxy is a derivative of modern technological advances for many reasons. Previously—before evidence-based medicine became widely practiced—doctors could do little that would change a patient's outcome in any meaningful way. This was back when pharmacies still dispensed leeches over the counter. When we first learned the sort of tricks of the trade that are our staple to this day—antibiotics, surgery, vaccines, etc.—we were too arrogant to consider a patient or his or her family member a voice worth listening to. There were also few situations in which a patient could not participate in his or her own medical decision making: patients were either fully alive or fully dead. Death was swift and fast and there was almost no time for dialogues to occur.

All roads, though, lead through the Karen Ann Quinlan case, which first highlighted on a national level just how much the process of dying had evolved. Situations such as those involving the Quinlans had been popping up ever since the advent of mechanical ventilators and CPR but had never been featured on the front pages of newspapers. How physicians dealt with these situations prior to it surfacing naturally was truly ad hoc and extempore: Sometimes they would reach an agreement with patients' families, and other times they would go and make important decisions without their express consent.

The patient-autonomy revolution, however, came at just the right time to turn things in the right direction before patients' rights were usurped for good. Advance directives were developed to extend patients' autonomy beyond the persistence of their own ability in order to provide prospective autonomy to patients. Advance directives therefore allowed patients to define their treatment preferences even when they were not physically or cognitively able to state them. The myriad shortcomings of living wills, however, resulted in the origin of health-care proxies, also called surrogates.

The first requisite for a proxy to be activated is if a patient in fact cannot make decisions for themselves. This means that patients have to lack what is called in medical lingo "capacity." Capacity is the ability of adults to possess insight into their medical and psychological state, to understand the various treatment options they may have and comprehend the consequences of not proceeding with recommended management, and then lastly to communicate their thoughts to others. Capacity evaluation, for which I always seek expert psychiatric consultation, is a spot check: a patient does not indefinitely lose capacity but needs to have capacity evaluated for each and every decision a physician feels is due to impaired cognition. For example, if a suicidal patient wants to leave the hospital emergently, I can have the psychiatrists make a capacity evaluation at that moment, but any subsequent attempts to leave would need a new capacity evaluation.

While many physicians assume that patients don't have capacity when they disagree with them, patients merely need an internally consistent mental machinery to demonstrate capacity. People are allowed to make stupid decisions that may not be in their best interest as long as they retain the brains needed to understand that. However, some patients will defer important decision making to surrogates even when they retain capacity.

States have varying levels of formal requirements for what it takes for a patient to be able to officially nominate someone as their proxy. While some require documents to be filled out in the presence of a notary, increasingly, especially to confer health-care decision making, patients can appoint one of their family or friends as a proxy with a minimum amount of paperwork and just two informal witnesses.

It's probably for the best that nomination of a surrogate should be easy for patients. Hospitals bombard patients with forms, materials, and junk mail, much of which is lawyer-authored or lawyer-mandated spam. Increasingly during the course of my training, I realized that the health-care-proxy nomination is most crucial to patients retaining their autonomy. While I improved my practice to have people fill out forms even when I am being pulled in myriad other directions, national rates for nominating surrogates remain depressingly low. In one study from an ICU in New York, among critically ill patients—who need surrogate decision making more than perhaps any other group—less than one in five patients had nominated agents.[1] Numbers in other studies aren't much higher.[2]

Once health-care proxies have been nominated, they come into play when patients lose capacity. They lose their executive function when the patient regains capacity, but while they wear the crown of thorns the scope of their powers is as vast as that of the patients themselves. All consents go through them, all lab tests and results are reported to them first, and all decisions require their affirmation. The principles underlying surrogate judgment, though, are not very well understood, even by those bestowed with this great responsibility.

If the patient has let their preferences be known in any material fashion, their proxy is obliged to follow those instructions. This tenet of proxy decision making is called subjective standard, meaning that if a patient has filled out an advance directive, their proxy is only loosely required to follow those instructions. In most cases, proxies agree with wishes patients may have put down in a living will, and this combination makes for a powerful and persuasive statement. When surrogates and living wills agree, physicians are more than 95 percent likely to agree as well with the patient's preferences.[3] However, there are instances when agents disagree with what may have been written by a patient in a will.

This is a physician's nightmare. Living wills are imperfect but represent the patient's own actual preferences—albeit without any context whatsoever. The health-care proxy is not a form—it is an actual living person, reacting to all the information around them, and frequently advocating for the patient and/or for the decision they think is best for the patient. Both are powerful in their own right. While this does not come up too often, it places the doctor in a pickle. When physicians in Switzerland were presented with clinical vignettes that showed disagreement between the surrogate and the living will, physicians were twice as likely to opt for the less aggressive option.[4]

When no evidence can be relied upon to guide decision making for surrogates, they are required to use the best-interest standard.[5] What this means is that if a patient left no evidence, whether material or circumstantial, about what their preference would be in a certain situation, surrogates need to shift their focus from patient autonomy to patient well-being. In this situation, therefore, surrogates need to think more like objective onlookers (i.e., the way physicians are technically supposed to think). Best interest requires surrogates to take into account how sick or debilitated the patient is, what the prognosis is, what the available options are, what degree of benefit the possible treatments offer, how much the patient will suffer in undergoing said treatments, and whether the benefits outweigh the possible harms.

The vast majority of situations at the end of life do not involve the subjective standard or the best-interest standard. Because advance directives are so rarely filled out, subjective standard rarely comes up, and when it does, it is rarely contested. Best interest matters mostly either in children or when the proxy has really no information about or relationship with the patient, which is uncommon. This leaves the vast majority of decision making under the shadow of the controversial umbrella of substituted judgment.

PATIENTS LOOK TO anyone in a white coat, whether a medical student, a senior physician, or even a pharmacist, for answers to fairly complex questions. Frequently much rides on the answers we give: life or death is certainly up there, but health-care decisions also have a great domino effect on finances. Medical bills are the single greatest cause of bankruptcy in the United States, affecting two million Americans annually.[6] How every question is answered affects how caregivers make important decisions, which makes almost every response high-stakes. I have been asked a lot of difficult questions: How long does my sister have to live? What are the chances my son will come out of this procedure alive? Will my father ever walk again? The hardest question, however, has always been, "Doc, if this were your mother, what would you do?"

This question is at once one of the smartest things a patient's loved one can ask a physician as well as one of the least. Doctors can frequently come across as android-like to patients; their responses don't reflect the sort of emotions that family and friends feel. Physicians overrely on numbers and percentages and technical terms when talking to caregivers, which can make them appear, perhaps rightfully, aloof.[7] Bringing up a physician's own family member, and using that as a prism to suffuse a physician's thoughts with emotion, makes sense given that it's a foolproof means to squeeze the humanity out of almost anyone.

On the other hand, though, this question goes against the central concept lying at the heart of the role of a health-care agent—substituted judgment. This principle truly encapsulates what a health-care proxy's role is. A health-care proxy is someone who extends a patient's voice to when the patient himself is voiceless. Their role is to provide physicians information about what a patient would have wanted were they capable of voicing that desire meaningfully. The expectation is that they will use whatever knowledge they have of the patient's preferences and values— personal, spiritual, medical, and ethical—to guesstimate what the patient's opinion would have been in a given situation. Therefore, in an interesting twist, after a patient loses capacity the most important answers don't come from physicians but from the agents patients appoint for themselves.

Substituted judgment therefore requires proxies to make a prediction—something human beings are terrible at. We are terrible on a large societal level at predicting political, financial, and sporting trends, and we are worse at an individual level. In their paper, titled "The Failure of the Living Will," Angela Fagerlin and Carl Schneider write, "People mispredict what posters they will like, how much they will buy at the grocery store, how sublimely they will enjoy an ice cream, and how they will adjust to tenure decisions."[8] Startling data shows that paraplegics aren't much sadder and lottery winners aren't much happier than anyone else.[9] While paraplegics suffer initially after the incident that cost them the function of their legs, within just a few weeks their predominant view of their lives is positive.[10] This, of course, while extremely counterintuitive, demonstrates how much our imaginations can lead us astray. Too frequently we paint an incorrect and incomplete picture of future events too lush or too muted. So, for example, while Midwesterners attribute their woes to not living in a warmer and more culturally rich area like Southern California, in reality their life satisfaction does not differ much from actual matched Californians.[11]

Patients are not that great at predicting their own future preferences and decisions. So you can imagine that when someone else is predicting patients' preferences on their behalf, inaccuracy would be rife. One study published in the *Annals of Internal Medicine* is particularly illuminating. In this meta-analysis, the authors compiled results from all the well-designed studies looking at how well surrogates compared with the patients themselves in accurately predicting what their treatment preferences might be. Surprisingly, just 68 percent of agents were able to accurately predict what decisions patients would make in a multitude of different situations ranging from surgery to antibiotics.[12] When the patient suffered from dementia or stroke, they were only accurate 58 percent of the time. While three studies demonstrated that surrogates were more likely to want more treatment than the patients themselves, only one study showed surrogates withholding treatment the patient would have preferred, suggesting that surrogates tend to be more aggressive about care they are not receiving themselves than the patients who end up receiving the care. Interestingly, surrogates who had been selected by the patients themselves were no better than those that had been arbitrarily appointed by the physicians.

The position that proxies occupy is compounded by the fact that frequently patients themselves don't know what they would want in a future kerfuffle. More than half of all patients change their decisions about treatments they would want over a two-year period; when researchers from Chapel Hill and Seattle studied around two thousand elderly patients, they found that over two years, on average there was a trend toward patients wanting less aggressive treatment.[13] In fact, patients who wanted the least amount of treatment at the start of the two years were the most stable group, with 85 percent still wanting the same after two years. Patients who wanted the most aggressive treatment were most likely to change their minds, and after two years more of this group was likely to be in the least-treatment preference group than those who still wanted most treatment. Patients who leaned toward more treatment after two years were poorer, were more depressed, and were less likely to have health insurance, though they were not actually sicker than patients who leaned toward less aggressive management.

This data, and multiple other studies that found surrogates to be no more accurate than flipping a coin, has caused a significant number of ethicists, physicians, and philosophers to cast doubt on the viability of substituted judgment, which makes for great ethical theory but is almost impossible to replicate in an actual clinical setting.[14] The holy grail of end-of-life decision making, substituted judgment, is drilled into the heads of unsuspecting medical students and residents, with little if any education about its shaky foundation. The question then is why we choose to continue to carry on with our reliance on substituted judgment to help guide conversations at the end of life.

Perhaps the most important reason we continue to ask proxies to channel their loved ones is that we really haven't come up with any other alternative. Physicians tend to fare even worse than proxies at predicting patient preferences.[15] Furthermore, given that making these important calls is tough on patients, when surrogates believe they are merely voicing someone else's desires, erroneous as they might be, they feel less vulnerable to the burdens of such crucial pronouncements as opposed to when they are solely required to be the deciders.[16]

While doctors may not have the answer to the question "What does Mr. or Mrs. Smith want?," there's much they can do to help the Smiths reach that answer in the best possible fashion. Traditionally, doctors always told the Smiths what Mr. or Mrs. Smith should have been thinking. More recently, physicians have been told to ask the anointed Smith to predict what Mr. or Mrs. Smith would want were they able to verbalize their desired treatment. These conversations usually cause more harm than good: Physicians and family members frequently end up talking about separate, disparate procedures as if they are putting together a sandwich at Subway.

So now when someone asks me the question "Doc, if this were your mother, what would you do?," I don't just reflexively blurt out what my own personal preference in that situation might be. Like the vast majority of people, I have never had an explicit discussion about what sort of specific life-sustaining interventions my mother would personally want for herself if they were up for consideration. But over the few decades we have spent together, I have learned a few things about her. She loves food, babies, and embroidered clothes in no particular order. What she loves more than anything else, though, are her children, and I know that the highlight of her day is being able to talk or Skype with me or one of my siblings even for a few minutes. I know her enough to know that no matter what, she would want more time, and it would be worth it for her.

No two parents are the same, though. So, back in that room on that stormy day, where I was standing next to Sven, with the two daughters and the father, with the elderly woman whose heart and kidneys had both decided to tank, and the older daughter asked me what I would do if this were my parent, I knew it was my cue to take this conversation where it needed to go. We had spent too much time talking about her dialysis, about her blood pressure, about her medications, but I still didn't feel like I knew anything meaningful about the person hiding inside my patient.

"Why don't you tell me more about your mother?" I asked.

The family looked at each other as if they really were caught off guard, so I continued, "I feel like we have spoken so much about her yet I really don't feel like I know her too well."

As if on cue, the daughters started talking: This family's matriarch was perhaps one of the kindest people ever. "She never hurt a bee . . . or ant," the older daughter told us. Perhaps her favorite thing was to make meals for those she loved. She was so warm, we were told, that she would invite strangers over to her home to make them dinner. Finally, the younger daughter, who had failed at holding back her tears, said, "She taught me everything I know, but never this. . . ."

As her voice trailed off, the room had taken a different feel. I couldn't believe my eyes, almost as if I were living a cliché, but the storm had cleared and it was ridiculously bright outside. The goodness of the woman had removed all of the tension that had preceded it. I asked them, "What was the one thing you would say was the most important for her to do?"

The father, who had thus far been quiet throughout, spoke up. "To her, a life in which she couldn't cook up a feast or go out with her friends would not be worth living."

They weren't expecting us to say anything, because it seemed like the answers they had sought from us had become self-evident through their own stories. They knew she wouldn't be able to cook at home anymore and they knew how important cooking was to her. They knew now that she wouldn't want to stay indefinitely in the hospital, shuttling between the ward and the ICU as she struggled to just get by. The family finally came to the conclusion that perhaps taking the focus away from aggressive and life-extending treatments was the course she would have opted for.

When I stepped out of the patient's room with the rest of the team, we all felt relief that the meeting had gone well after a rocky start. I looked around and saw Sven standing behind everyone. I went up to him to find him flushed, with watery eyes and all. He said, "I have never experienced anything this intense before."

PERHAPS WHAT IS more crucial than patients picking what treatment they would want, where they would like to die, and when would they want to not pursue further interventions is who they would want to make choices for them when they are incapacitated. Mostly, though, patients appoint surrogates without giving their choice the kind of thought it needs. The question then is: Who makes a great health-care proxy?

To answer this question, it's worth reiterating what the role of a proxy is. A proxy has two primary roles: In the first, they are supposed to follow wishes patients may have expressed or implied about how they would like to live out the end of their lives. In the second, when they lack any evidence whatsoever, actual or circumstantial, they need to think about what would be in the patient's best interest based on accepted medical standards.

To be able to help forecast a patient's thoughts, a surrogate has to be someone who knows the patient intimately. The relationship a proxy has with the patient is thus of paramount importance in the selection process. Vincent was only forty-two years old when he had a massive bleed in his brain, lost his pulse, and received CPR thrice. While his heart regained some function, his brain didn't; a CAT scan revealed that his brain had become so gooey and swollen that it was starting to push its way out through his skull.[17] His doctors performed neurologic testing on him and found him to be brain dead. Doctors were moving toward removing Vincent from the ventilator when his extensive and complicated social history surfaced. Raised with ten adopted siblings, Vincent now was survived by two ex-wives and five children, two of whom were adult sons. Both of his sons, Ted and Will, were twenty-one years old. Will was estranged from his father and hadn't spoken to him in years. Ted knew Vincent well, but Ted was born from an affair Vincent's wife had when she was still married to him. Will was blood on paper but a stranger in the flesh, while Ted was raised by Vincent as a son, though he shared none of his DNA. In this case, Vincent's doctors rightly assigned Ted as the decision maker, highlighting the importance of bond over blood.

An ideal agent would also be someone who, when faced with untouched territory, would be able to adjudicate what lies in a patient's best interest. This is much harder than it seems and is perhaps where most proxies stumble in carrying out their responsibilities. One issue with best interest is that it risks harking back to the paternalism of medical practice in prior times. In an article in the *Atlantic,* published November 6, 2013, titled "My Mother Deserved to Die Comfortably," a writer described the difficult course her mother endured during her prolonged struggle with lung cancer. The writer described a tense relationship with her father, who was the primary caregiver of the mother, and was at her side at all times. However, he had thrown a shroud of denial around his wife, as he attempted to shield her from all bad news and her grim prognosis. To him, it was in his wife's best interest to have as much hope as possible, and to do everything possible to prolong her life. The daughter could not bear the sight of her mother so "miserable, frowning up at the ceiling, mouth ajar as if to cry out." In one instance, while she was not her mother's health-care proxy, she filled out an advance directive on her mother's behalf in which she stated she did not want any further treatment. This, to the daughter, was in her mother's best interest, but nowhere did she mention anything about what her mother herself wanted, what she valued, what she would have said were she able to say so.

The best proxies are those who have a way of homing in on what the patient valued above all other things. One moment I will never forget came one day when a patient with chronic lung disease from emphysema was admitted to the ICU with worsening of his lung disease. I went about with my usual history taking, with the family at the bedside. He was accompanied by his entire family; his daughter was the health-care proxy and she was the one driving the boat. Her father wasn't saying much; he was wearing a Red Sox shirt, so I figured I could talk about that. He had an encyclopedic knowledge of the woes of our team that had led to their season being cut short just a few days ago. Beyond baseball, though, the patient knew very little about why he was in the hospital, what time of year it was, or even where he was at that point. "The only thing he still knows about are the Sox," his daughter confirmed. When the question about his preferences for life-sustaining treatments arose, the daughter spoke up: "With the baseball season over, he has nothing to look forward to." I had never heard a preference quite like this, but the moment I did, its earnestness made sense. We deescalated care immediately.

A proxy may be very close to the patient but may not necessarily be able to judge what is in their best interest. When I think of myself, I know that no one knows me as well as my wife. For many years, we have shared every intimate detail one can imagine, and I trust completely that if anyone were to forecast what I would want or how I would react in any given situation, she would do as good a job as any. Yet if a time were to come when she could no longer rely on information I might have explicitly put down, would she be the one to say enough is enough, if enough truly was excessive? Would her love for me allow her to ever "give up" and call in the reaper?

The centrality of using agents to make health-care decisions about patients rests on their assumed selflessness and benevolence. "Not all proxies fit the model of loving, caring people who specially cherish the patient's interests," wrote well-known oncologist and writer Ezekiel Emmanuel in response to an article favoring proxies over advance directives.[18] Financial conflicts of interest arise fairly commonly at the end of life, though frequently surrogates are careful not to bring them up in front of physicians.[19] However, I do remember an instance when I was taking care of a man who had finally succumbed to heart and lung disease; his sister had durable power of attorney, and when we talked to her it was very clear that the patient would not want any aggressive management at all, so we started to make a transition toward withdrawing life support. While everything was all set, the sister did not appear quite ready and requested more time. This was something I happily acquiesced to, because transitioning from full-guns-blazing to a cease-fire can be traumatic; the constant flow of data, the beeping alarms, the staff shuttling in and out of the room, the sight of blood and secretions, while grim and taxing, can confer a false sense of progress. Take that away, and when you just have the patient lying in their room in peace, no longer can loved ones be distracted by noise and they have to face the end head-on. This, as you can imagine, is hard, which is why giving families time to adjust is the humane thing to do.

As the days clicked by, though, the sister seemed to be doing fine, but continued to request deference. I noticed that the only visitor she received was a middle-aged man in a suit carrying a leather briefcase. When I went up to meet the two together, it turned out that the visitor was in fact a lawyer; the sister was requesting time so that she could get the paperwork ready to transfer her brother's properties into her name. Needless to say, I convinced her that it was unethical to make the patient suffer needlessly against his wishes.

Another question that patients need to ask themselves is whether it is even fair to place the burden of decision making on a loved one. I will never forget a forty-year-old woman who was admitted to the medical service after throwing up blood from vessels in her stomach that had gotten enlarged from years of drinking. Because of her inability to reach sobriety, she did not meet the requirements to be placed on the transplant list. However, she was hoping that she would be able to get a big chunk of liver from her daughter instead of having to get one from someone else. I was looking forward to meeting the daughter to discuss treatment options further, but when she showed up, I was left in utter shock. The daughter, who had been appointed the health-care proxy by the single mother, was a fifteen-year-old high-school student. Not only had the mother placed the entire burden of her liver disease and what were surely the last few months of her life on a girl who was not yet old enough to be considered an adult, but she had also convinced her that she should donate her liver to her, in an operation that places the donor's life at considerable risk. So many aspects of their relationship seemed to be cannibalizing at heart that it left me very disturbed.

At least in theory, with a patient close to death and unable to participate in their management, the discussions are linearly approximated between the health-care proxy and the physician. An ideal health-care proxy would therefore be someone who knows the patient well enough that they would be able to channel their thoughts and preferences and would also be able to keep their best interest in mind even if that might mean paying the heaviest emotional price and letting go. They would be someone who would listen to physicians but also advocate loudly for the patient. Furthermore, it would be important for them to have some basic medical knowledge about the patient's condition, treatment options, and prognosis. Studies in both the United States and Europe, however, have shown that even among those surrogates who self-report good comprehension of the medical issues pertaining to their loved one, half lack adequate knowledge about the patient's condition and severity of illness.[20] Interestingly, a college education does not improve objective understanding of relevant medical issues. As can be easily imagined, very few patients have access to any one person who embodies all of these requirements.

Surrogates are smart, though, and knowing this reality they frequently employ a zone-defense approach. Health-care proxies are rarely by themselves and are frequently one of several family members and friends deeply involved in the final deathly dialogue. Surrogates leverage resources, emotional and intellectual, from many people to help move things along. Every family, though, is different, and nowhere do these differences come into sharper focus than when they are negotiating the final rites of one of their own.

Why Families Fall

When an elderly patient comes to the hospital, he or she leaves behind a family unfinished. In many cases, the family loses a voice, which usually occupies a central role. But when a matriarch or patriarch falls, the family usually regroups, frequently at the bedside. Few things galvanize a clan like impending doom, and at least over the past few decades, doom has taken residence in the hospital.

When I walk into a patient's room and find a crowd assembled, I start with introductions. I introduce myself, allow my team to introduce themselves, and then have the family do the same. I struggle to remember names but I take care to identify who is who in the family. Just meeting a family member for the first time, I can tell who is the one burning the midnight oil, changing diapers, giving medications, and remembering appointments. For a lot of elderly patients, the primary caregiver, usually the spouse, is also very elderly, with their own medical issues to bog them down. While the caregivers might be the ones with diaries charting the patient's glucose, their blood pressure, and other data points, they may not necessarily be the ones who are most in touch with what the patient may necessarily want. However, many caregivers have difficulty relinquishing their responsibilities to the hospital staff, given that they are so invested in the day-to-day care of the patient. To me, though, they are an invaluable resource, uncovering nuance in care otherwise inaccessible.

While the health-care proxy is the official decision maker, proxies differ in their decision-making style. Some are totalitarian, while others are populist; some are decisive, while others are irresolute; some are collaborative, while others are lone wolves. Some go mad with power, while others wilt under the pressure. Some proxies have an iron grip on the loudspeaker, while some eagerly pass it on to someone else. It is important to recognize who the family's spokesperson is, because in many cases it may not be the proxy. Sometimes it is someone else because of personality, sometimes because of availability, and sometimes because the decision maker doesn't speak English and leaves the communications to whomever is the most fluent speaker.

The spokesperson is an important member of the patient's family. Some ICUs will actually require families to declare a single spokesperson with whom all communications will occur and who will then disseminate bullet points through the several degrees of friends and relatives who might be involved. This to me is detached from reality; having one spokesperson sounds great, but hanging around a patient's bedside all day is hard for any one person. Families take breaks, arrange shifts, and therefore I end up talking to whomever will lend me an ear and the patient acquiesces to.

All family members have unique relationships to the patient and that relationship frequently bears increasing significance as life ticks away. A lifetime of history sculpting complex and overlapping layers of love, resentment, guilt, and all sorts of other feelings conflate into a slurry of thoughts and desires that define the relationship between one family member and another. No one defines this complex relationship better than the seagull. The seagull is the distant and remote relative who seems to fly in only when the situation couldn't be more acute and, in many cases, brings a completely new and different perspective to the situation. As the blog Crashingpatient.com put it, "They fly in, crap on everything, and fly away."

The seagull is a surprisingly common member of the families I have encountered, and their spatial displacement adds complexity in their relationship not only with the patient but with the rest of the family and the medical team. Guilt is a characteristic often demonstrated by seagulls: Many feel guilty that they haven't been around to take care of the patient. That remorse, though, frequently turns into an overzealous desire to be the "savior." Even family members recognize this, with one brother describing his sister as "the child from out of town. She is the one that feels that she has to have the whole thing fixed before she can go home. She is the one that doesn't have the time to wait it out. This illness is a wait out."[1] Too many times, I have seen patients in the ICU who are literally on maximal life support until the out-of-towner can fly in, usually from California, with the whole team and the rest of the family holding tight until the arrival. Seagulls will usually bring in their unique viewpoint and may differ not only from the clinicians but from the other family members who are much more involved in the care of the patient. "Look, I'm with Mom all the time; I know what she wants. You see her twice a year. How do you know what she wants," said one sister to another in front of the medical team in a family meeting.

A frequent presence in many families is the medical expert. The medical expert isn't necessarily an expert: I have met family experts who ranged from deans of medical schools to technicians working in a dialysis center. The medical expert is frequently the one translating jargon into English (or Spanish or another language) and frequently takes up the role of the interlocutor. Even when the medical expert may not be the proxy, their word carries a lot of weight with the family members. Many times, just as a patient is being rolled into the hospital, a family member hands me the phone to speak to a distant relative who happens to be a physician. Sometimes, these experts can also begin to micromanage the team. A sister of one of my patients, who happened to be a physician, would loudly demand additional and unnecessary testing, badger the interns, and hover over us in the team's workroom, and she even volunteered to write the medical notes for him, which I had to politely refuse given that it was a gross violation of dozens of patient-privacy and hospital-credentialing laws. Nevertheless, having someone with any amount of background in medicine greatly facilitates communications between doctors and families and is a great resource for the patient.

Research has shown that unlike the law, which prefers a single proxy making substituted decisions inferred from previously expressed patient values or wishes, patients themselves prefer the family coming to a decision based on their own judgment.[2] In the largest study of its kind, the vast majority of patients desired families to make decisions together without necessarily taking into account their wishes.[3] In many ways, that view is far more entrenched in reality than those espoused in ethics classes. Even though we like to reassure families and health-care proxies that they are not so much making a decision as transmitting wishes from their loved ones, to most families it certainly feels like they are making the most important decision of their lives. Too many times, like scripture or literature, patients' values can end up meaning whatever families want them to mean. That a patient could never sit in the house for a single day could be interpreted by family members to mean that the patient would never want to be tied down under any circumstance, especially to a hospital bed. However, another interpretation of someone with a wanderlust could be that they need more intensive treatment to reach a point where they would be able to fulfill that desire. Which way families go is them deciding actively and not just swaying to the winds. Furthermore, while ethicists would argue that surrogates and families should not take their own values under consideration when carrying out substituted judgment, they are blinding themselves to the fact that few people would ever be comfortable with directing management at odds with their own belief system.

The discordance between theory and reality, differences in opinion between families and physicians and within families and within the medical team, and a plethora of other misapproximations are some of the reasons the end of life has become a battleground. As of today, the

United States finds itself embroiled in what has been described as an "epidemic of physician-family conflict in the ICU."[4]

THE PROSPECT OF death ferments many emotions: for some, hope that suffering will end; for most, fear of the unknown, of either not being or hellfire. It is an emotional minefield: Sorrow, despair, hope, satiety—one never knows what one will trip on. For doctors, though, it's always just another day at the office. This discordance is one of the reasons conflicts between families and physicians have exploded.

The physician-family conflict is also a relatively modern phenomenon and is actually the greatest achievement of the patient autonomy revolution. When doctors acted like monarchs, they handed down decisions like decrees, leaving little room for negotiation. In many economies, such a relationship continues to this date, but it has terrible consequences. In China, physicians continue to exert great power over patients, and their uncontested diktats can leave family members distraught and enraged. That is one reason patients violently attack and kill physicians there at such an alarmingly frequent rate—about twenty-seven attacks per year per hospital.[5]

In Pakistan, being a doctor can be quite dangerous as well. Kidnappers hoping to net a hefty ransom frequently target doctors, particularly successful ones. Terrorists attack hospitals treating victims of terrorism. Health-care workers assisting with vaccinating children are killed despite being provided police escorts, as the Taliban believe vaccinations are a Western conspiracy to sterilize Muslim children.[6] Some Shiite physicians in my medical school actually hired bodyguards to stay with them at all times, given the spate of sectarian violence in which the Shiite minority was singled out by extremists.

The nature of family-physician conflict in the United States is altogether different, and while not many lives are lost, the frequency with which conflict occurs at the end of life in the United States is shocking in its own right. One study surveyed doctors and nurses in the ICUs of four Boston hospitals and asked them whether there had been a conflict regarding the care of patients who had spent a prolonged period of time in the ICU.[7] In four Harvard Medical School–affiliated institutions, some of the best hospitals in the world, physicians reported conflicts with families on a third of all cases. In fact, in this study physicians underreported conflicts compared with nurses, who were much more sensitive to family-and-physician discord. Furthermore, in a survey that studied doctors and patients concordantly, physicians were half as likely as patients to report a conflict. Just to show the degree to which doctors and families differed, in only 20 percent of the cases did both even agree there had been a conflict to begin with.[8] Additionally, conflicts escalate to a crescendo as the end of life approaches. A study conducted in Duke University Hospital showed that among patients for whom withdrawal or withholding of care was considered, 78 percent experienced a conflict.[9]

These numbers should shock anyone—dying is stressful, always has been—but the degree of conflict noted in American wards and ICUs suggests that the way things are currently structured in medicine isn't helping. To better understand why families and doctors grate against each other, it is useful to break down the major causes of clashes at the end of life.

Of all the things that come up in healthcare, decisions surrounding life-sustaining treatment account for a lion's share of what puts patients and doctors at odds. Almost half of all conflicts surround decisions regarding withdrawal of care, with surrogates six times more likely to want more "aggressive" care as opposed to doctors.[10] This jars with what we know about what patients want when people fill out advance directives: The overwhelming majority do not want aggressive care for themselves.[11] To me, how end-of-life conversations are set up has only made things worse.

When a family member was asked to describe his predicament, he said, "It's a lot like being on a jury in a murder trial, and you've got to determine whether this guy's going to go sit on death row . . . it's a horrible burden upon the juror." This description of a surrogate's role, while being a complete misrepresentation and misinterpretation of substituted judgment, is nevertheless a very prevalent thread. The burden surrogates face when making binary decisions of the highest magnitude are considerable and well documented.[12] Surrogates deviate frequently from their stated roles and often make judgments based on their own values and with interests in mind other than the patient's.[13] One mother told her doctor, "She's always said she wouldn't want to live on a machine. But right now, I'm making the decision that it's best for her to be on the machine."[14]

Physicians, on the other hand, are well versed in the ethical principles that are supposed to be followed: Not only have they been studying these principles since medical school days, they experience these conversations on a regular basis, while patients' families do so much less frequently. Physicians also may not have many emotional investments in patients, allowing them at least in theory to maintain some semblance of objectivity. However, physicians contribute to conflicts, primarily by communicating poorly. Despite years of communication-skills training, many physicians lack basic insight and self-awareness; in addition, patients uniformly complain about how little time physicians spend talking to families and patients, and there are high rates of burnout among physicians. All in all, overinvolved family and underinvolved doctors unsurprisingly make for a particularly caustic combo.

Not all conflicts occur between patients and families. The medical team itself is made of many moving parts, and frequently the pieces don't align optimally. You don't need to see the television series *Scrubs* to realize that medicine can be unbelievably tribal. Surgeons disagree with internists, who disagree with radiologists, who disagree with emergency physicians, whom it seems everyone disagrees with. Intrateam differences rarely occur over the use of life-sustaining treatment; they mostly center on differences in the management plan. One adage that holds true for the most part is that doctors are always more aggressive about procedures they don't have to do themselves. Thus nurses recommend more medications to physicians, who worry about their side effects; physicians recommend procedures to surgeons, who worry about their complications; and surgeons recommend imaging studies while the radiologist worries about the risks of the tests. Nurses frequently and rightly feel they are not adequately involved in patients' management.

Nothing is more distressing to a family than to see a medical team in disarray. If the stream-of-consciousness flow of medical information in their direction is not bad enough, disruptions in that current can be very disturbing. The worst meetings I have had with families are not the ones in which the family fights but the ones in which the doctors do. It is vital for all teams involved in the patient's care to be present in the meeting at the same time, so that any possible questions that arise can be answered simultaneously without any loose ends. Therefore, without fail, before every meeting I conduct a huddle in which I want all the stakeholders to discuss their positions and their roles. I also nominate someone as the marshal, who introduces the team, and guides the family and the physicians, helping maintain narrative flow and ensuring that all burning issues are addressed.

Families also spar among themselves. Different family members have different relationships with the patient, and that can affect the chances of conflict occurring. A study showed that the more congruent surrogates were with the patient's preferences the less conflict occurred in the family. Spouses were much more in accord with the patient, while adult children seemed to be pretty much guessing and were more likely to be involved in conflict than spouses.[15] Having a spouse has been found to be protective against interfamily conflict, and that makes sense, because the spouse then holds the family together.[16] A physician describing a messy family meeting painted a scene that is fairly representative: "There was dissension between family members. There was a lot of baggage that they came in with, a lot of family conflicts, and they used it as a forum for control issues, as in who was gonna make what decisions and who proves to Mom that they loved her more and that sort of thing. That was a problem."[17] Relatives frequently use these situations to demand increasingly aggressive treatment as a mechanism of "loyalty signaling."[18]

While consensus is not supposed to be something that guides surrogates, it is frequently strived for in reality. In truth, patients want their families to achieve a unified decision, and surrogates want the same. Part of it is a defense mechanism: Given the difficulty of the decision, proxies want to both consult other family members for advice and help spread the burden among the others. "I can't make the decision on my own when I got five sisters," said a proxy describing why he wanted to make a joint decision with the rest of his siblings.[19] "I'm not taking responsibility to say, well you should have did everything and they should have did this and they should have did that, and I said no, I'm not taking that responsibility. . . . We either all make the decision or none make the decision."

When family members differ, it is the proxy who suffers most, even when he or she is following the patient's wishes. In the words of a son, "Just trying to deal with the pain that everybody's [feeling] . . . with . . . what she [the patient] would feel if we kept her alive . . . because I know she's not going to be happy. What my dad feels, if we let her go, 'cause I know he's not going to be happy. And my brother's not going to be happy, and um . . . just trying . . . to keep a happy medium, but it's such a hard situation, that there really isn't one."

When fights do occur, physicians are rarely formally equipped to deal with conflict resolution. Given how frequently they encounter it, especially in an intensive-care setting, lack of such training is a gaping oversight. Mediation is a voluntary dialogue that frequently involves an unaffiliated third-party peacemaker. A mediator's primary role is to inquire what the warring parties' *positions* are (what they want) and what their *interests* are (why they want what they want), and to do that the most important tool at the mediator's disposal is just listening intently.[20] While physicians usually concern themselves with families' position (they want "everything"), they don't do as good a job of delving into their interests (they want to absolve themselves of the guilt of "giving up"). Simply clarifying roles and elucidating interests is sometimes all that's needed to get opposing groups on the same page.

The best means to deal with conflicts in the face of death is to prevent them from occurring in the first place. Families with a prior history of conflict, those facing a language barrier, and those belonging to a minority have been shown to have a higher prevalence of subsequent conflict in statistical models.[21] Spouses are protective against fights, and the lack of a spouse should therefore alert physicians. Nevertheless, given the very nature of the subject matter, some amount of contention will remain inevitable.

In the vast majority of cases, families are the greatest resource that could ever exist for a patient or for their physician. Families humanize patients and provide physicians a person to interact with and talk to as opposed to staring blankly at a computer screen when the patient is incapacitated. Talking to families is a big reason doctors become doctors, and while the current ethical framework surrounding substituted judgment is imperfect, it keeps physicians away from difficult value-laden decisions. This is precisely why my personal nightmare is not when a patient is wheeled in with an entourage in tow, but when the only person accompanying the patient is a bored transporter. Patients who lack families are a particularly challenging group to manage at the end.

I REACHED MY workroom one day on the medical wards to find it immersed in the aroma of fresh, warm brownies. It was a greeting far more inviting than that of disinfectant and diarrhea. As I partook of the cocoa-laden delicacies, I inquired about who had brought these in. Turns out it was the family of an elderly lady who had just been admitted overnight. I walked to her room to find it exploding with joy and energy. She was surrounded by family members of all ages and was chatting away, making me almost wonder whether she even needed to be in the hospital or not. On that very day, another lady was admitted to my medical service who came in by herself. Her room was like most other rooms on the floor: sterile and pulseless. I asked her whether she had ever thought about what she would want in case of a serious life-threatening illness; she told me she had never talked to anyone about it. I asked her if she had a health-care proxy; she told me she didn't. I asked her if there was anyone who would know her treatment preferences; she told me there wasn't. She was all by herself, all alone, and she wasn't the only one.

As people age, as they beat the odds, friends and family start falling like autumn leaves around them. It is estimated that by 2030, there will be two million Americans who will have outlived all of their family and friends.[22] In addition, the past few decades have seen major changes in our social networks. Modern-day Americans have seen a substantial culling of their societal webs: the average number of confidants that an average American has dropped from three to two since the 1980s.[23] Significantly, almost a quarter of Americans don't have a single confidant. Couple this with the fact that 44 percent of nursing-home residents lack decision-making capacity and it has huge implications, especially as life erodes and the end beckons.[24]

Loneliness is an interesting, ubiquitous, and highly subjective feeling that almost everyone can relate to. Loneliness is the evil twin of solitude: while a hundred years of solitude evokes feelings of eternal contentment and untampered-with peace, even a second of loneliness has a hollow and bleak air to it. Loneliness's subjective nature has made it an especially devious target for researchers as they try to come up with measures to better delineate it. While initially scientists merely used binary variables such as living alone or marital status to assess the degree of loneliness, increasingly the focus has moved to complex measures of social interaction that look at the size of one's social network and the degree of network participation. There remains considerable debate about the assessment of loneliness, but there is one thing everyone agrees on: Loneliness is dangerous. So dangerous, in fact, that across 148 studies that included more than 300,000 participants, loneliness was found to increase mortality by a whopping 50 percent.[25] This, just for reference, is greater than established risk factors such as smoking, lack of exercise, obesity, and alcohol consumption. This relationship was stronger when complex measures of social integration were assessed as opposed to simpler metrics.

No matter how many people one is surrounded by, how many bouquets litter one's room, how many retweets every last 140-character morsel generates, the truth is that everyone experiences death alone. Death separates us fully from everyone around us in a way that nothing else can. Death is an experience we can't share with anyone else; it is something poets and writers infer, songwriters serenade, but only from projection and extrapolation. No one who experiences death lives to tell the tale.

The loneliness of death creates an uncrossable bridge between us and everyone and everything else. Much of what we achieve in our lives is an attempt to offset the sheer terror that the existential loneliness of dying arouses when the cover of meaning is lifted. The chief defense we erect against nothingness is family, and up until just before the end, it holds up quite well.[26]

No one knows exactly why loneliness kills. Researchers are split along two lines. One hypothesis is that loneliness exposes one to stress that would otherwise have been eased by social interactions. The other, more plausible hypothesis is that social integrations promote behaviors that are amenable to good health. Family and friends, to most, are a big reason to live on and to live well. My father, left to his own devices, would likely smoke, eat, and laze his way through life. While my siblings and my mom haven't been able to completely curtail his bad habits, I believe it is because of our constant nagging that he watches his diet, goes out for a walk, takes his medications, and, after forty or fifty long years, has finally stopped smoking.

Watching the contrasting situations in my two patients' rooms was a shattering sight; while a fairly common occurrence, the duality of their experiences sensitized the team to their contrasting yet similar trajectories. The next day, in a lovely gesture, my attending physician brought a bouquet of fall flowers and a copy of the *New York Times* for my lonesome patient. Perhaps more than the antibiotics we were giving her, it was that gesture which was the most significant intervention that we made for her.

On the totem pole of horror, though, this lady's case doesn't even show up. On that very floor, an elderly lady, pale as sand, with platinum blond hair, was admitted after she developed a urinary-tract infection. Not only did this lady not have a single friend, family member, or acquaintance, she didn't even have herself anymore. She had end-stage dementia and hadn't spoken a single word for years now. She was emaciated to the point that the skin covering her bones was almost translucent. While her eyes were wide open, she wasn't really looking. No one could grab her attention, not even if anyone mashed their fist in her chest or yelled into her ear.

When a patient becomes incapacitated, a health-care proxy by default is appointed. These proxies are restricted to family members and usually go down a sequence starting with the spouse and then moving to children, parents, and siblings. Many states allow same-sex partners to also serve as the first-choice proxy by default. Because so few people nominate proxies when they are well, default proxies are actually the most common surrogates.[27] However, while spouses are most frequently appointed proxies by default, studies have shown that not everyone thinks their spouse is best suited to be their proxy. African Americans and Hispanics prefer to nominate their daughters as agents.[28] When family isn't present or there is a conflict in the family and there is no urgency to make a decision, a court-appointed guardian is sought.

Things are much more complicated when time is not in abundance. Patients who lack both capacity and surrogates constitute a significant challenge and constitute a fourth of patients who die in the ICU.[29] No one really knows how crucial end-of-life decisions ought to be reached for these patients. States have yet to reach consensus about what to do in these situations, with some actually offering no guidance about what physicians should do. There is disagreement even within medical professional societies about how best to proceed in these situations: while the American Medical Association and the American College of Physicians recommend that these cases be referred to the courts for review, the American Geriatrics Society prefers review of these cases by physicians and institutional committees.[30] Both options are subpar: Judicial review is time-consuming and cumbersome and is not as responsive as needed by the time constraints of the ICU. Hospital committees, on the other hand, often don't add meaningful independent input, given that they are constituted mostly of hospital employees and physicians, without many independent and unaffiliated voices. Perhaps for these reasons, physicians rarely consult either of these resources when a decision is needed.

When faced with a critically ill patient without a voice, an advance directive, or an agent, most physicians usually look inward or consult their colleagues. Ostensibly, this is not a bad choice: Every patient is unique and complex and no one knows them inside out at that moment the way the physician taking care of them does. Docs also get a lifetime of training in bioethics and are familiar with the issues surrounding patients close to death. Many vulnerable patients without proxies prefer to have a physician choose treatments for them rather than leave that choice to a court-appointed guardian.[31] Patients who let their doctors decide don't have any worse outcomes than patients making collaborative decisions and actually tend to worry less about their health.[32]

On the other hand, physicians differ about what to do in certain situations; this variation can occur based on the patient's health status but also on things that have nothing to do with the patient.[33] Medical decisions are based as much on a physician's style and values as the clinical evidence base. Any time there is only one voice in a conversation, it's a recipe for disaster, even if that voice is that of the doctor taking care of the patient. Establishing a proxy for patients before they lose capacity is therefore critical. I have worked in some ICUs that mandate that a health-care proxy be established for each and every patient who is admitted, and it made subsequent decision making much smoother.

When I called the nursing home, I found out that the lady with dementia had a court-appointed legal guardian. The patient was getting sicker, and it didn't seem like she was going to turn around even after her infection had been treated adequately. I called the number the nursing home had given, and it led me to the office of the lawyer who had been serving as the patient's guardian. I explained to him the situation, that the patient was getting sicker, that given how sick she had been to begin with, if she got worse we had no chance of meaningful recovery. The guardian, though, was not very forthcoming—he had not seen the patient in years, was very hard to pin down, and was satisfied with the status quo. He told me that he wanted the patient to remain full code. He didn't come see the patient in the hospital, citing his busy schedule.

Just a few days after, I was paged around noon that the patient's blood pressure had plummeted and it seemed as if she had entered a terminal spiral. Reflexively, I called the ICU team to come evaluate the patient. Even as I stood at the foot of her bed, barking orders, I could see that none of the nurses or the rest of the team was comfortable with this situation. Sending a patient such as her to the ICU and subjecting her to a cascade of traumatic procedures sounded like a horrible idea, especially when none of us were sure whether she herself would want this for herself. I realized that perhaps where I could make a greater difference was not here. I told my colleague to take over the bedside management and went to the nursing station and called the lawyer once more.

Luckily, he picked up the phone. As I spoke to him, nurses, social workers, and the ethics support team, which we had earlier consulted, surrounded me in anticipation. I felt like a turn-of-the-century surgeon performing in an amphitheater. I told him that the ICU team was here to take the patient for what were almost surely futile and excessive interventions. Trying to stall, he initially told me that he didn't think he was legally allowed to change the patient's code status to DNR/DNI. When I pressed him, he suggested, "What if a relative pops up from somewhere who disagrees?" When I told him that that was both unlikely and unimportant at this stage, he finally agreed that it was in the patient's best interest to not escalate management any further. Within moments, the signed DNR/DNI form started to wriggle out from the fax machine.

When I got off the phone, everyone was still looking at me. Before this conversation, we had been talking to the lawyer for many days, and he had finally relented. Legal guardians are not free of potential conflict of interest; they get paid on an annual basis and therefore it is the patient's longevity, not their quality of life, that sends a check to their desk.[34] In that moment, though, I felt an elation I had never felt before, not even after a successful procedure or presentation. The only goal of the assembled team was the patient's best interest, and for the voiceless in our midst, the most vulnerable population of them all, that small moment meant a lot to me and all those who were there to encourage me on.

BY DAY A hospital is bustling, busy, full of life despite the obvious subtext. By night it morphs into something else. It's quieter, darker, and darker still. The darkness doesn't just permeate the walls and the floors; it seeps into the occupants as well. The hospital staff working nights is also a unique breed. There are many nurses who almost exclusively work night shifts, and they are characterized by their relish for autonomy. The number of physicians in a hospital at night is probably a tenth of the number during the day, and the few physicians who do work nights are usually at the bottom of the pecking order. It would be incorrect to say that I am immune to the darkness.

On one such night, when I was covering sixty or so patients, I was paged by a nurse that one of the patients on the bone-marrow transplant service had died. This was not unexpected; the elderly patient had been battling lymphoma for many years, and the family had finally decided that there was no use to keep pushing forth and had opted to go the "comfort route" and not pursue any life-prolonging treatments. The interns, anticipating the patient's demise, had in fact already filled out a death certificate for me in case she died.

When I entered the room, it was completely dark until I turned on a pair of deep yellow bulbs at the head of the bed. The lights revealed a hollowed-out face, with her eyebrow ridges covering her face in deep shadows. She was as pale as the bedsheets she was wrapped in, and her cheeks were so indented that I wondered whether they were touching each other in her mouth. It was really strange to me that the first time I had ever met her was when she had *just* died.

After I declared her death, I had to make the worst phone call of someone else's life. I found the phone number of her husband and called him. His voice was rushed—I am sure when he saw the hospital number on his cell phone he had already prepared himself for the worst. After I introduced myself, I let him know that his wife had passed away.

My pronouncement was followed by silence. Out of the silence emerged the words I least expected to hear: "Thank you, Doctor. Thank you for letting me know." I was humbled. I really had nothing to say other than to let him know that she died without any pain. I went back to filling out paperwork, sending e-mails to the patient's physicians, and figuring out whether the case needed to be referred to the state medical examiner. As I was working on this, the husband arrived with his son. They were both wearing pajamas, and had the look of people who had just jumped out of bed and found themselves standing in front of a speeding truck. The nurses led them into the room, which they had tidied up.

I entered the room behind them and put a hand on the husband's shoulder and let him know I was sorry. He broke down, saying, "Me, too." The nurse, who knew the family much better than I did, squeezed his hand, and I reached out for the closest box of tissues. The nurse pulled out her phone and showed the husband a picture of his now-deceased wife, from just a week ago, wearing patient clothes, lying with her poodle on top of her. Just last week, in what seemed like a logistical nightmare for the transplant team, they had arranged for her dog to come see her in the hospital. "She fought for so long, and I guess after that, she had decided she was done," the husband told me.

Just as I was about to respond, my pager went off and I had to attend to another situation. I left the room and never saw that family or the deceased again. Soon the nurse had the patient transferred to the morgue and the room was cleaned and made available for the next patient. When the team arrived in the morning and I let them know that the patient died, the intern let out a sigh but had little time to reflect since she had so many other patients to worry about.

In contrast to our obsession with preventing, averting, delaying, or ameliorating death, medicine doesn't really have a plan for what to do for patient's families after a loved one dies. This goes back to the fact that doctors do not have any legal responsibility for caregivers and family. This may not matter as much after a peaceful death as it does after a traumatic one. What this ends up looking like is frequently the family being stranded out at sea after sailing through the most intense storm ever.

For the longest time, when the end was near and it wasn't looking pretty, the curtains would be drawn, the doors would be closed, and the family would be asked to leave while the doctors and nurses got on with their jobs. For most patients who want all possible treatment, the end usually involves a nurse or physician pounding on their chest with their elbows locked and hands clutched. This of course is the dominant sensation that comatose dying people don't feel in addition to the myriad needles penetrating their bodies, the masks on their faces pushing oxygen. Needless to say, it's a violent, morbid, chaotic end, which for years doctors have tried to shield families from, hoping that this won't be the lasting imprint that stays with them.

To date, two-thirds of physicians in North America and Europe believe it is not appropriate for families to witness attempts at resuscitation.[35] Broadly, the two main reasons doctors are opposed to families being at the bedside during CPR attempts are that they fear that families will interfere with a process already prone to bedlam and that they don't want to traumatize them.

I have seen many things during my residency that would shock anyone, and few stick long enough for me to remember them vividly; they are overtaken by something else and then something else after that. Few things, though, have the staying power of cardiopulmonary resuscitation.

In the face of this reality, there has been gathering interest in providing family members a front-row seat in this horror show. The French study we previously discussed showed that four in five family members opted to witness CPR when asked and that family members who witnessed CPR demonstrated much lower rates of anxiety and post-traumatic stress disorder than family members who refused to observe it, even among family members of patients who survived.[36] That goes against the grain of a mantra that dates back to when CPR was first developed. The study, though, is far from closing the debate on whether family members benefit from this vantage point. If anything, it shows what ought to be done after any patient passes away. While the outcomes were telling (only 3 percent of patients were alive a month after CPR), all family members were exposed to fully trained physicians following a preset protocol, had another person explain to them details about CPR, and finally had physicians conduct a debrief after the CPR.[37] This is far from routine practice, and that, to me, was the take-home message from this study: It is not enough to train health-care professionals in how fast to compress someone's sternum. At the same time, though, with physicians being asked to see more and more patients, their ability to effectively counsel might be limited without the help of dedicated social workers and counselors.

Here's what I have been taught about CPR: Initially, CPR was recommended to be administered at around 100 compressions a minute, in time with the Bee Gees' "Stayin' Alive," and a subsequent study actually showed that doctors did better CPR when thinking about that disco sensation.[38] So, because I was trained to think of this song, this is what is going through my mind when I am pushing down on a patient in their last moments on earth. While recent data indicate that faster CPR, at around 125 compressions a minute, is better[39]—similar to, say, Metallica's "Enter Sandman" or Guns N' Roses' "Welcome to the Jungle"— something about the irony of a song called "Stayin' Alive" being the soundtrack of a procedure which confers a survival rate of 3 percent when it occurs outside a hospital is too ironic to pass up.

While I have received very structured training about how to resuscitate, and what to do when it succeeds, I never sat through a class teaching me what to do when CPR fails. That leaves me to my own improvised means. I was the intern in the cardiac-care unit when a patient came in after a cardiac catheterization. The cardiologist accompanied the patient and told the waiting family that the procedure had been a rousing success: His heart, which hadn't seen blood for hours as he clutched his chest, was now fully perfused. There was so much comfort in his voice that I could never have imagined that that moment would ever enter my book of horrors. The family was chatting in the room with the patient, in a festive and celebratory mood, when his blood pressure started to fall. I saw a code coming and asked the wife if she wanted to stay or leave. She chose to stay as others retreated to the family solarium. Just before his final heartbeat, one of the cardiologists found that the heart attack had left a hole in his heart.

As I invariably found myself designated as the chest compressions guy at any code blue, I caught a glimpse of the wife as she looked on, surrounded by hospital staff. I started having flashbacks from just minutes ago when we were all congratulating her husband and the family about the successful procedure. In what seemed like an eternity and a flash, it was over. As was my training, which had equipped me well up to that point, but not beyond.

I walked toward the glass door and slid it open as nurses covered her husband in white sheets. I walked toward her without the courage to look her in the eyes. I told her we failed her husband, but she spoke before I was finished: "You did your best." Left with nothing to say, with my higher brain emitting only white noise, I did what my brain stem instructed me to do. I hugged her and cried.

When Death Is Desired

Several hours into our meeting, Rafael started to read the piece aloud. I was handed a Xeroxed copy of a single-page essay from the *Journal of the American Medical Association*, published in 1988. A poet and physician, Rafael Campo, had invited myself and several other medical residents to his home for a writing workshop. We were interested in writing powerful, moving essays, and Rafael picked out what he thought was a particularly strong piece. The essay was titled "It's Over, Debbie," and it seemed to us that the most intriguingly unusual thing about it was that the author's name had been "withheld by request."[1] But that was before we read the piece itself.

The essay started like many other personal anecdotes penned by physicians and routinely published in medical journals: a sleep-deprived resident was paged in the middle of the night. The author, a gynecologist in training, was informed on a call night that a patient was having difficulty "getting rest." As he proceeded to check what was going on, contrary to his expectation of finding an elderly female, he found a twenty-year-old girl named Debbie. Experiencing "unrelenting vomiting" and "labored breathing," the young patient had terminal ovarian cancer. A dark-haired nurse was standing next to her, holding her hand and comforting her till the doctor on call arrived. "Hmmm, I thought," wrote the author, "very sad."

He then went on to describe scenes that anyone on a cancer ward has seen innumerable times. "The room seemed filled with the patient's desperate effort to survive . . . it was a gallows scene, a cruel mockery of her youth and unfulfilled potential." However, it was what happened next in the essay that sent the first shiver down my spine, all the way to my toes.

"Her only words to me were 'Let's get this over with.'" The author returned to the nursing station with thoughts circling his head. "I could not give her health, but I could give her rest," he wrote. He then drew up twenty milligrams of morphine in a syringe, walked back to her room, and injected the morphine into her vein. "With clocklike certainty, within four minutes, the breathing rate slowed even more, then became irregular, then ceased," wrote the author.

The article was not a long read, only a word over five hundred. It must have been difficult for Rafael to read the piece, but nothing would have been harder to write or say than the three very last words: "It's over, Debbie."

Few things have left me feeling as soulless as those last three words. I would learn later that I was far from the only one shaken to my being. The essay generated a firestorm at *JAMA* (*Journal of the American Medical Association*). They received more letters in response to this one piece than to any other article published in the journal's more-than-a-century-long history.[2] Overwhelmingly, physicians opposed the piece and what it purportedly represented far and wide. A comment published in the *JAMA* in the aftermath of "It's Over, Debbie" was perhaps the most scathing:

> By publishing this report, he [the *JAMA* editor] knowingly publicizes a felony and shields the felon. He deliberately publicizes the grossest medical malfeasance and shields the malefactor from professional scrutiny and judgment, presumably allowing him to continue his prac-

tices without possibility of rebuke and remonstrance, not even from the physician whose private patient he privately dispatched. . . . Decent folk do not deliberately stir discussion of outrageous practices, like slavery, incest, or killing those in our care. . . . The very soul of medicine is on trial.[3]

The firestorm didn't remain buried in the back pages of the *JAMA*. Ed Koch, the irascible mayor of New York, was incensed, calling the article "a confession." He went on to demand that Attorney General Edwin Meese III force the journal into releasing information pertaining to the submission.[4] "This is not a case of an informant. This is a case of a confessed murderer." The Illinois State attorney general Richard Daley took action and issued a subpoena to the American Medical Association, which is based in Chicago and oversees the journal, requesting that all documents related to the article, including the name of the author, be released. A Cook County grand jury ordered that all records be turned over to the state for further prosecution.[5]

Conspiracy theories swirled, with many not even believing the account to be true. Forensics experts doubted that twenty milligrams of morphine could in fact end someone's life—least of all within the reported four minutes.[6] Clinicians found the scenario implausible. Some doubted that any physician would make such a decision about a patient they didn't know too well.[7] Pressure was piled on George Lundberg, who was the editor of the journal at the time, and who had gone ahead with publishing the piece even after some of his editorial staff objected to it.[8] Some even suggested that Lundberg's wife, an English professor, had penned the piece.[9]

After the firestorm that "It's Over, Debbie" ignited, pressure kept piling on the American Medical Association from all directions to out the author and rescind the article. Yet the piece also generated a second wave, one that came from perhaps the most important stakeholders in this debate: patients and the public. A young woman whose mother had lost her mother to lung cancer wrote, "I feel very strongly that if such a patient wants to end her life by being injected with morphine or any other drug that will end her pain, then she should have the right. No one should have the right to make them suffer."[10] Others said that they "applaud that physician as one caring more about a patient's pain than about cruel, outdated professional ethics and laws." Alex Hardy, a patient who had been diagnosed with terminal metastasized cancer, wrote the most moving account:

> I have traveled down a road filled with evasion, equivocation and moral hypocrisy. Most physicians don't want to face the fact that one of their patients is going to die. Very few will even discuss death. It is often claimed by physicians that they can't "play God" and remove life support. Aren't they "playing God" when the life support is ordered? . . . My only concern is that some misguided physician will try to keep me alive against my wishes. Being alive is not merely existing on a machine or with massive drug doses. A person must have the ability to think, function, and participate (even in a small way) in the everyday flow of human events.[11]

Alex Hardy died less than a month after writing this commentary. What the author of "It's Over, Debbie" described has been called many things, ranging from physician-assisted suicide, euthanasia, and mercy killing to flat-out cold-blooded murder. In many ways it crystallized what is one of the most passionately debated issues in modern culture.

THE HISTORY OF euthanasia and physician-assisted suicide is littered with unhinged characters, such as the Chicago-based surgeon Harry J. Haiselden. A public advocate for euthanasia and eugenics in the early twentieth century, he assumed the national spotlight when he convinced the parents of a syphilitic child, John Bollinger, to allow the baby to die. While the Chicago Medical Society threatened to strip him of his clinical privileges, he was acquitted by a grand jury, which let him continue allowing sick children to die.

But like any self-respecting promoter of eugenics, Haiselden didn't just stop there; he went on to produce the magnum opus of his life, a film called *The Black Stork*. In the semifictional depiction of his life and endeavors, Haiselden plays himself as a righteous surgeon crusading to rid the world of lesser beings. A scene from the grainy black-and-white film starts with the camera centered on a dark-haired, pale woman, her eyes surrounded by dark halos of smudged makeup, who wakes up abruptly with a nurse sitting by her side, stroking her hair. It dawns on her suddenly what had just happened: She has just given birth to a baby, and the baby is lying half covered in a blanket across the room.

Standing next to the baby is a tall white man in a dark suit with slick jet-black hair. This is Haiselden, playing himself, stroking the baby with his massive hands. He doesn't say a word, but he doesn't have to, with hands such as his. As he strokes the infant, whose only visible deformity is malnutrition, he alternates between the loving and caring way a physician generally touches a newborn and a cruder grip, turning the child's head from side to side like the head of a rag doll, examining the child like a piece of steak. When the nurse offers to cover the neonate, he admonishes her, and his words appear as text on the screen: "There are times when saving a life is a greater crime than taking one."

Haiselden's actions granted his cause national exposure, and even though authorities criticized his practices, he was allowed to continue them.[12] When the Chicago Medical Society voted to terminate his membership, it was more because of his hunger for publicity than for the ethics of his actions.[13] His film was shown under different names, such as *Are You Fit to Marry?*, to state legislators, and was in cinemas until the 1940s, long after Haiselden's death, in 1919.

Euthanasia and physician-assisted suicide are sometimes used interchangeably, but there is a crucial difference: While euthanasia involves the physician himself committing the act that leads to the premature demise of the patient, in physician-assisted suicide the doctor provides the patients the means, usually a lethal prescription of sedatives, to commit the act of their own volition. Of the two, euthanasia has a far longer history and tradition than physician-assisted suicide, which is a more recent development and emphasizes patient autonomy.

The precursor of euthanasia—suicide—has an ancient history. While for most of time, particularly in Western traditions, suicide has been thought of as a sinful and despicable act. In some cultures suicide was not only tolerated but in odd instances encouraged. Take, for example, the ancient Hindu practice of sati, which started in the Vedic period, between 1500 BC and 500 BC. Suttee involves a widow immolating herself in her husband's funeral pyre.[14] The practice was banned by the British, when they colonized the subcontinent. However, this ban actually caused a lot of resentment from locals in the late 1800s. To date, even though the practice has been banned, some women voluntarily present themselves to be burned at their husbands' funerals.[15]

In Western traditions, we infer attitudes toward suicide through their descriptions in ancient Judaic texts. An analysis of all deaths that can be classified as self-inflicted in Judaic literature shows that suicide was portrayed in two differing lights—Samson's heroism and Saul et al.'s disgrace. When Samson, the Israelite judge with superman strength, crushed the pillars of the Philistine temple that was the site of his trial, he did so knowing that while it would bring about his demise, it was the only way to deal defeat to the Philistines; this death of his was presented as incredibly heroic.[16] For the most part, though, suicide was depicted as an act of the disgraced and fallen; many cruel kings of Israel, such as Saul, Zimri, and Abimelech, died by their own sword.[17] Despite these depictions, no specific position on the moral balance of taking one's own life was held.

The society of the ancient Greeks was the first in which euthanasia and physician-assisted suicide became mainstream. While the ancient Greeks valued health above all other virtues, they did not consider prolonging life at all costs to be a duty of the physician unless it was specifically desired by the patient. According to Pausanias, a Spartan king in the fifth century BC, the best physician was the one who would bury the patient quickly rather than letting them linger. Describing prevailing attitudes toward the terminally ill,[18] Celsus, a second-century Greek philosopher, wrote in his seminal text, *De Medicina,* "For it is the part of a prudent man first not to touch a case he cannot save, and not to risk the appearance of having killed one whose lot is but to die."

In Ancient Greek society, there was widespread acceptance of suicide, with physicians aiding patients with bladder stones and headaches in ending their lives by cutting their veins. In the seventh book of his treatise *The Natural History,* Pliny the Elder described the ignominious end of one Jason of Pherae in the first century, who was diagnosed with an abscess in the chest and, having "been given up by the physicians, determined to end his life in battle, where he received a wound in the chest, and found, at the hands of the enemy, a remedy for his disease."[19]

THE HIPPOCRATIC OATH is considered by many the seminal text defining what it means to be a physician. Not only has it managed to pervade medical-school curricula in the Western world, but reciting it is part of the initiation of medical students around the world, alongside other rituals, such as white-coat ceremonies. Ostensibly, the message of the oath can be simplified to the adage "Do no harm," but it is in the details where a more complicated face emerges. Not only is it unclear how much of the Hippocratic oath was written by the man whose name it bears, but estimates of the time at which it was written range between the fifth century BC to the first century BC.

Relevant to the euthanasia debate, one of the more famous stipulations of the oath is "I will neither give a fatal draught [drug] to anyone if I am asked, nor will I suggest any such thing."[20] The oath, in its original form, also prohibits doctors from performing surgeries and abortions. These statements suggest that the beliefs of Hippocrates were very likely similar to the beliefs of the Greek mathematician Pythagoras. Pythagoras and his followers believed in the transmigration of souls and the sanctity of life and that a voluntary end to one's life could never be justified.[21] This also led them to feel that surgery should be prohibited.

While evidence is sparse, it is clear that the oath did not gain much acceptance among Greek physicians during the ascent of the Roman Empire. If anything, with the advent of Stoicism, a subset of Hellenistic philosophy, the anti-euthanasia mandate of the oath went further underground. The Stoics believed that to ascertain the order that determines the universe and to achieve freedom, life ought to be guided by reason. To the Stoics, overcoming death's design was the ultimate goal. According to the Stoic Seneca, "What is evil is to live in necessity; but there is no necessity to live in necessity. . . . Let us thank God that no one can be forced to remain alive."[22] The Stoics followed through on their beliefs. Marcus Porcius Cato (95 BC–AD 46), also called Cato the Younger, was one of Julius Caesar's greatest enemies and is associated with the quote in the play *Cato, a Tragedy*, "Give me liberty or give me death."[23] Upon his defeat by Caesar in the Battle of Thapsus, Cato, up-ended with dishonor, attempted to kill himself with a sword but was unable to do so and ended up severely injuring himself. He then ripped at his wound until he died a grim and gruesome death.[24] Zeno, the founder of Stoicism (335 BC–265 BC), also led by example. One day on his way home from a lecture, he tripped and broke his toe. Taking this to be a cosmic nudge, Zeno held his breath until he died.[25]

The real game changer was Constantine the Great (272–337), the Ro-man emperor who converted to Christianity and brought Christian val-ues to the fore in mainland Europe. Christianity has always held that human life is the property of God, a gift that we must preserve under all circumstances. Saint Augustine (354–430) categorically stated, "Nay, the law, rightly interpreted, even prohibits suicide, where it says, Thou shalt not kill."[26] So dominant was the Christian influence that the whole idea of deliberate or rational suicide, so widely propagated by the Stoics, was wiped off the European landscape. During the Middle Ages, Saint Thomas Aquinas (1225–1274) further advocated against suicide, saying it was unnatural, sinful, and unconstructive to society.[27] There-fore, for almost two millennia not only was suicide, assisted or other-wise, illegal, it was a punishable offense. The properties of people who committed suicide were confiscated, and people who committed sui-cide were dissolved in ignominy.

It wasn't until the Renaissance that the status quo was questioned. Just as the Renaissance put all prevailing customs and practices to the fire, the Renaissance also challenged religion's stance toward man's right to die. Thomas More, Lord Chancellor during the reign of Henry VIII and a prominent member of the Catholic Church, wrote a book in 1516 called *Utopia*. In *Utopia*, More described what he envisioned as a perfect society. *Utopia*'s perfect society jarred with many of the strongest of Christian beliefs: priests could be either male or female and were allowed to marry; all religions would be tolerated, including disbelief; and divorce would be easy to acquire. The Utopians' attitude toward the dying was also quite advanced: "They console the incurably ill by sitting and talking with them and by alleviating whatever pain they can. Should life become unbearable for these incurables the magistrates and priests do not hesitate to prescribe euthanasia.... When the sick have been persuaded of this, they end their lives willingly either by starvation or drugs, that dissolve their lives without any sensation of death. Still, the Utopians do not do away with anyone without his permission, nor lessen any of their duties to him."[28]

The Renaissance not only saw a revival of conversations about euthanasia but also saw the debate get more nuanced. Francis Bacon in 1605 made a distinction between inward euthanasia, which represented a peaceful passing of the soul, and outward euthanasia, which represented a pain- and distress-free death of the body.[29] He recognized that clergy and family members helped provide inward euthanasia, and he suggested that doctors do more to provide the dying outward euthanasia. It appears, however, that what Bacon was suggesting was not *active* euthanasia, in which a drug was administered or a procedure was carried out to hasten death, but to alleviate pain and suffering through *passive* euthanasia.

Enlightenment philosophers such as David Hume, proponents of empiricism, who emphasized evidence and lived experience over everything else, also came out in favor of self-determination. Hume (1711–1776) had strong views about suicide. He first published his essays "On Suicide" and "On the Immortality of the Soul" in 1775 but decided to have them physically removed from the collection they appeared in because of the controversy they generated. It wasn't until after his death that the essays were posthumously republished under his byline.[30]

While Hume's influential essays do not expressly discuss euthanasia, he skirts the issue intimately. "That suicide may often be consistent with interest and with our duty to ourselves, no one can question, who allows that age, sickness, or misfortune, may render life a burden, and make it worse even than annihilation." He questions the great significance placed on the value of human life in very concrete terms: "The life of man is of no greater importance to the universe than that of an oyster. . . . A hair, a fly, an insect is able to destroy this mighty being whose life is of such importance. . . . It would be no crime in me to divert the Nile or Danube from its course, were I able to effect such purposes. Where then is the crime of turning a few ounces of blood from their natural channel?" Hume was also joined by others who, while not approving of suicide, were strongly opposed to the laws making suicide illegal.

At the same time, though, objections to euthanasia remained steady, though nowhere close to how severe they were during the Dark Ages. Hume's fellow empiricist John Locke (1632–1704) did not view self-harm favorably, holding that since humans were created by God, self-harm would amount to infringing on the property rights of God, and therefore he consistently opposed suicide in any shape or form.[31] Humans were considered stewards of the body, which was entrusted to them by God, and therefore had no express right to bring harm upon it. Locke equated his argument against suicide with his reticence to slavery: "Nobody can give more power than he has himself; and he that cannot take away his own life cannot give another power over it."[32] Immanuel Kant (1724–1804), the German philosopher, like Locke, also considered "the willed disposal of personhood" morally decrepit.[33]

The Renaissance and the Enlightenment did much to unshackle opinions about euthanasia. But it was the nineteenth century, which saw the development of anesthesia, the widespread use of opiate painkillers, the advent of surgery, and all sorts of other medical advances, that brought the debate about euthanasia from philosophers' dissertations to patients' bedsides. However, this was also a time when the debate about the right to die became intertwined with something much more sinister—*the right to kill.*

THE WORD "EUTHANASIA" is derived from two Greek roots: "*eu*" means "good" or "well," while "*thanatos*" means "death," and "euthanasia" therefore quite literally means "good death." Yet if you talk to the average person, they do not carry a positive view of the word "euthanasia." In fact, euthanasia for most people probably sounds like the opposite of a good death. This perception, though, was not always the case, and it is events that occurred during the nineteenth century and the first half of the twentieth century that have come to define how people these days feel about it.

The start of the nineteenth century saw morphine being successfully extracted from opium by the German pharmacist Friedrich Sertürner. Morphine found widespread application, though its use was critiqued in some instances. For example, some Christians objected to the use of morphine at childbirth, given that it contradicted the biblical decree "I will greatly multiply thy sorrow and thy conception; in sorrow thou shalt bring forth children."[34] However, these hurdles were overcome, with the first half of the nineteenth century seeing multiple advances around the world culminating in the successful use of ether as a general anesthetic. These advances gave physicians control over both pain and consciousness. While the most immediate applications of anesthetics and analgesics were in surgery it became apparent that, for the first time, pain of all sorts could be alleviated.

John C. Warren, a founder of the *New England Journal of Medicine,* came from a family of physicians. His father served Thomas Jefferson in the Revolutionary War and founded Harvard Medical School in 1782. Warren's most famous operation was the first public demonstration of general anesthesia used during a surgical procedure. Warren, however, also realized that applications of ether existed beyond surgery. In his book recounting his experiences with etherization, Warren recommended expanding the use of ether to ease the passage of those in the final stages of dying: "Since the establishment of ethereal practice in surgical operations, its former utility in mitigating the agonies of death has led me to employ its influence in a more free and decided manner. . . . The value of the discovery will be greatly enhanced since the number of those who are called on to suffer in the struggle between life and death, is greater than that of those who are compelled to submit to the pain of surgical operations."[35] Warren found great value in alleviating suffering at the end of life, remarking, "If we find the means of preventing or relieving these pains, the great change may be viewed without horror, and even with tranquility."

In fact, according to Warren, anesthesia had become a deterrent to euthanasia in some cases. "As soon as a patient is condemned to the knife, what terror does his imagination inflict. . . . No wonder many people are unable to bring themselves to submit—no wonder that some, wrought to desperation, are led to anticipate their sufferings by a voluntary death. Horror of the knife led a gentleman in this city afflicted with a stone in the bladder to commit suicide."[36]

While John Warren never prescribed ether, chloroform, or morphine to expressly end someone's life, there was a sense that it was only a matter of time before someone would. As was going to become a pattern in subsequent history, it was a nonphysician who favored active euthanasia.

The Birmingham Speculative Club was a clique of thinkers and philosophers who gathered to discuss topics of general interest. Lectures delivered there were subsequently published. The most influential of these lectures was delivered in 1870 by a hitherto unknown gentleman, Samuel D. Williams, who asked his audience, "Why should the patient about to be operated upon by the surgeon always have a refuge from suffering open to him, and yet the patient about to suffer at the hands of Nature the worst she has to inflict, be left without help or hope of help?"[37] He then went on to lay down his assertion "that in all cases of hopeless and painful illness it should be the recognized duty of the medical attendant, whenever so desired by the patient, to administer chloroform . . . so as to destroy consciousness at once, and put the sufferer at once to a quick and painless death," adding the preconditions that "all needful precautions being adopted to prevent any possible abuse of such duty; and means being take to establish, beyond the possibility of doubt or question, that the remedy was applied at the express wish of the patient."

This lecture given in a cozy hall was widely circulated and was reprinted in the influential magazine *Popular Science Monthly*. Other nonphysicians who raised their voices at the turn of the century in favor of active euthanasia included the Harvard art professor Charles Eliot Norton and the prominent lawyer Simeon E. Baldwin, who would later be nominated president of the American Bar Association.[38] These views in part influenced the bill presented to the Ohio state legislature seeking to legalize euthanasia. While the bill was quashed, it was only the first such bill that would be presented to elected representatives in the United States.

The leading medical journals of the time, which have maintained their prominent positions to this day, dug in their heels and vehemently opposed any suggestion that doctors should assist in letting their patients die. In separate editorials, both the *Journal of the American Medical Association* and the *British Medical Journal* used the word "executioner" to describe what the role of physicians would amount to were euthanasia to be made legal.[39]

At the same time, while the medical community categorically rejected active euthanasia, they cozied up to an even darker and morally bankrupt concept: eugenics. Eugenics found life after Darwin published *On the Origin of Species,* per which, "medical men exert their utmost skill to save the life of everyone to the last moment . . . thus the weak members of civilized societies propagate their kind. No one who has attended to the breeding of domestic animals will doubt that this must be highly injurious to the race of man."[40] A particular point of emphasis of the eugenics movement was to target children or individuals who were "feeble-minded" or with "subnormal intelligence." Eugenics was widely embraced in post–World War I Germany, and in the United States as well. By 1926, twenty-three states had passed legislation legalizing sterilization.[41] Many of the states with voluntary sterilization did not require consent from the person to be sterilized, making sterilization practically involuntary.[42] Furthermore, sterilization was heavily directed toward minorities and foreigners.[43] By 1944, more than forty thousand people had been documented to have undergone sterilizations, and a further twenty-two thousand underwent sterilizations between 1943 and 1963.[44]

These sterilizations weren't clandestine events; they occurred with the express approval and encouragement of the most prominent medical associations as well as the courts. An editorial in 1933 in the *New England Journal of Medicine* proclaimed, "The burden on society resulting from this increase in feeble-mindedness is tremendous. For one thing, persons with subnormal intelligence are always potential criminals. . . . We should . . . recognize this danger that threatens to replace our population with a race of feeble-minded."[45] The editors saw the potential solution in Nazi eugenics: "Germany is perhaps the most progressive nation in restricting fecundity among the unfit. . . . The individual must give way before the greater good."[46]

The courts weren't far behind, and nowhere is that better represented than in the "landmark" case *Buck v. Bell* (1927).[47] Carrie Buck was placed into the care of foster parents after her mother was interned for promiscuity. She was just seventeen when she was raped by her foster mother's nephew and became pregnant. To protect the family from embarrassment, Buck's foster parents had her committed to the Virginia State Colony for Epileptics and Feeble Minded, where she was to be sterilized in accordance with the Virginia Sterilization Act of 1924. When the case went to the Supreme Court, they voted eight to one in favor of the state's right to sterilize her. In his decision, Oliver Wendell Holmes wrote, "It is better for all the world, if instead of waiting to execute degenerate offspring for crime, or to let them starve for their imbecility, society can prevent those who are manifestly unfit from continuing their kind. The principle that sustains compulsory vaccination is good enough to cover cutting the Fallopian tubes."[48] It wasn't until the late 1970s that the Virginia Sterilization Act, the basis of this ruling, was formally overturned.

While the eugenics movement lost steam after the Second World War, to many it remains synonymous with euthanasia. Much of the battle over euthanasia has been about framing, with one side constantly trying to tie euthanasia in with eugenics and other terms like "death panels," while the other side tries to separate euthanasia from them. The audibles and optics of euthanasia are very important to understanding where we are today in this unending debate.

THE DECADES AFTER the Great War saw an explosion in medical technology, including the development of mechanical ventilation, cardiopulmonary resuscitation, and other technologies that could sustain life almost indefinitely. The public didn't catch up to these advances until the Karen Ann Quinlan case, which became the seminal incident involving patients regaining a semblance of autonomy. While the Supreme Court ruled in favor of the patient's right to be left alone, it didn't comment on a patient's right to die.

While the Quinlan ruling was a big victory for pro-euthanasia groups, they had a massive challenge in front of them. Just the word "euthanasia" would evoke the most horrifying images in people's minds. While there has always been public support for some of the principles that pro-euthanasia groups supported, such as autonomy, the right to live free, and the right of self-determination, there were very few people who liked any of the actual details that came with it.

This set in motion a massive rebranding operation, an epic campaign of verbal engineering. The Euthanasia Society of America changed its name first to the Society for the Right to Die and subsequently to Choice in Dying. While it was initially called "merciless release" by a pro-euthanasia campaigner, "aid-in-dying" became the moniker of choice in the 1980s and 1990s, particularly during the failed campaign in Washington State in 1991 to legalize euthanasia.[49] However, the defeat of both campaigns in both California and Washington State at the ballot box meant that euthanasiasts had to go back to the drawing board. A poll conducted by the Euthanasia Research Guidance Organization resulted in the emergence of the term most in vogue in current times: "death with dignity."[50] Not only was this the term potential voters found most agreeable (or euphemistic, depending on which side you are on), it also implied that patients who die either with severe disability or after the failure of aggressive resuscitation do so without dignity.[51]

Words are so crucial that commentators can hardly agree on a specific definition for euthanasia. Words such as "suffering," "painless," and "relieve" carry the same amount of moral skew that words such as "mercy killing" and "suicide" do. These words aren't just important to philosophers and social advocates; they are deeply influential to voters and patients. I was working in a cancer center when I learned about this firsthand. In that hospital, when patients or their families wanted to forego any further life-sustaining treatment, they could opt to go down a route called "comfort measures only." This path, frequently instituted for patients getting hospice care, can mean different things to different people. For the vast majority of patients, it means that anything that doesn't directly provide symptomatic relief, such as lab checks, vital-sign monitoring, antibiotics, hydration, etc., is not considered, while for other patients drips of medications to keep the heart beating stronger or to keep fluid from accumulating in the lungs may be considered as "comfort measures."

When I was working in the cancer center, I was taking care of a patient with pulmonary fibrosis. The patient had lived with the disease for many years; in her case it was hereditary, and she had seen her two sisters develop it and take their last breaths at its hand. In pulmonary fibrosis, the lung loses its elasticity, and is gradually replaced with a stiff fibrous material that cannot exchange oxygen. Patients increasingly become dependent on oxygen tanks to help them breathe, and the irreversible disease continues to progress until the patient dies from being unable to breathe anymore or something else comes along to take them away. In my patient's case, something else did come along, and it was lung cancer. She was admitted to the hospital and got chemotherapy and was made to wear a huge breathing mask for almost three weeks before she decided she couldn't do it anymore.

At this point, I called on the palliative care team to come and help us make the transition. When I told the palliative care specialist that the patient was likely to opt for comfort measures only, the specialist told me she didn't like that term. She preferred "intensive comfort measures." "Rather than patients feeling we are holding something back, they should know that we are doing more," she told me.

The visuals matter, too, and no one understood that better than Jack Kevorkian. Jack Kevorkian was a pathologist and the most famous supporter of euthanasia during the second half of the twentieth century. Jack Kevorkian confessed to helping dozens of patients carry out euthanasia. He was taken to court four times between 1994 and 1997 but was always acquitted until in 1998, when he went on the television show *60 Minutes* and showed the world a video of him injecting a patient suffering from amyotrophic lateral sclerosis with a cocktail of lethal medications to help him end his life. While, predictably, the video landed Kevorkian in jail for manslaughter, he had won the visual war. He showed a patient suffering to the extent that he couldn't take a single breath with comfort, gave him a few medications, and within moments, he was not grimacing, he was not laboring, he was sitting limply in a chair, dead. The televised death was followed by an interview with the deceased's wife, who said, "I don't consider it murder, I consider it humane. I consider it the way things should be."

To some Kevorkian was a villain and a murderer,[52] but to others he was a hero.[53] Even supporters of euthanasia, like the comedian and talk show host Bill Maher, felt that he was not the best advocate for the cause and on more than one occasion had been his own worst enemy. But Kevorkian brought euthanasia back into the open and provided it the sort of coverage and publicity that euthanasiasts had always hoped for. The newspaper stories that he generated and the pieces on television in some ways normalized assisted death.

Despite resolute resistance, mostly from physician groups, campaigners around the United States have been relentless in their push to make active euthanasia legal. The greatest setback they faced was when active euthanasia was declared illegal by the US Supreme Court in their decisions on *Vacco v. Quill*[54] and *Washington v. Glucksberg* in 1997.[55] It was made clear that there was no constitutional right to die. When the focus moved to state-based changes, failure awaited them at the start; initiatives in both Washington State in 1991 and California in 1992 were defeated at the polling booth. However, 1994 would be the turning point: Oregon became the first state in the United States to pass a ballot measure legalizing physician-assisted death and so became the test case for euthanasia in the United States.

WHILE SOCIETAL ACCEPTANCE of euthanasia and physician-assisted suicide has waxed and waned one generation after another, it wasn't until very recently that this practice was actually legally recognized. However, it wasn't in the United States, where these issues have remained a point of great contention, or in Europe, where society has traditionally been very accepting of human apoptosis. The first territory to fully formalize the right of terminally ill people to take their own lives was the remote and rural Northern Territory in Australia.

The state legislature in the Northern Territory reasoned that there was no need for terminally ill patients to suffer any more than they already had at the hands of their diagnosis. The physician had to ascertain that the patient was terminally ill, that the patient would die of the disease, that there was no alternative treatment available, and that the patient was of sound mind. This information had to be corroborated with another physician. The chief proponent of physician-assisted suicide in Australia was a physician, Philip Nitschke, who enacted all of the legal suicides in the Northern Territory. His motivation to become a physician was to overcome his self-professed hypochondria. While he failed to unworry, he found his calling in championing euthanasia.[56]

The legalization of physician-assisted suicide in the Northern Territory lasted for only two years, from 1995 to 1997, when the Rights of the Terminally Ill Act was overturned in federal parliament. Seven people committed assisted suicide during that time, but those seven cases present a very insightful view of euthanasia and the people who seek it.[57]

Many patients who seek euthanasia suffer from depression. The first patient who sought physician-assisted suicide in the Northern Territory was a woman with breast cancer who was completely alone, divorced from her husband and estranged from her children. She had tried and failed to commit suicide earlier and now wanted to avail herself of the act. She declared to the media that her prognosis was limited, though doctors disputed that assessment. But before the law could be formally enacted, she committed suicide on her own.

The second patient who sought physician-assisted suicide was also someone who lacked any relatives or any social support. He was single and lived in a small cottage in the outback. "I'm just existing, I can't see the point anymore. I've seen my time. I'm ready for the sweet long sleep," he told reporters. He decided to put his affairs in order and made what I can only imagine would be the longest three-thousand-kilometer car journey ever undertaken in history. What awaited him in Darwin, the capital of the Northern Territory, was more pain: The law was appealed by legislators, and physicians were advised against assisting with any suicides. He eventually had to make what must have seemed an even longer journey back home, where he died in a local hospital. Social isolation is another recurring theme; another patient was an elderly man who had moved from England, had never married, and had no relatives in Australia. He was delivered the lethal medications in his home, which had previously been boarded up.

The first patient to succeed in obtaining the means to commit assisted suicide was an elderly man with prostate cancer. The cancer had weakened his bones to the extent that he once suffered a fractured rib from a hug. He was undone by nausea, frequent infections, diarrhea, and an inability to urinate on his own. The end occurred with his wife by his side, holding his hand. While a great deal of emphasis, particularly in the United States, has been placed on pain, other considerations seem to be important for some patients. One woman who had intestinal cancer had to poop in a bag, and the odor forced her to limit her social activity. When she decided to go ahead with physician-assisted suicide, the act had been revoked, and instead she was started on a morphine drip at a very high dosage, which was escalated exponentially along with multiple other additives, until she finally met her maker after an agonizingly long final ordeal.

The most intriguing of the seven cases was that of Janet Mills.[58] Mills had lived a tough nomadic life, raising three children in caravans. She was forty when she developed an itchy rash, eventually diagnosed as a rare form of lymphoma called mycosis fungoides. For over a decade she underwent chemotherapy and all sorts of treatments to control her itching, but to no avail. She was frequently hurting herself scratching and causing infections. She could barely get any sleep and lost all interest in life. She told a psychiatrist, "I scratch day and night. My hands and feet blister. . . . I can't take anymore. It's so hopeless. You want to get something to help, but you can't." Her husband reported that every night she woke up and wanted him to help her die. When Nitschke helped her die with an automated lethal injection device, she was accompanied by her son and her husband.

While Australia was the first place to legally (and briefly) allow physician-assisted death, to most the Netherlands is the mecca of modern euthanasic death. While euthanasia wasn't technically legal in the Netherlands until 2002 and could be punished with up to twelve years in prison, it had been openly practiced since at least the 1970s. In fact, the Dutch medical society had provided guidelines for how to perform both euthanasia and physician-assisted suicide. The decades' worth of data available from the Netherlands provides an example of what a society where euthanasia finds wide acceptance looks like. That picture provides ammunition for both advocates and detractors of legalizing physician-assisted suicide.

Before we take a look at euthanasia in the Netherlands, it is important to highlight some of the factors that define it as a nation and a health economy. Since the Renaissance, the Netherlands has been a bastion of liberalism. When philosophers such as Descartes feared persecution, they made their way to the Netherlands to be able to freely express their views. While the Dutch suffered much under Nazi occupation, they rebounded from the Second World War and instead of recoiling from their identity, they embraced it with greater fervor. One aspect that they distinguished themselves with was championing the right of patients to end their lives.

Truus Postma and her husband, Andries, met when they were medical students, and set up a family practice in the 1950s in the tiny rural village of Noordwolde.[59] They were dedicated to their community, and nothing about either would suggest that they would become the pioneers of euthanasia in the developing world. But as this preface would suggest, their heart-wrenching circumstance would be the sentinel case as the Netherlands sought to face willful death head-on. In 1971, Truus's mother was suffering. In the wake of a bleed in her brain, she was left deaf, unable to speak properly or even control her bodily movements. She had to be restrained in a chair to prevent her from falling to the ground. Repeatedly, she would request that Truus end her life, and Truus eventually relented. Truus injected two hundred milligrams of morphine into her mother's vein. Her mother became unresponsive, and her breathing slowed down until it stopped and she passed. Truus informed the nursing home's staff, who informed the authorities, who sent the case to the courts. The district court in Leeuwarden found Truus guilty of killing her mother on request but punished her with only a per-functory week of jail time. At the same time, the court also laid down guidelines under which a physician could hasten a patient's death: The patient had to be suffering from a terminal incurable sickness and had to formally request for euthanasia to be carried out.

The Postma case, and a few other notable court cases, along with widespread public support for euthanasia, allowed physicians free rein to do as they willed, but given that there was no formal requirement for physicians to report an assisted death, no one really knew what the ex-tent of the practice was until the Remmelink Commission released its findings in 1991. The commission conducted an anonymous survey of Dutch physicians and found that in 1990, of the 130,000 deaths that oc-curred in the Netherlands, 2,300 patients (1.8 percent) died as the result of euthanasia, while an additional 400 patients (0.3 percent) died of physician-assisted suicide.[60] While the sheer number of patients getting euthanasia was quite low, the focus of critics of euthanasia was an ad-ditional 1,000 patients who were reported to not be competent at the time they underwent euthanasia. These 1,000 patients were the evi-dence that detractors needed, which to them demonstrated that the Dutch were well down a slippery, slippery slope. One of the core argu-ments against euthanasia has always been that it would creep into the involuntary execution of elderly and disabled patients.[61] The argument was that once you start down this path, the threshold will lower for physicians to take a patient's life in their own hands. As one Israeli phy-sician described a Dutch physician telling him, "The first time it was difficult."[62]

Upon digging deeper, a more nuanced picture stared to emerge: Most patients had previously expressed an interest in euthanasia, and their life expectancy was very limited regardless. A second survey, in 1995, showed that the rate of patients getting euthanasia had plateaued, with a slight reduction in patients getting euthanasia without their ex-press consent.[63] Data from 2001 showed a further flattening of cases of euthanasia, suggesting that the line had truly run out of gas and had steadied out, with about ninety-seven hundred requests a year, five thousand of which were completed.[64] Over the same time, palliative care continued to improve, with a very steady decline in patients requesting euthanasia owing to unbearable pain. Therefore, proponents of euthanasia also use this data to argue their case that legalizing euthanasia allows patients to retain autonomy even under the most horrifying of circumstances without exploding into a mass culling of the old and weary.

While countries such as Belgium[65] and Luxembourg[66] have also since legalized euthanasia, and countries including Germany, Switzerland, and Japan have legalized physician-assisted suicide, the landscape is truly different in the United States.[67] Americans are a much more conservative populace, but there is another great difference, which makes comparisons somewhat meaningless: All these other countries have universal healthcare. In the Netherlands, for example, while medical costs are considered either "normal" or "exceptional," patients don't have to pay anything out-of-pocket. This, of course, has great implications for this debate.

Although large parts of the country consider euthanasia and physician-assisted suicide equivalent to murder, one state took the lead in bringing this aesthetic to American shores. While Oregon is just the twenty-seventh-most-populous state, it has become the face of the most modern of American deaths.

When the Plug Is Pulled

Brittany Maynard had just gotten married when the headaches started. A headache is the most ubiquitous of symptoms: it's hard to live through any amount of life, sometimes even a caffeine-deprived day, without having one. While many live a long life span without ever having a heart attack or a stroke or even getting a urinary-tract infection (especially men), almost everyone gets a pain in the noggin at some point. Of the almost forty million patients in the United States who have recurring headaches every year, only a few have a life-threatening cancer. After an extensive workup, including an MRI of the brain, it turned out that Brittany was one of those people.

A Bay Area resident, Brittany did what anyone else with a potentially curable cancer would—she went ahead with neurosurgery, which involved removal of part of her skull. Yet the cancer came back, and when it did, it was stage-four and incurable. With or without treatment, patients with her diagnosis live for less than a year. "After months of research, my family and I reached a heartbreaking conclusion," she wrote. "There is no treatment that would save my life, and the recommended treatments would have destroyed the time I had left."[1] She considered traditional palliative hospice care but felt that she "could develop potentially morphine-resistant pain and suffer personality changes and verbal, cognitive and motor loss of virtually any kind." It was thus that she decided that she would not leave the end in the control of her disease or her doctors. She and her family packed their bags and drove to Oregon.

"I want to die on my own terms."

OREGON'S JOURNEY TO become the first state in the United States to allow physician-assisted suicide began in the 1990s, when the right-to-die movement was at its most heated and fraught. Starting with the publication of "It's Over, Debbie," in 1988, and Jack Kevorkian's first assisted suicide, in 1990, euthanasia and physician-assisted suicide were debated in medical conferences, legislatures, courts, and the realm of public opinion. By a tight margin of just 2.6 percent in 1994, voters in Oregon made it the first state to allow terminally ill patients to take their own lives with the assistance of a doctor. Almost immediately, before it could be implemented, a federal district judge barred the act with an injunction, reasoning that it failed to offer the same "protections against suicide" to those applying for assisted suicide as it did to the general population. That injunction, however, was lifted in 1997, and physician-assisted suicide had finally arrived in the United States.

The rules that Oregon laid down were fairly similar to those being used in other parts of the world. The petitioner had to be an adult over eighteen years of age, have capacity to make medical decisions, be a resident of Oregon, and have a terminal illness with an expected survival of less than six months. Patients who met these requirements needed to make one written request to be given a lethal prescription, cosigned by two witnesses, and two verbal requests to the prescribing physician. The prescriber and another consulting doctor had to confirm both the terminal illness and the expected survival of less than six months. If either felt the patient didn't have capacity or had some psychiatric disorder, a referral to a psychiatrist was made. After apprising the patient of any other alternatives that might be available, physicians also were required to inquire if the patient would want to notify their next of kin or not.

For a debate where the middle ground has always been a vanishing space, the Death with Dignity Act was a bomb. Surveys conducted in the 1990s showed that the vast majority of physicians opposed physician-assisted suicide and euthanasia.[2] While some physicians from some religious denominations (Jewish, unaffiliated) were more open to euthanasia, the majority still remained opposed.[3] While doctors in Oregon were more likely to be open to it,[4] physicians in other states were far more skeptical. The surveys, however, also revealed that physicians in the United States were receiving requests for euthanasia from their patients and a small percentage of physicians, despite it being illegal, were complying with these requests. A national survey showed that about 5 percent of physicians had delivered a lethal dose, compared with 7 percent in Oregon.[5] A survey of intensive-care nurses, too, found that one in five had delivered a lethal dose of medication to a patient at their request with an express desire to terminate their lives.[6] Given that euthanasia and its variants were illegal and practitioners could be tried for manslaughter, it is likely that the surveys underestimated just how prevalent the practice was, but it still surprised most.[7]

On the other hand, though, the public was more open, but still seemed to be split down the middle.[8] The group of people most in favor of legalizing either euthanasia or physician-assisted suicide has always been and remains the few to whom these measures are most directly relevant: patients with terminal diseases.[9] To me this is the group most significant to this debate, yet they frequently fail to find a seat on the table. Compared with the public and physicians, patients with terminal diseases are much fewer in number, and frequently their diagnosis leaves them in no condition to be able to actively pursue a life outside of the hospital, the nursing home, or the hospice where they spend most of their time.

When physician-assisted suicide did become legal in Oregon, the expectation was that Oregon would become a veritable final home for patients flocking from across the United States to take control of their final days. Another fear, perhaps more justifiable, was that the brunt of this initiative would be economically disadvantaged patients, such as minorities and the uninsured, who couldn't afford treatments and would therefore choose this route. Unlike the Netherlands, where health insurance is universal, Oregon had around a half million uninsured people at the time the act was passed.

Sixteen years of rigorously collected data from when the act was put in place in 1997 has now refuted most of those fears.[10] Over sixteen years, 1,173 patients requested lethal prescriptions and two-thirds of these, 752, filled and used them. This comes to just about a handful of patients per every ten thousand deaths. The average age of the patient is seventy-one years, with 77 percent of patients being between fifty-five and eighty-five years of age. Only six patients have ever been younger than thirty-five, as Brittany Maynard was. The vast majority of patients are white (97.3 percent), have insurance (98.3 percent), die at home (95.3 percent), are enrolled in hospice (90.1 percent), have a high-school education (94.1 percent), and have cancer (79.8 percent). Just about half of patients are male (52.7 percent), are married (46.2 percent), have a baccalaureate or higher (45.6 percent), and die without a physician at the bedside (44.7 percent). Notably, only one patient since 1997 ever died in a hospital. While there was concern that vulnerable populations would be more likely to go ahead with assisted suicide,[11] only one African American male and twelve people without insurance have ever gone ahead with it in Oregon.

What motivates terminally ill Oregonians to go ahead with their decisions? The top three reasons stated by patients are losing autonomy (91.4 percent), being less able to engage in activities making life enjoyable (88.9 percent), and loss of dignity (80.9 percent). Inadequate pain control was stated as a reason by only 23.7 percent of the patients. This should be surprising, given that 65 to 85 percent of patients with advanced cancer experience significant pain.[12] This is important for many reasons; many critics of physician-assisted suicide point to it representing a failure of palliative care and pain control. Yet as demonstrated in the Netherlands,[13] legalization only highlights end-of-life care, making physicians more aware than ever before about fulfilling their duties to patients who are dying.

It has been postulated that depression drives most of the requests for patients wanting to end their lives themselves. Yet studies from Oregon suggest that depression is one of the least important factors driving patients to make their decisions.[14] Part of it might be just receiving the prescription. "Now that I've had the prescription filled and it's in my possession," Brittany wrote, "I have experienced a tremendous sense of relief."[15] A third of patients don't even use their prescriptions, and of those that do, when they do it varies between 15 days and 1,009 days from when they first requested a lethal dose.[16]

When Oregon first allowed assisted suicide, comparisons with Nazi experiments were made very frequently. It can now be argued that there are few places where death is better than in Oregon, and not just for those who choose to end their lives themselves. Far from being a cautionary tale about the slippery slope toward eugenics, the Oregon model has been accepted by several other states. In 2008, voters in Washington State passed an act similar to the one in Oregon, paving the way for physician-assisted suicide to be legalized there.[17] This was followed by Montana, where in 2009 the Supreme Court asserted that there existed no law prohibiting physicians from helping their patients deliberately expedite death.[18] In 2013, the state legislature in Vermont passed the Patient Choice and Control at End of Life bill,[19] which was quite similar to previous acts. Most recently California made this option available for its residents in 2016; and outside the United States, Canada has also passed an aid-in-dying bill.

Just a few days before Brittany Maynard died, it seemed like she had a change of heart. In a video released on October 29, 2014, she said, "I laugh and smile with my family and friends enough that it doesn't seem like the right time."[20] Hearing this, I wrote her an e-mail, hoping to know what was going through her mind. Before I heard back, news broke on the second of November that she had taken her life just as she had always intended to. "Goodbye world. Spread good energy. Pay it forward," she posted on her Facebook page, her last words.[21]

While five states have legalized physician-assisted suicide, that leaves forty-five others where it remains illegal, and even within the states where it is legal, it continues to be used by only a small minority of patients. Yet there are perfectly legal and much more common practices that can greatly hasten a patient's death and that skim awfully close to active euthanasia. On many nights, I have been asked, and have complied, with requests to double up on a morphine drip, until the line on the heart monitor ran flat, flat, flat. . . .

FOR MANY PHYSICIANS who trained or worked during the AIDS epidemic, that experience has come to define them not only as doctors, but as people.[22] Rafael Campo, the physician-poet, was a resident in the early 1990s at the University of California, San Francisco; he practiced in the heart of the epidemic. "HIV was very instructive to me in the limits of what we could do," he told me one day, reminiscing about those days.

One of the defining encounters of his training came, of course, in the middle of the night. The patient in question was a transvestite performer who was in excruciating pain and "was drowning in her own secretions." While the patient was experiencing extreme discomfort from her Kaposi sarcoma, a cancer involving the skin, what really shook Rafael was that she was having difficulty breathing. "When patients cannot breathe, it is one of the most awful experiences of suffering that I have witnessed," he said.

Being exposed to such pain can make anyone question their core beliefs. "We all formally take the Hippocratic oath and we wear white coats and profess to do no harm. . . . Doing no harm should not mean sitting silently next to someone who is suffering. . . . It's a form of harm to allow that person to suffer without relief," he said.

Open to her suffering, Rafael "sensed a deep connection with her." Short of euthanasia, he wanted to provide her the comfort she needed, also knowing that this relief could come at a cost. As he delivered what would prove to be a fatal dose of morphine to ease her pain, he crystallized that moment in a poem—"Her Final Show"—which ended with him "pronouncing her to no applause."[23]

If you feel that this instance of terminal sedation bears an eerie similarity to euthanasia, you are not alone. Terminal sedation, the act of giving medications such as benzodiazepines or opiates until unconsciousness is achieved at the end of life, to relieve otherwise unrelenting pain or distress, is a common practice that has one very big difference from euthanasia—it is legal.

Despite advances in medications that can help alleviate symptoms associated with modern death, such as pain, difficult breathing, delirium, nausea, vomiting, anxiety, and distress, in many cases symptoms go unmitigated.[24] In addition to physical symptoms, many patients experience significant existential suffering stemming from imminent death. The most common reported such symptoms include feelings of meaninglessness, feelings of being a burden on others, and death anxiety.[25] With some amount of variance, patients whose deaths are imminent are provided terminal sedation at their or their appropriate health-care proxy's request.

The guiding ethical principle at the heart of terminal sedation is that of the double effect. The double effect finds its origin in Christian tradition during the Middle Ages; it holds that if an action is performed with a good intention, then even an adverse outcome is acceptable, provided that the intention was good.[26] What this means is that if a physician prescribes a drug such as morphine to relieve pain, any side effects stemming from that, such as slowed breathing, are acceptable, provided that the physician gave the medication with the purpose of symptom relief.

Terminal sedation received the blessing of the law in the landmark trials *Washington v. Glucksberg* and *Vacco v. Quill* in 1997.[27] While ruling against physician-assisted suicide, the US Supreme Court realized that there were many patients who suffered from intractable symptoms close to death. The American Medical Association came out fighting against supporters of physician-assisted suicide and presented an amicus brief, which stated, "The pain of most terminally ill patients can be controlled throughout the dying process without heavy sedation or anesthesia. . . . For a very few patients, however, sedation to a sleeplike state may be necessary in the last days or weeks of life to prevent the patient from experiencing severe pain."[28] This allowed the court to provide terminally ill patients demanding physician-assisted suicide an alternative with many similar features.

While supporters have tried to rechristen the provision of a deep sleep before death as "palliative sedation," avoiding the ominous "terminal" bit, much of the criticism of terminal sedation has come not only from physicians but from the physicians who are supposedly experts in all matters of death—palliative care experts. Susan Block, a palliative care expert at the Dana Farber Cancer Institute, coauthored an article in which she dubbed the administration of a morphine drip at the end of life as "slow euthanasia."[29] But far from using that analogy to dissuade the practice, she and her coauthor, Andrew Billings, make the argument that de-euphemizing terminal sedation might make the public and physicians more open to euthanasia and physician-assisted suicide in the appropriate context.

Timothy Quill is also an important voice in this debate. A palliative care specialist in Rochester, New York, Quill made his first foray onto the national stage in a big way. In a piece in the *New England Journal of Medicine* in 1991, he "confessed" to prescribing a lethal dose of barbiturates to one of his patients, Diane.[30] When she was diagnosed with leukemia, Diane refused any chemotherapy. While she was offered hospice care, Diane wanted a means to fully control her end. "She had known of people lingering in what was called relative comfort, and she wanted no part of it," wrote Quill. "When the time came, she wanted to take her life in the least painful way." Diane wanted Quill to help her commit suicide. Quill prescribed her the medications under the cover of treating insomnia. A few months later, she ingested the medications early in the morning on her couch, covered in her favorite shawl. The response to his disclosure was immense. "The huge outpouring of support from families who had struggled with similar issues was way out of proportion to the amount of opposition," he told me.

Quill finds fault with the underlying principle of the double effect that allows physicians to give at times escalating doses of painkillers and sedatives at the end of life. To Quill, human intentions are complex, and we, as a society, "would do well to look beneath the idealized, sanitized intentions espoused by many medical ethicists to the actual experience of doctors and patients."[31] This statement really rings true with me. Even when I was an intern on the wards or in the intensive-care unit, there were times when I increased the dose of a patient's sedation until they were pretty much comatose, when the goal of the patient's care was to achieve comfort at all costs. Every time I asked the nurse to increase the dose, I knew that this would push the patient closer to death, and in some cases perhaps my unconscious intention was to expedite their final passage.

In the view of one commentator, at least, the US Supreme Court, in its rejection of physician-assisted suicide and acceptance of terminal sedation, endorsed a practice much closer to euthanasia. In physician-assisted suicide, the physician is not directly involved in the ingestion of the lethal medications, and therefore the patient proceeds with complete autonomy. On the other hand, patients who receive terminal sedation are usually much more actively sick, and frequently lack the capacity both to make the decision and to have surrogates make the decision for them. Because all of the control in terminal sedation lies in the hands of the providers and not the patients, in many ways this practice is indeed quite close to euthanasia.[32]

Even more controversial is the application of terminal sedation among patients who desire it not to relieve physical ailments but to smother the psychological anguish associated with an inevitable death.[33] Studies have shown that the proportion of people making requests for terminal sedation or euthanasia not driven by physical symptoms is growing. The reduction in such requests being driven by uncontrolled symptoms likely represents an improvement in how we are managing these symptoms at the end of life. However, the provision of opiates or other drugs for psychological stressors such as death anxiety rather than symptoms is not very well established. In fact, the American Medical Association stated that "palliative sedation is not the way to address suffering created by social isolation and loneliness."[34]

Studies, however, have shown that the provision of sedatives or opiates does not shorten survival in terminally ill patients.[35] Patients receiving these medications are generally the sickest of the sick and mostly their underlying illnesses are so advanced that they drive the agenda regardless of what else is at play.[36] Furthermore, the acceptance of the double effect is one of the greatest factors that provide physicians the peace of mind to relentlessly battle suffering without having to worry about inadvertent or advertent consequences. While it may represent a rebranding of euthanasia, the euphemization also serves an important purpose. Two physicians wrote about how the double effect helped them better provide comfort to their patients in an article, calling it "a great aid to those of us who care daily for patients who are very ill and dying."[37] The double effect provides a modicum of softness to what might otherwise be perceived as a cold act of mercy killing under other circumstances.

"If you have any pain, we will give you something to get rid of it," said a nurse, but she went on to add, "Ninety-nine percent of the time, that's right. But, when you get that one patient, it makes you realize that there's not a cure for everything, not all the time."[38] The entire debate about all these practices—euthanasia, physician-assisted suicide, and terminal sedation—does only pertain to that 1 percent of the population who face an awful death. Increasingly, physicians do a good job of managing the rattle of death, and that is largely because of the great attention that issues such as euthanasia have directed toward helping patients achieve a good death.

Most patients, though, die not from adding interventions such as painkillers and sedatives, but by the active withdrawal of life-sustaining interventions. Sometimes these are as advanced as ventilators or heavy-hitting medications, but at other times they are the most basic of things—food and water. While active euthanasia, even in parts where it is legal, accounts for a vanishingly small percentage of deaths, it is rare for people to die in hospitals these days without life-sustaining treatments having been withdrawn.

THE ADVENT OF technology far beyond our imagination not only brought hope for many patients who would have otherwise succumbed to their ailments but also raised ethical questions the like of which had never been asked in the past. While the case of Karen Quinlan provided the first precedent for when treatment could be withdrawn by guardians on behalf of a patient if they had expressed such a wish in the past, the situation came to a head not in a courtroom but with a desperate parent with a loaded gun at the bedside of his intubated infant in an intensive-care unit in April 1989.

Eight months before Rudy Linares pulled out a .357 Magnum revolver in the pediatric ICU, a routine day went terribly awry. Samuel, Rudy's fifteen-month-old child, accidently swallowed a balloon at a birthday party and started to suffocate. Rudy tried his best to revive his child. When he started to fade, Rudy lifted Samuel into his arms and ran to the closest firehouse, screaming, "Help me! Help me! My baby is dying!"[39] While Samuel was eventually revived, his brain never recovered and he had plunged into a persistent vegetative state.

Months into the ordeal, Rudy requested that the doctors disconnect Samuel from life support. They agreed, but the hospital's lawyer warned them against going ahead, citing that they could face possible criminal charges. As time went by, despair turned to frustration, which then turned to rage. When the hospital left a message on Rudy's voice mail saying that they were transferring Samuel to a nursing home, something inside him broke, and he headed to the hospital with the gun in his possession. When he pulled out the revolver in the ICU, he declared, "I'm not here to hurt anyone. I just want to let my son die."[40]

Rudy pulled the tube from his son's throat. Within seconds, Samuel became motionless, but Rudy kept cradling him in his arms for at least twenty minutes. A physician slid him a stethoscope to confirm that Samuel's heart had in fact stopped beating. Eventually, he gave up his gun, was arrested, and had murder charges filed against him.

In the court of public opinion, Rudy was a hero: A poll by the *Chicago Tribune* showed that six thousand callers favored him thirteen to one.[41] Neither the hospital nor the courts wanted to punish Rudy, despite the legal gray area that he had unearthed. Neither did the jury; they let him walk. And while Rudy was not the perfect poster child to highlight the ethics of withdrawing life-sustaining treatments—he had been arrested multiple times for battery, and just two weeks after being declared not guilty of murder, barely survived an overdose of PCP, cocaine, and alcohol[42]—he did more than most bioethicists ever have to highlight the role of technology at the end of life.

The late eighties, punctuated as they were by the Rudy Linares drama, were a time in history when the American people revolted against the machines keeping them alive to perpetuity in hospitals and nursing homes. "'Life sustaining' becomes 'death prolonging'; patients do not

recover, nor do they die. Instead they become prisoners of technology,"
wrote a physician, capturing the mood of the times.[43] The right of
people to withdraw or withhold life-sustaining treatment reached the
Supreme Court again. Taking on the mantle from Karen Quinlan was
another young girl now horribly removed from her prior self—Nancy
Cruzan, whose tragic end, too, was fought out on the national stage.

Nancy's first death occurred in January 1983, when she lost control
of her car on a deserted road and ended up facedown in a water-filled
ditch. Paramedics arrived on the scene and helped resuscitate her with
CPR. But while her pulse returned fifteen minutes after she had first lost
it, her person never did. She slipped into a persistent vegetative state and
never came back. After four years went by with her wilting away in a
nursing home in Missouri, her parents petitioned to have her feeding
tube removed, only to hit a snag. While the parents relayed that in conversations she had expressed a desire not to be artificially animated, the
state required more concrete proof. While a trial judge agreed, the Missouri Supreme Court overturned that decision, stating that while Nancy
did have the right to withdraw treatment, that decision could not be
made by someone else on her behalf. The court gave the state the right
to require documentation, although at that time only Missouri and New
York had strict requirements for documentation, mostly in the form of
advance directives. The Cruzans found millions of sympathizers, with
one parent, whose own daughter was in a coma, writing, "Throughout
my daughter's life I made many a decision to guide her into adulthood
and now, when she's incapable of deciding for herself, the state wants to
take the place of her father." He went on to add, "Walking into her room
is like entering a funeral parlor. . . . Could it be that Rudy Linares, who
held off the medical staff at a Chicago hospital and the police at gun-
point so that he could 'rescue' his dying infant from a ventilator, was so
much wiser than our courts?"[44]

What the court did yield was that it declared artificial nutrition and
hydration as forms of medical treatment. While they agreed with prevailing perspective shared by medical and bioethical organizations, they
found staunch opponents who argued that food and water were not
medical treatments and their withdrawal amounted to a euthanasic

murder. "Even a dog in Missouri cannot be legally starved to death," said Reverend Joseph Foreman, an Atlanta-based pro-life advocate.[45] Not only did these protesters challenge the ruling multiple times in court, they even stormed the medical facility housing Nancy in an attempt to reconnect her with the feeding tube.

Eventually, though, the court admitted the testimony of coworkers of Nancy Cruzan's, who described her desire to not be in a vegetative state, and authorized the Cruzans to go ahead with taking out the feeding tube. About two weeks after this separation, Nancy completed the long and agonizing death that had taken almost eight years to unfold. It didn't take long for her legacy to be realized. In contrast to 1987 and 1988, when about half of all deaths in ICUs were preceded by a decision to withdraw or withhold life support, that number was 90 percent in 1992 and 1993, as shown by a study from investigators at the University of California, San Francisco.[46] This is reflective of a modern state of affairs in which it is really difficult for someone to fully pass without a physician almost allowing it to happen. As one of my senior critical-care attending physicians once told me, "No one should die in the ICU without a physician's order [to withdraw life support]."

The controversy over physician-assisted suicide and euthanasia has made many people consider alternatives, and terminal dehydration is one that has piqued considerable interest. A particularly personal story was shared by David Eddy, a physician who was asked by his mother to share her dying: "Write about this, David. Tell others how well this worked for me. I'd like this to be my gift."[47] Virginia was eighty-four, but her age was only a number to her. At seventy, she had traveled alone across Africa, and at eighty-two had survived a capsized raft in Wyoming's Snake River. Yet after her husband passed away, she started to look at life differently: "I know they can keep me alive a long time, but what's the point? If the pleasure is gone and the direction is steadily down, why should I have to draw it out until I'm 'rescued' by cancer, a heart attack, or a stroke? . . . Is the meaning of life defined by its duration? Or does life have a purpose so large that it doesn't have to be prolonged at any cost to preserve its meaning?"

Mulling her choices, she thought about physician-assisted suicide but didn't go ahead with it given the fact that it was illegal. While thinking her options through, she had a brain wave, and her family went along with it. After her eighty-fifth birthday, "she relished her last piece of chocolate, and then stopped eating and drinking." Six days later, her family could not wake her, and she passed.

While Eddy presented a five-star review of terminal dehydration, this does not represent the majority view either. Death from terminal dehydration can take between days and weeks, leaving patients and families trapped in uncertainty.[48] Furthermore, terminal dehydration places the entire onus on the patient to starve themselves to a prune—a task that could be too difficult for someone who is already suffering.

While treatment withdrawal has now become ubiquitous, it is still controversial. After all, this is where "pulling the plug," originated from, and just that phrase itself reflects an active aspect of treatment withdrawal. At times when patients are fully dependent on life support—such as, say, if they are intubated and connected to a ventilator—withdrawing life support can cause almost instantaneous death.

A patient who had end-stage heart failure, who had become tired of the complications, requested that his physicians turn off his left ventricular assist device, a turbine in his heart keeping blood flowing through his body after his heart failed to keep up. Within moments of it being turned off, he died. When differentiating between euthanasia and treatment withdrawal, scholars frequently cite that while euthanasia is an act of commission, withdrawal represents an omission. The moral basis of this argument is flimsy, and frequently, withdrawing treatment is as much a deliberate act as injecting lethal drugs is.[49]

Another central argument against euthanasia harks back to the Hippocratic oath, which states that a physician's main role is to prolong life. Yet this statement does not take into account what the patient's preference might be. When a terminally ill person decides that they don't want any life-prolonging medications, procedures, or resuscitative measures, they are effectively stating their desire to not want to live on as long as medically sustainable. Why do we rightly allow patients to shorten life in one manner that might involve a lot more uncertainty, loss of autonomy, and suffering rather than another? If preventing suicide is the aim, nowhere in time have we been able to successfully prevent suicidal people from going ahead with their plans. In fact, patients who are depressed or even suicidal can refuse any future treatment or withdraw ongoing treatment, while they might not qualify for physician-assisted suicide.[50]

Even as our society, courts, and physicians have all made their peace with treatment withdrawal, it is interesting to note how indistinct the line between passive or semi-active euthanasia and more active forms of euthanasia really is. While as doctors we draw clean and sharp lines in our heads to allow us to function and do our jobs, the truth is far murkier. In the course of writing this book, I have learned many things about myself. Most surprising is to realize that, knowing what I know now, I have come to the conclusion that we must do more to discuss and support competent terminally ill patients' right to demand and acquire the means to end their suffering with the aid of a physician.

WHILE EVERY LIFE is unique, death remains consistently disempowering, harrowing, and, for the most part, undesired. Most people who seek death through suicide do so more to end life rather than achieve death. This is true of all patients at the end of life; to date I have not had a single patient who expressly wanted to die just for the sake of it. If anything, life is valued ever more as it strains to leave.

Some claim that modern medicine has done more to prolong death than to extend meaningful life. While I disagree with this notion, there are many patients whose demise is preceded by an extended period of debility and suffering. When nurses and physicians look at these patients, they frequently assess them as having a much poorer quality of life than the patients themselves may think. This is not surprising, as patients frequently adapt to the inconveniences that come with their illnesses. The vast majority of patients want to do everything reasonably possible to prolong life for as long as they can.

In a few harrowing and tragic cases, the very act of living itself comes to be defined by distress and despair. The underlying disease, whether it be cancer or sepsis or cirrhosis, invades the true essence of the patient's life.

At this time, physicians can provide relief on many levels. Opiates for pain, benzodiazepines for anxiety, antiemetics for nausea can all be easily dispensed by physicians or by nurses specializing in end-of-life care. These medications, though, are far from perfect. Opiates cause people to be sleepy, groggy, and confused, and while they may ensure pain relief, too frequently they take a toll on the patient's animation. Opiates also create their own need: As soon as the body sees opiates, it reacts by increasing the number of receptors in the neurons, meaning that a higher dose will be needed to achieve a similar effect the next time.

When the end draws closer, it is usually preceded by an acute escalation of medical interventions. A third of elderly Americans undergo a surgical procedure in the hospital in the last year of life, with a fifth undergoing such procedures in their last month of life.[51] Given that these procedures are done so close to dying, it isn't clear if they provide any meaningful benefit. A fifth of patients also undergo life-sustaining interventions such as intubation, CPR, and artificial nutrition in the last six months of life.[52] The crescendo of hospital visits, medical interventions, medication prescriptions builds up and up and up, and just before it seems like the storm will never ebb, the realization hits that there is nothing left for the tsunami to destroy. The majority of these patients or their family members then decide to withdraw life-sustaining procedures, as they finally embrace an end they fought so hard to defer for so long.

The same way that, in the old world, the trajectory at the end would entail people lying in their beds after a short but rapidly progressive illness, the de facto mode of modern death looks something like this: Person falls sick, gets better, but never gets back to baseline, accumulating diagnoses and procedures until it becomes clear (usually quite belatedly) that more will not necessarily do any good. This makes sense for the vast majority of people, and perhaps with good reason, but a select few patients don't want to go down this trodden path. There are states that have created pathways, laid down rules, and for the most part, for the few that choose to do so, it has turned out to be, if not a happy ending, the ending they wanted.

Why have physicians provided the greatest opposition to assisted suicide throughout history? Physicians are trained, as soldiers are to fight, sailors are to sail, and politicians are to politick, to treat. Whether it's trying to quell a symptom or correct someone's electrolyte imbalance or cut out a mass or open up a blood vessel, over years and years of busy days and long nights, rigorous preparation and draining didactics, physicians are trained to *do*. Just as it is hard for patients and their families to let go, doctors are not always ready to not do more.

To many physicians, incorporating suicide assistance in their practice repertoire also risks sending mixed messages to patients. Physicians argue that trust is the cornerstone of the patient-doctor relationship, and giving physicians the power to kill might alter what goes through the mind of a patient when they see a physician approach them in the middle of the night.

The truth is that, to a great extent, both ordinary people and the medical community have accepted practices very close to, if not indistinguishable from, euthanasia. Terminal sedation, terminal dehydration, even garden-variety withdrawal of care and the withholding of lifesaving treatments—while to physicians the distinction between these practices and euthanasia is self-evident, to the untrained eye the difference is blurry at best.[53] If anything, by obfuscating the issue, control over how patients die has been taken out of patients' hands and placed into the control of proxies and physicians, who are notoriously bad at predicting patients' preferences.

During my medical training I was taught that the ethics of our profession took shape by placing the patient on the pedestal. But as I researched for and wrote this book, talked to patients, physicians, nurses, caregivers, and researchers, contemplated what was routine and unquestioned, it became clear that much of what is now considered standard in end-of-life care came to be for expediency's sake. It was the evolution of medical technology and techniques that drove the conversation, while patients and even physicians strove to keep up.

Central to the discussion and yet somehow unresolved is the definition of harm. The central theme expounded by those who rally against assisted suicide is the historically durable maxim "Do no harm." But what is harm? Is a patient who gets treatments they would not want harm? Are not excessive unbeneficial procedures harm? Is a death far away from a place one would want not harm? And, perhaps most importantly, is a death that one would not have wanted not harm?

When the ancient Greeks coined the word "euthanasia," they sought to answer a question that we still struggle to answer: What is a good death? It is perhaps the most important and difficult question of all: How can the single greatest loss a life can experience ever be good? With what seems like an organized machine standing in the way, patients fight an uphill battle not to prevent death but to experience it in a reasonable way. On its front page, the *New York Times* ran the story of Joseph Landry, describing the inability of the medical system to grant him his only wish—to die at home, the way he would have wanted. The piece, which described his daughter's efforts to help her father during this time, was titled "A Father's Last Wish, and a Daughter's Anguish."[54] What patients' wishes are about, how they would want their lives to conclude and, importantly, what can be done to help them achieve that in the way they would want, are some of the most pressing questions of our time. And despite all our progress, they haven't been fully addressed.

#WhenDeathIsShared

Loneliness is about as much of a hallmark of how we die today as anything else is. As we age, we walk up the steps of a pyramid. With every level, the air gets just a tad thinner, and as the pyramid shrinks, so does our circle of friends and family. Roger Angell, now in his nineties, wrote in the *New Yorker,* "We geezers carry about a bulging directory of dead husbands or wives, children, parents, lovers, brothers and sisters, dentists and shrinks, office sidekicks, summer neighbors, classmates, and bosses, all once entirely familiar to us and seen as part of the safe landscape of the day."[1]

While much of this is a side effect of the radical extension in life span that humanity has achieved, most isolation experienced by the dying is an artifact of how the health system has evolved. Most folk, as soon as they fall sick, end up in hospitals, nursing homes, rehab facilities, and for quite a few, that is where they stay for vast swaths of what will be the remainder of their lives.

The disability that precedes death impedes people from going on about their lives the way they would want to. They can't go down to the bowling alley, or the park, or the bar, to talk to old friends, or to make new ones.

This, however, has begun to change, and unsurprisingly it is patients who are driving this shift. Increasingly, people have begun to document their journeys through illness, remission, and recurrence virtually—on the internet. Whether in the form of blogs, Facebook posts, tweets, or videos, patients facing what appears to be the end take to the internet to share their thoughts. I was taking care of a young man, just in his early twenties, who was diagnosed with a rare, malignant tumor. Every day I went to see him during morning rounds, he seemed lost. He would rarely acknowledge my presence, preferring to stare into his laptop, and once told me that he wasn't much of a morning person. And then one day, to my utter surprise, he was sitting up in bed, cheerfully greeting me at seven in the morning. When I asked him what was behind the sudden positivity in his disposition, he told me that he had to leave the hospital later that day. I was surprised—he had an active infection, was getting antibiotics through an intravenous line, and had tubes draining pus from his gallbladder. From a purely medical perspective, it was a most absurd request. Before I could tell him that, though, he turned his laptop around so that the screen was facing me. He had a Web page open, which displayed a picture of him in patient clothes giving two thumbs-up and a wider smile than I had ever managed to eke out of him. It was a fund-raising Web site, and he had an event planned later that day. I realized then that the only thing that gave him joy was playing out somewhere else, somewhere he wasn't being poked incessantly with syringes, having high-grade fevers, and negotiating pain medication with nurses and doctors.

I had to get creative to help him make it to his fund-raiser. We decided to time his antibiotics such that he had a window wide enough that he could go and then come back to the hospital the same day.

Nowadays, countless patients with life-threatening illnesses take to the Web to log their pain, their suffering, and of course, the peaks that dance with the troughs, the moments of elation and escape. One such blogger was a twenty-something girl, who went by the pseudonym Oblomov, the name of an underappreciated Russian novelist. She would write about her journey with cancer through diagnosis, remission, and then, ominously, recurrence. In a post titled "The Diary of Another No-body," she wrote, "My blogging and note-keeping is . . . an empowering gesture of defiance against the march of time, people's short memories and the indifference of the universe."[2] Her blogs, though, precluded her from being a nobody. Recognized by Clive James in a profile in the *New York Times*,[3] she had accumulated numerous followers, many of whom cheered her on as they would a marathoner, holding out bottles of water and Gatorade as she panted along. Her real name was Shikha Chabra, and by the time I got around to getting in touch with her, she had stopped blogging. She had passed away.

Spurred by the internet, patients and their family members have be-gun to talk about death in a way that it has never been talked about before. If anything, it is the medical establishment that stands in the way of an even broader conversation. In response to a piece I wrote for the *New York Times*[4] describing what people's final moments in the hospital look like, a physician wrote in the comments section, "As a practicing oncologist, I find it a bit strange to explore these thoughts in such a public forum (yes, I understand the irony involved in myself doing the same at this moment). If death is sacred, and the moment so private, why write a book or drama-tize something that literally thousands of healthcare providers do every year?" Immediately, another reader retorted, "Why publicize it in a book? Precisely for the reason that death is NOT 'sacred,' it's inevitable. Yet we as Americans have pushed death so far away that horrific, futile efforts and procedures are inflicted on dying patients without either real thought, or clear understanding, because somehow, modern medicine is going to save the day. Modern medicine can NOT ever save the inevitable day, but can only postpone it. Patients and their family members need to KNOW what can & does happen as loved ones come close to death. They need to know, exactly what may happen, what it can mean in terms of longevity, and what it can mean to the patient in terms of their quality of life."

To date, death has been shrouded in mystery, sometimes because no one knew any better and sometimes on purpose. In most cultures, talk-ing about death has been shunned, thought to be a bad omen. Death is now being engaged with in a way it has never been before, by people faced with imminent death as well as by those far from their mortal ends. It is this cultural shift that may help more than any scientific innovation to improve how we die.

USING SOCIAL MEDIA and the internet, people are starting to give others an intimate and personal view of death. When Scott Simon tweeted, "Heart rate dropping. Heart dropping," on Monday, July 29, 2013, at 7:27 p.m. to his million-plus followers, he took anyone who had come across that tweet to the side of his mother, who lay dying in a Chicago facility. Though he was a correspondent for NPR who had lived a fairly public life, this was by far his most public moment, as he live-tweeted his mother's passage. The stream of texts were both lighthearted ("I know end might be near as this is only day of my adulthood I've seen my mother and she hasn't asked, 'Why that shirt?'") and heartbreaking ("Nurses saying hearing is last sense to go so I sing & joke"). When the end came, at 8:17 p.m., he wrote, "The heavens over Chicago have opened and Patricia Lyons Simon Newman has stepped onstage."

Increasingly, rather than being pushed to the periphery, people facing death are pushing back and occupying center stage. While I could never communicate directly with Shikha Chabra, I was able to talk to one of her best friends, Kriti, who first encouraged Shikha to start blogging. "Shikha had never been too keen on social media," Kriti told me. "However, during her illness she became a voracious Facebook user—partly to share her blog posts with people, but mostly to stay in touch with friends because she didn't get to see many of them."

When Shikha posted about death, many of her family and friends didn't really know how best to respond. "People aren't very good at talking about things like that," Kriti said. As Shikha's illness grew, social media became the only way she could touch the outside world. "My last proper conversation with her was on Whatsapp . . . my messages went unanswered for a few days until I finally got a response: she said she wasn't well but would write when she was better—this was the last one I got from her." Her last post on Facebook was a hilarious video mashup of scenes from the *Star Trek* series transposed onto a song by the pop star Ke$ha. Kriti said, "Her last few days were torturous, though I think she did send a few farewell messages on Whatsapp and her mom said she was browsing Facebook when she could."

Unbeknownst to their physicians, many patients prefer to "face the reaper" head-on via social media. In England, a thirty-year-old man, who worked in retail, developed a headache and difficulty walking. An MRI revealed an aggressive brain tumor. The tumor progressed despite treatment, and he lost the function of the entire right side of his body as well as the ability to speak. Bound to his hospital bed and left with only a few other avenues to communicate, he took to an iPad to blog about his experience. Distressed to be leaving behind a one-year-old son, he hoped that his son would get to know him better through this blog. The blog, by its dynamic nature, gave doctors insight into just what an emotional firestorm approaching the end of life can be. In a paper, his doctors wrote, "One day he would plan his funeral, the following day he would request transfer to the acute hospital for further chemotherapy."[5] While acknowledging the blog's cathartic value, the team also pondered whether "doctors have the right to edit or respond if they feel unjustly represented? . . . Do they have any real right of reply?" They ended their piece by asking, "Electronic dissemination of these records is likely to become the social norm. Are we ready?"

Other aspects of death and dying as they relate to social-media use raise difficult questions. Family members have at times found out about loved ones' deaths through Facebook, causing obvious unforeseen trauma. There was one instance in which the family of a young patient dying of a brain tumor were incensed when his friends set up a Facebook page with pictures of his children, asking for donations for their education.[6] The family became inundated with messages from distant friends who had only gotten in contact with him after years in absentia after the public display. The reaction was particularly severe among family who were not used to using social media themselves.

Social media have also become a powerful medium for activism, but even this can be a double-edged sword. Joshua Hardy was only seven and was dying of a rare cancer, which he had been fighting since infancy. After receiving a bone-marrow transplant, he acquired a viral infection, which was very serious given how weak his immune system was. Desperate to get an experimental treatment not yet approved for clinical use, the family launched a social-media campaign and were able to collect thousands of signatures to pressure the company into getting Josh the medication. After they were able to acquire the medication for Josh, their efforts elicited a backlash, with many saying that this caused a disparity, because not everyone has the resources to leverage social-media crowdsourcing at a similar level.[7]

Social media's role extends past one's last living moment. A few days after I found out that a friend of mine from school had died in a swimming accident, I was surprised to see a post from his Facebook account pop up in my newsfeed. It was a picture of him with his family, and it seemed that his sister was now posting on his behalf. Strange as it seemed, the sister, hurting with loss, would post from his account about how she saw him alive in her dreams, how she still imagined the whole thing being conjured by her imagination. Reading these posts from my departed friend's account would put my stomach in a lurch, juxtaposed as they were with cat videos and vacation pictures. Eventually, they made me so uncomfortable that I decided to block the posts from my newsfeed.

Almost a million Facebook users have passed away, and people have coined the term "Facebook ghosts" for such accounts.[8] Facebook allows profile pages to be transformed into memorial pages, giving a very public face to the expression of grief.

Social media allow people to leave behind a trove of thoughts, feelings, and moments captured in words, photographs, and videos that can be accessed presumably for generations to come. While in older times, it was within the purview of only a select few to have their lives documented in the way of an autobiography, all of us who use social media are actually creating the most intimate of accounts of our lives. Several companies have developed ways for social media to remain part of one's life long after the curtains are drawn and the lights dimmed. One of these, Dead social.org, allows members to curate messages that are sent out from their social-media accounts in the event of their deaths. Members, for no charge, can have audio and video messages posted from their Facebook or Twitter profiles at scheduled times long after their deaths, which per the Web site could "have a significant impact on [their] legacy."

Social media, it is fair to say, are no passing storm, and are here to stay. As people age, as their movement gets restricted and the isolation of illness consumes them, the role the internet plays in allowing them to communicate only increases. As computer systems become even more intelligent, we will surely develop ways to broadcast our thoughts just by thinking them. Whatever one's opinion of the impact digital connectivity has had on our social lives, the benefits that can potentially be derived by people facing the end of life are undeniable. More than many of the advanced medical treatments that we have developed, it is the internet that gives me hope that we might be able to ease some of the existential suffering people experience when they face their mortal end.

Physicians have many blind spots, but the lives patients live outside the hospital might be the biggest. For doctors, it is important to see patients as patients, but sometimes it helps to just see them as people, stuck in a place they would never want to be in. As a community, we have only started to feel out what new media can do to help people with terminal illnesses. Programs are being proposed that, among other things, will use social media to help patients not only with connectivity but with their actual medical care.[9] With Skype and other video-chat services now commonplace, they could be used for virtual meetings not only with friends and family, but with caregivers. Online forums, such as the Cancer Experience Registry, are already being used to record the emotional toll chemotherapy can have on patients. The opportunities for innovation are truly endless.

SCIENTIFIC ADVANCES HAVE revolutionized the practice of medicine, yet it remains important to also realize that in many ways medical practitioners are intractably rooted in ancient and lapsed practices. Physicians, after all, are some of the few remaining professionals who continue to use pagers to communicate. The technology underlying many of the things we use on a daily basis, such as stethoscopes and electrocardiograms, is over a hundred years old. Many developments considered to be cutting-edge are based on much older treatments, such as the malaria treatment that garnered its discoverer the Nobel Prize in Physiology or Medicine in 2015, which was based on a treatment first used five hundred years ago.[10]

Even the electronic-health-record software that powers most modern hospitals is clunky, incoherent, and archaic by current standards. Much of how medicine is learned and practiced and how physicians interact with patients also remains frozen in time.

Unsurprisingly, physicians, while active on social media for personal use, have largely not incorporated new media into their practice. This is understandable: Many physicians are wary of trampling over patient-privacy regulations, which have become increasingly stringent over the years. Yet the lack of active physician voices has left a huge void. People are more interested in their health, particularly close to the end, and frequently seek to interface on platforms other than the brief interactions they have with physicians in the flesh. The space physicians leave is filled by hackneyed self-promoting quacks and con artists who are only too happy to cash in on people's fears and curiosity.

The discrepancy between people's interest and doctors' silence has been uniquely filled by a special group who straddle both worlds—doctors who also happen to have terminal illnesses. Kate Granger was twenty-nine, a physician training in geriatrics—the care of elderly patients—when the anvil dropped. While vacationing in California in 2011, thousands of miles away from her home in Yorkshire, England, she fell sick, and her husband, Chris, took her to a local emergency room. It was revealed there that her kidneys were failing. Further investigation revealed that there was something in her belly blocking urine from leaving her kidneys. That "something" was the rarest of cancers—a sarcoma that affects one in two million people. Initially, it was thought to be restricted to her abdomen and potentially treatable with surgery. How Kate learned otherwise may not sound too foreign to many patients.

"I'm in a side room. I can hear everything that's going on outside. I'm in pain and alone," she was quoted in the *Daily Mail* as saying.[11] "A junior doctor [came] to see me to talk about the results of the MRI scan I'd had earlier in the week. I'd never met this doctor before. He came into my room, he sat down in the chair next to me and looked away from me. Without any warning or asking if I wanted anyone with me he just said, 'Your cancer has spread.'"

Kate did not take her illness lying down. It was clear that she had no plans to suffer in solitude. She started writing a blog and took to Twitter shortly after, where she accumulated more than thirty-five thousand followers. She started an acclaimed campaign called #mynameis, encouraging more doctors and nurses to introduce themselves to patients and family members and build relationships with them. Even though she was brought back from the brink with chemotherapy, her cancer remained incurable and could recur at any moment. But Kate had plans for when that happened: She planned to live-tweet her final moments. "#deathbedlive will include tweets about my symptoms, treatment, fears, anxiety, expectations and how Chris is coping," she wrote to me. "I hope to reflect on my life as a whole, my favorite memories and have an opportunity to thank everyone for everything they've done for me. In the process I hope #deathbedlive will start a conversation about death in society in general and provoke some discussions around end of life wishes within families."

As a physician, Kate felt that access to a patient's social-media output could be very valuable to their physicians. "I would be very interested in their writing in case it helped me understand their experience of dying better. . . . If the patient is not receiving good care, this real-time feedback is invaluable in addressing concerns and improving things."

Despite going public about her illness and wanting to live-tweet whatever the future has in store for her, Kate was still torn between sharing and holding back. "I think dying is an intensely personal experience and perhaps it should be just a time for the person and their loved ones, away from sight of the wider world. I may feel pressure to share experiences as an expectation from the Twitter community, when perhaps I should be focusing on myself, Chris and my family." Her views evolved as she had also been hounded by internet trolls. On one occasion she "was told [she] was 'not fit to practice as a doctor.'" When the end did come for Kate, who passed away in July 2016, she didn't end up live-tweeting her death. It was her husband, though, who announced her death, appropriately, on Twitter: "Peacefully & surrounded by loved ones @grangerkate passed away yesterday. RIP my soulmate & TY. Love u 4ever. . . ."

Physicians have become more open about confronting their mortality in public spaces. One of the greatest writers of our time, Oliver Sacks, who recently passed away, wrote several pieces after he was diagnosed with a terminal illness. After soaking in the splendor of the night sky, he wrote, in a piece in the *New York Times Magazine* on July 24, 2015, a month before his passing, "It was this celestial splendor that suddenly made me realize how little time, how little life, I had left. My sense of the heavens' beauty, of eternity, was inseparably mixed for me with a sense of transience—and death."

Doctors haven't done a great job, however, of leveraging new media to their patients' benefit, although there are some who hope to change that. Dan Miller, a professor of anthropology at University College London, is conducting a multiyear project looking at the use of social media by hospices.[12] Among other things, Miller wants to break away from thinking of communications within the barriers of individual modalities such as Facebook, Twitter, and Skype. "We need to move beyond getting fixated on this media or that media alone," he wrote to me in an e-mail. "One person sees texting as ruling everything else, so you can speak by voice phone, meet face to face, organize an appointment but always text first to check if that is ok. Another person can't respond to a doctor face to face but can write pages of e-mail at midnight." During the course of his research, Miller has found doctors to be particularly rigid in what they regard as the optimal way to communicate with patients: "Many of the doctors really don't like to hear such suggestions and have very firm opinions as to what media should or should never be used. This is a problem for patients."

Social media are opening up new avenues of communication for those close to death. It would not surprise me if people start using services like Skype to broadcast their deaths. To Miller, such an airing wouldn't be very radical. "Why would your Skype example be different from the traditional death bed scene that for many cultures is almost compulsory? It just allows people to be present who otherwise could not be."

In my opinion, anything that opens a window into the dark room of death and dying in our society would be welcome. Anything that provides patients and family members more channels to communicate would be a step in the right direction. Medical people are always trying out new instruments, new procedures, and new medications, yet when it comes to new modes of communication, the only way a patient can see a physician is by finding a spot in a clinic or, worse, when they are admitted to the hospital.

If death is the enemy, it fights best in darkness. Death stealthily commands and controls every aspect of our lives. Many talk about defeating death with drugs or devices, but these have only served to delay death and prolong dying. Perhaps the best way to beat it is to talk it to death.

DEATH, THE GREAT enemy, is now seeing many facing off with it using unusual means and on very public forums. Death cafés[13] and death salons,[14] where people converse about death over drinks and food, have started opening up. People like George Carlin jabbed death with jokes, once unthinkable. College courses about death are becoming increasingly popular.[15] One can even buy a watch, called a Tikker, that provides wearers a reminder of how much estimated time they have left to live. In Japan, young people can even go and have their pictures taken inside caskets, to see which one they would prefer if and when one becomes necessary. All of this forms part of what has been called the "death positive" movement, which seeks to open up death not only to those who are actually facing it, but to a younger generation who have not yet had to come to terms with their mortality.[16]

Awareness of our mortality does more than remove the shroud of fear from death—it makes us kinder. One study showed that people who thought more about death were more likely to participate in selfless activities such as blood donation.[17] Other research has shown that people who reflect about dying are more likely to donate to charities and have enhanced gratitude. And lastly, thinking of death, almost counterintuitively, reduces stress,[18] and reducing stress is known to lead to a longer and healthier life.[19]

While physicians do talk about death, they do so more candidly among themselves than outside their circle. We are trained to think of death as the greatest failure of all. I was once in the ICU when a fellow resident of mine was placing a feeding tube in a patient. The patient was very sick but seemed to be turning the corner. Midway during the placement, the patient became unresponsive. The monitor showed that his heart had gone into a malignant arrhythmia, and when the resident felt for the pulse, she found nothing. CPR ensued, but the patient could not be revived.

My friend, overcome with emotion, started to cry in the corner of the room. I walked her out into the waiting embrace of other residents. I knew how she felt. She felt that she had failed, and to this day I know that memory.

In every research study performed and every treatment evaluated, the only endpoint that determines success or failure is death. A treatment may make people feel much better, but if it doesn't prevent death, it is shelved.

When it comes to themselves, doctors certainly don't consider death the worst possible outcome. In fact, the vast majority of physicians value the quality of their life far more than the length of their life. This is reflected in the fact that physicians rarely want to have CPR performed on them if the need arises. This is true in young[20] and older[21] physicians. Certainly when it comes to themselves, physicians prefer a swift death to protracted dying.

Perhaps it is time that physicians, like some of their patients, start to have more honest and open conversations about death. This is easier said than done. Death has become highly politicized in the United States, and politicians frequently use things people fear to control them. While at one time physicians often spoke over their patients, the pendulum has now swung and physicians choose to stay mum at a time when their opinion would be of greatest value.

People have always talked of conquering death, and it has been assumed that death can be conquered by somehow averting it. To me, death derives its power from the deafening silence it induces whenever it enters a discussion. We would benefit from resuscitating many of the aspects of death that we have lost. Death needs to be closer to home, preceded by lesser disability and less isolation, but there is an important aspect of death that we have to do away with. The deaths we die cannot be truly modern until we bring the subject of death within the pale of conversation and start having calm, educated conversations about it in classrooms, bars, restaurants, backyards, and, of course, in the clinic.

NOTES

HOW CELLS DIE

1. Wenner M. Humans carry more bacterial cells than human ones. *Scientific American.* 2007.

2. Salzberg SL, White O, Peterson J, Eisen JA. Microbial genes in the human genome: lateral transfer or gene loss? *Science.* 2001;292(5523):1903–6.

3. Everson T. *The Gene: A Historical Perspective.* Greenwood Publishing Group; 2007.

4. Tuck S. The control of cell growth and body size in Caenorhabditis elegans. *Exp Cell Res.* 2014;321(1):71–76.

5. Kramer M. How worms survived NASA's Columbia shuttle disaster. Space.com, www.space.com/19538-columbia-shuttle-disaster-worms-survive.html. 2013.

6. Sulston JE, Brenner S. The DNA of Caenorhabditis elegans. *Genetics.* 1974; 77(1):95–104.

7. Kerr JF, Wyllie AH, Currie AR. Apoptosis: a basic biological phenomenon with wide-ranging implications in tissue kinetics. *Br J Cancer.* 1972;26(4):239–57.

8. Hotchkiss RS, Strasser A, McDunn JE, Swanson PE. Cell death. *N Engl J Med.* 2009;361(16):1570–83.

9. Lotze MT, Tracey KJ. High-mobility group box 1 protein (HMGB1): nuclear weapon in the immune arsenal. *Nat Rev Immunol.* 2005;5(4):331–42.

10. Festjens N, Vanden Berghe T, Vandenabeele P. Necrosis, a well-orchestrated form of cell demise: signalling cascades, important mediators and concomitant immune response. *Biochim Biophys Acta.* 2006;1757(9–10):1371–87.

11. Taylor RC, Cullen SP, Martin SJ. Apoptosis: controlled demolition at the cellular level. *Nat Rev Mol Cell Biol.* 2008;9(3):231–41.

12. Narula J, Arbustini E, Chandrashekhar Y, Schwaiger M. Apoptosis and the systolic dysfunction in congestive heart failure. Story of apoptosis interruptus and zombie myocytes. *Cardiol Clin.* 2001;19(1):113–26.

13. Melino G. The sirens' song. *Nature.* 2001;412(6842):23.

14. Horvitz R. Worms, life and death. In: Frängsmyr T, ed. *Les Prix Nobel.* Stockholm; 2003.

15. Gompertz B. On the nature of the function expressive of the law of human mortality, and on a new mode of determining the value of life contingencies. In: *Philosophical Transactions of the Royal Society of London.* 1825;115:513–83.

16. Caserio at the guillotine. *New York Times.* August 16, 1894.

17. Comroe JH Jr. Who was Alexis who? *Cardiovasc Dis.* 1979;6(3):251–70.

18. Moseley J. Alexis Carrel, the man unknown: journey of an idea. *JAMA.* 1980; 244(10):1119–21.

19. Moseley, Alexis Carrel.

20. Weismann A. *Essays upon Heredity and Kindred Biological Problems.* Poulton EB, Schönland S, Shipley AE, eds. 2nd ed. Oxford: Clarendon Press; 1891–92.

21. Carrel A. On the permanent life of tissues outside of the organism. *J Exp Med.* 1912;15(5):516–28.

22. Friedman DM. *The Immortalists: Charles Lindbergh, Dr. Alexis Carrel, and Their Daring Quest to Live Forever.* Ecco; 2007.

23. Carrel A. *Man, the Unknown.* Halcyon House; 1938.

24. Witkowski JA. Dr. Carrel's immortal cells. *Med Hist.* 1980;24(2):129–42.

25. Hayflick L. The limited in vitro lifetime of human diploid cell strains. *Exp Cell Res.* 1965;37:614–36.

26. Shay JW, Wright WE. Hayflick, his limit, and cellular ageing. *Nat Rev Mol Cell Biol.* 2000;1(1):72–76.

27. Carrel, *Man, the Unknown.*

28. Watson JD. Origin of concatemeric T7 DNA. *Nat New Biol.* 1972;239(94):197–201.

29. Blackburn EH, Gall JG. A tandemly repeated sequence at the termini of the extrachromosomal ribosomal RNA genes in Tetrahymena. *J Mol Biol.* 1978;120 (1):33–53.

30. Cooke HJ, Smith, BA. Variability at the telomeres of the human X/Y pseudoautosomal region. *Cold Spring Harb Symp Quant Biol.* 1986;51: 213–19.

31. Moyzis RK, Buckingham JM, Cram LS, Dani M, Deaven LL, Jones MD, et al. A highly conserved repetitive DNA sequence, (TTAGGG)n, present at the telomeres of human chromosomes. *Proc Natl Acad Sci U S A.* 1988;85(18): 6622–26.

32. Harley CB, Futcher AB, Greider CW. Telomeres shorten during ageing of human fibroblasts *Nature*. 1990;345(6274):458–60.

33. Greider CW, Blackburn EH. Identification of a specific telomere terminal transferase activity in Tetrahymena extracts. *Cell*. 1985;43(2 Pt 1):405–13.

34. Bodnar AG, Ouellette M, Frolkis M, Holt SE, Chiu CP, Morin GB, et al. Extension of life span by introduction of telomerase into normal human cells *Science*. 1998;279(5349):349–52.

35. Jaskelioff M, Muller FL, Paik JH, Thomas E, Jiang S, Adams AC, et al. Telomerase reactivation reverses tissue degeneration in aged telomerase-deficient mice. *Nature*. 2011;469(7328):102–6.

36. Lopez-Otin C, Blasco MA, Partridge L, Serrano M, Kroemer G. The hallmarks of aging. *Cell*. 2013;153(6):1194–217.

37. Kim NW, Piatyszek MA, Prowse KR, Harley CB, West MD, Ho PL, et al. Specific association of human telomerase activity with immortal cells and cancer. *Science*. 1994;266(5193):2011–15.

HOW LIFE (AND DEATH) WERE PROLONGED

1. Clark A, ed. *Aubrey's Life of John Graunt (1620–1674)*. Oxford at the Clarendon Press; 1898.

2. Jones HW. John Graunt and His Bills of Mortality. *Bull Med Libr Assoc*. 1945; 33(1):3–4.

3. Smith R, lecturer. John Graunt, the law of natural decline and the origins of urban historical demography. Part of conference: Mortality Past and Present: John Graunt's Bills of Mortality—Part One. Barnard's Inn Hall, London. November 29, 2012.

4. "Old Medical Terminology." www.rootsweb.ancestry.com/~usgwkidz/oldmedterm .htm.

5. King JA, Ubelaker DH, eds. *Living and Dying on the 17th Century Patuxent Frontier*. Crownsville, MD: The Maryland Historical Trust Press. www.jefpat.org /Documents/King, Julia A. & Douglas H. Ubelaker-Living and Dying on the 17th Century Patuxent Frontier.pdf.

6. Abstract of the Bill of Mortality for the Town of Boston. *N Engl J Med Surg*. 1812:1:320–21.

7. Howe HF. Boston and New England in 1812. *N Engl J Med*. 1962;266:20–22.

8. Death-rates for 1911 in the United States and its large cities. *Boston Medical and Surgical Journal*. 1912;CLXVI(2):63–64.

9. The state of US health, 1990–2010: burden of diseases, injuries, and risk factors. *JAMA*. 2013;310(6):591–608.

10. Hsiang-Ching Kung DLH, Xu J, Murphy SL. *Deaths: Final Data for 2005*. National Vital Statistics Report. Centers for Disease Control and Prevention; 2008.

11. Bodenheimer T, Chen E, Bennett HD. Confronting the growing burden of

chronic disease: can the U.S. health care workforce do the job? *Health Aff* (Millwood). 2009;28(1):64–74.

12. Narayan KM, Boyle JP, Thompson TJ, Sorensen SW, Williamson DF. Lifetime risk for diabetes mellitus in the United States. *JAMA*. 2003;290(14):1884–90.

13. Jones DS, Podolsky SH, Greene JA. The burden of disease and the changing task of medicine *N Engl J Med*. 2012;366(25):2333–38.

14. Ziv S. President Harding's mysterious S.F. death. *San Francisco Chronicle*. December 9, 2012.

15. Gladwell M. *Blink: The Power of Thinking Without Thinking*. Back Bay Books; 2007:72–75.

16. Stewart J. *America (The Book): A Citizen's Guide to Democracy Inaction*. Grand Central Publishing; 2004:378–84.

17. Voo J. America's 10 unhealthiest presidents. *Fitness Magazine*. January 2009.

18. Taylor M. A mystery of presidential proportions; new book analyzes Warren G. Harding's death in S.F. *San Francisco Chronicle*. August 1, 1998.

19. Wilbur RL, ed. *The Memoirs of Ray Lyman Wilbur 1875–1949*. Stanford University Press; 1960.

20. Ford ES, Ajani UA, Croft JB, Critchley JA, Labarthe DR, Kottke TE, et al. Explaining the decrease in U.S. deaths from coronary disease, 1980–2000. *N Engl J Med*. 2007;356(23):2388–98.

21. Rago J. The story of Dick Cheney's heart. *Wall Street Journal*. July 11, 2011.

22. Shane S. For Cheney, 71, new heart ends 20-month wait. *New York Times*. March 24, 2012.

23. Go AS, Mozaffarian D, Roger VL, Benjamin EJ, Berry JD, Blaha MJ, et al. Executive summary: heart disease and stroke statistics—2014 update: a report from the American Heart Association. *Circulation*. 2014;129(3):399–410.

24. National Cancer Institute, National Center for Health Statistics, Centers for Disease Control and Prevention. *SEER Cancer Statistics Review 1975–2005*. 2008.

25. Marelli AJ, Mackie AS, Ionescu-Ittu R, Rahme E, Pilote L. Congenital heart disease in the general population: changing prevalence and age distribution. *Circulation*. 2007;115(2):163–72.

26. Isaacs B, Gunn J, McKechan A, McMillan I, Neville Y. The concept of pre-death. *Lancet*. 1971;1(7709):1115–18.

27. Whitney CR. Jeanne Calment, world's elder, dies at 122. *New York Times*. August 5, 1997.

28. Genesis 5:27.

29. Burger O, Baudisch A, Vaupel JW. Human mortality improvement in evolutionary context. *Proc Natl Acad Sci U S A*. 2012;109(44):18210–14.

30. Ruse M, ed. *Evolution: The First Four Billion Years*. The Belknap Press of Harvard University Press; 2009.

31. Schwartz L. 17th-century childbirth: "exquisite torment and infinite grace." *Lancet*. 2011;377(9776):1486–87.

32. Gurven M, Kaplan, H. Longevity among hunter-gatherers: a cross-cultural examination. *Population and Development Review.* 2007;33(2):321–65.

33. Griffin JP. Changing life expectancy throughout history. *J R Soc Med.* 2008; 101(12):577.

34. Riley JC. *Low Income, Social Growth, and Good Health.* University of California Press; 2007.

35. Oeppen J, Vaupel JW. Demography. Broken limits to life expectancy. *Science.* 2002;296(5570):1029–31.

36. Wilmoth JR, Deegan LJ, Lundstrom H, Horiuchi S. Increase of maximum life span in Sweden, 1861–1999. *Science.* 2000;289(5488):2366–68.

37. Olshansky SJ, Carnes BA, Cassel C. In search of Methuselah: estimating the upper limits to human longevity. *Science.* 1990;250(4981):634–40.

38. Wilmoth et al., Increase.

39. Hayflick L. "Anti-aging" is an oxymoron. *J Gerontol A Biol Sci Med Sci.* 2004; 59(6):B573–78.

40. Olshansky et al., In search of Methuselah.

41. Hutchison ED. *Dimensions of Human Behavior: The Changing Life Course.* 4th ed. Sage Publications; 2010.

42. Weon BM, Je JH. Theoretical estimation of maximum human lifespan. *Biogerontology.* 2009;10(1):65–71.

43. *Ageing in the Twenty-First Century: A Celebration and a Challenge.* United Nations Population Fund (UNFPA), New York and HelpAge International, London; 2012.

44. Burger et al., Human mortality improvement.

45. Cohen AA. Female post-reproductive lifespan: a general mammalian trait. *Biol Rev Camb Philos Soc.* 2004;79(4):733–50.

46. Jones OR, Scheuerlein A, Salguero-Gomez R, Camarda CG, Schaible R, Casper BB, et al. Diversity of ageing across the tree of life. *Nature.* 2014;505(7482): 169–73.

47. Validated Living Supercentenarians Super Centenarian Research Foundation: Gerontology Research Group; 2014. www.supercentenarian-research-foundation .org/TableE.aspx.

48. Hamilton WD. The moulding of senescence by natural selection. *J Theor Biol.* 1966;12(1):12–45.

49. Kim PS, Coxworth JE, Hawkes K. Increased longevity evolves from grandmothering. *Proc Biol Sci.* 2012;279(1749):4880–84.

50. Johnstone RA, Cant MA. The evolution of menopause in cetaceans and humans: the role of demography. *Proc Biol Sci.* 2010;277(1701):3765–71.

51. Outhwaite RB. Population change, family structure and the good of counting. *The Historical Journal.* 1979;22(1):229–37.

52. Bird DW, Bird BB. Children on the reef. *Human Nature.* 2002;13(2):269–97.

53. Jones BJ, Marlowe FW. Selection for delayed maturity. *Human Nature.* 2002; 13(2):199–238.

54. Institute for Health Metrics and Evaluation. *The State of US Health: Innovations, Insights, and Recommendations from the Global Burden of Disease Study.* Seattle, WA: Institute for Health Metrics and Evaluation, University of Washington; 2013.

55. Whelan D. Cranking up the volume. *Forbes.* February 8, 2008. www.forbes.com /forbes/2008/0225/032.html.

56. United States Census Bureau. Fairfax County, Virginia. quickfacts.census.gov /qfd/states/51/51059.html. 2013.

57. United States Census Bureau. McDowell County, West Virginia. quickfacts .census.gov/qfd/states/54/54047.html. 2013.

58. Kochanek KD, Arias E, Anderson RN. *How Did Cause of Death Contribute to Racial Differences in Life Expectancy in the United States in 2010?* NCHS data brief, no. 125. Hyattsville, MD: National Center for Health Statistics; 2013.

59. Riley, *Low Income.*

WHERE DEATH LIVES NOW

1. Ariès P. *Western Attitudes toward Death: From the Middle Ages to the Present.* Johns Hopkins University Press; 1975.

2. Boston Mortality Statistics. *Boston Med Surg J.* 1912;CLXVI(2):66.

3. Hunt RW, Bond MJ, Groth RK, King PM. Place of death in South Australia. Patterns from 1910 to 1987. *Med J Aust.* 1991;155(8):549–53.

4. Katz BP, Zdeb MS, Therriault GD. Where people die. *Public Health Rep.* 1979; 94(6):522–27.

5. Brock DB, Foley DJ. Demography and epidemiology of dying in the U.S. with emphasis on deaths of older persons. *Hosp J.* 1998;13(1–2):49–60.

6. Flynn A, Stewart DE. Where do cancer patients die? A review of cancer deaths in Cuyahoga County, Ohio, 1957–1974. *J Community Health.* 1979;5(2):126–30.

7. Cartwright A. Changes in life and care in the year before death 1969–1987. *J Public Health Med.* 1991;13(2):81–87.

8. Zander L, Chamberlain G. ABC of labour care: place of birth. *BMJ.* 1999; 318(7185):721–23.

9. Illich I. *Medical Nemesis: The Expropriation of Health.* Pantheon Books; 1976.

10. Distress of dying. *BMJ.* 1972;3(5820):231.

11. Brock and Foley, Demography.

12. Where do people die? *J Coll Gen Pract.* 1960;3(4):393–94.

13. Broad JB, Gott M, Kim H, Boyd M, Chen H, Connolly MJ. Where do people die? An international comparison of the percentage of deaths occurring in hospital and residential aged care settings in 45 populations, using published and available statistics. *Int J Public Health.* 2013;58(2):257–67.

14. Decker SL, Higginson IJ. A tale of two cities: factors affecting place of cancer death in London and New York. *Eur J Public Health.* 2007;17(3):285–90.

15. Gomes B, Higginson IJ. Where people die (1974–2030): past trends, future projections and implications for care. *Palliat Med.* 2008;22(1):33–41.

16. Higginson IJ, Sen-Gupta GJ. Place of care in advanced cancer: a qualitative systematic literature review of patient preferences. *J Palliat Med.* 2000;3(3):287–300.

17. Solloway M, LaFrance S, Bakitas M, Gerken M. A chart review of seven hundred eighty-two deaths in hospitals, nursing homes, and hospice/home care. *J Palliat Med.* 2005;8(4):789–96.

18. Gruneir A, Mor V, Weitzen S, Truchil R, Teno J, Roy J. Where people die: a multilevel approach to understanding influences on site of death in America. *Med Care Res Rev.* 2007;64(4):351–78.

19. Weitzen S, Teno JM, Fennell M, Mor V. Factors associated with site of death: a national study of where people die. *Med Care.* 2003;41(2):323–35.

20. Gomes B, Higginson IJ. Factors influencing death at home in terminally ill patients with cancer: systematic review. *BMJ.* 2006;332(7540):515–21.

21. Bell CL, Somogyi-Zalud E, Masaki KH. Factors associated with congruence between preferred and actual place of death. *J Pain Symptom Manage.* 2010; 39(3):591–604.

22. Fischer CS, Hout M. *Century of Difference: How America Changed in the Last One Hundred Years.* Russell Sage Foundation; 2008.

23. Silverstein M, Bengtson VL. Intergenerational solidarity and the structure of adult child–parent relationships in American families. *Am J Sociology.* 1997; 103(2):429–60.

24. Bianchi S, McGarry K, Seltzer J. *Geographic Dispersion and the Well-Being of the Elderly.* Michigan Retirement Research Center, University of Michigan; 2010.

25. Moinpour CM, Polissar L. Factors affecting place of death of hospice and nonhospice cancer patients. *Am J Public Health.* 1989;79(11):1549–51.

26. Gooch RA, Kahn JM. ICU bed supply, utilization, and health care spending: an example of demand elasticity. *JAMA.* 2014;311(6):567–68.

27. Broad et al., Where do people die?

28. Munday D, Petrova M, Dale J. Exploring preferences for place of death with terminally ill patients: qualitative study of experiences of general practitioners and community nurses in England. *BMJ.* 2009;339:b2391.

29. Finkelstein A. The aggregate effects of health insurance: evidence from the introduction of medicare. *Q J Econ.* 2005;122(3):1–37.

30. Sampson WI. Dying at home [letter]. *JAMA.* 1976;235(17):1840.

31. Flory J, Yinong YX, Gurol I, Levinsky N, Ash A, Emanuel E. Place of death: U.S. trends since 1980. *Health Aff* (Millwood). 2004;23(3):194–200.

32. National Center for Health Statistics. *Health, United States, 2010: With Special Feature on Death and Dying.* Hyattsville, MD: National Center for Health Statistics; 2011.

33. Flory et al., Place of death.

34. Hanchate A, Kronman AC, Young-Xu Y, Ash AS, Emanuel E. Racial and ethnic

differences in end-of-life costs: why do minorities cost more than whites? *Arch Intern Med.* 2009;169(5):493–501.

35. Smallwood N. Poorest people are more likely to die in hospital. *BMJ.* 2010; 341:c4518.

36. Bigger than Marx, *Economist.* May 3, 2014.

37. McEwan I. *The Cement Garden.* Anchor; 1994.

38. Smithers D. Where to die. *BMJ.* January 6, 1973;1(5844):34–35.

HOW WE LEARNED NOT TO RESUSCITATE

1. Mills J, ed. *Body Mechanics and Transfer Techniques.* 4th ed. Philadelphia, PA: Lippincott Williams & Wilkins; 2004.

2. Turk LN III, Glenn WW. Cardiac arrest; results of attempted cardiac resuscitation in 42 cases. *N Engl J Med.* 1954;251(20):795–803.

3. 2 Kings 4:34 (KJV).

4. Mitka M. Peter J. Safar, MD: "father of CPR," innovator, teacher, humanist. *JAMA.* 2003;289(19):2485–86.

5. Kacmarek RM. The mechanical ventilator: past, present, and future. *Respir Care.* 2011;56(8):1170–80.

6. Perman E. Successful cardiac resuscitation with electricity in the 18th century? *BMJ.* 1978;2(6154):1770–71.

7. Delgado H, Toquero J, Mitroi C, Castro V, Lozano IF. Principles of external defibrillators. In: Erkapic D, Bauernfeind T, eds. *Cardiac Defibrillation.* InTech; 2013.

8. Beck CS, Pritchard WH, Feil HS. Ventricular fibrillation of long duration abolished by electric shock. *JAMA.* 1947;135(15):985.

9. Cohen SI. Resuscitation great. Paul M. Zoll, M.D.—the father of "modern" electrotherapy and innovator of pharmacotherapy for life-threatening cardiac arrhythmias. *Resuscitation.* 2007;73(2):178–85.

10. Zoll PM, Linenthal AJ, Gibson W, Paul MH, Norman LR. Termination of ventricular fibrillation in man by externally applied electric countershock. *N Engl J Med.* 1956;254(16):727–32.

11. Nadkarni VM, Larkin GL, Peberdy MA, Carey SM, Kaye W, Mancini ME, et al. First documented rhythm and clinical outcome from in-hospital cardiac arrest among children and adults. *JAMA.* 2006;295(1):50–57.

12. Vallejo-Manzur F, Varon J, Fromm R Jr, Baskett P. Moritz Schiff and the history of open-chest cardiac massage. *Resuscitation.* 2002;53(1):3–5.

13. Hake T. Studies on ether and chloroform, from Prof. Schiff's physiological laboratory. In: Anstie F, ed. *The Practitioner: A Journal of Therapeutics and Public Health.* London, UK: Macmillan and Co; 1874.

14. Eisenberg MS. *Life in the Balance: Emergency Medicine and the Quest to Reverse Sudden Death.* Oxford University Press; 1997:110.

15. American Medical Association. Section on Surgery and Anatomy. *Transactions of the Section on Surgery and Anatomy of the American Medical Association at the 57th Annual Session.* American Medical Association Press; 1906:518.

16. Kouwenhoven WB, Jude JR, Knickerbocker GG. Closed-chest cardiac massage. *JAMA.* 1960;173:1064–67.

17. Lawrence G. Tobacco smoke enemas. *Lancet.* 2002;359(9315):1442.

18. Satya-Murti S. Rectal fumigation. A core rewarming practice from the past. *Pharos Alpha Omega Alpha Honor Med Soc.* 2005;68(1):35–38.

19. Relman AS. The new medical-industrial complex. *N Engl J Med.* 1980;303(17): 963–70.

20. Tracking progress toward global polio eradication—worldwide, 2009–2010. *MMWR.* 2011;60(14):441–45.

21. Drinker P, Shaw LA. An apparatus for the prolonged administration of artificial respiration, I: a design for adults and children. *J Clin Invest.* 1929;7(2): 229–47.

22. Lassen HC. A preliminary report on the 1952 epidemic of poliomyelitis in Copenhagen with special reference to the treatment of acute respiratory insufficiency. *Lancet.* 1953;1(6749):37–41.

23. Andersen EW, Ibsen B. The anaesthetic management of patients with poliomyelitis and respiratory paralysis. *BMJ.* 1954;1(4865):786–88.

24. Watson JD, Crick FH. Molecular structure of nucleic acids; a structure for deoxyribose nucleic acid. *Nature.* 1953;171(4356):737–38.

25. Symmers WS Sr. Not allowed to die. *BMJ.* 1968;1(5589):442.

26. Emrys-Roberts M. Death and resuscitation. *BMJ.* 1969;4(5679):364–65.

27. Oken D. What to tell cancer patients. A study of medical attitudes. *JAMA.* 1961;175:1120–28.

28. Fitts WT Jr, Ravdin IS. What Philadelphia physicians tell patients with cancer. *JAMA.* 1953;153(10):901–4.

29. Kelly WD, Friesen SR. Do cancer patients want to be told? *Surgery.* 1950;27(6): 822–26.

30. Is the medical profession inevitably patriarchal? *Lancet.* 1977;2(8039):647.

31. Curtis JR, Rubenfeld GD. *Managing Death in the Intensive Care Unit: The Transition from Cure to Comfort.* Oxford University Press; 2000:11.

32. Gazelle G. The slow code—should anyone rush to its defense? *N Engl J Med.* 1998;338(7):467–69.

33. McFadden RD. Karen Ann Quinlan, 31, dies; focus of '76 right to die case. *New York Times.* June 12, 1985.

34. Kennedy IM. The Karen Quinlan case: problems and proposals. *J Med Ethics.* 1976;2(1):3–7.

35. Testimony begins in Karen Quinlan case. *Observer Reporter.* October 21, 1975.

36. Lepore J. *The Mansion of Happiness: A History of Life and Death.* Alfred A Knopf; 2012:153.

37. Pope Pius XII. *The Prolongation of Life.* November 24, 1957.

38. *In the Matter of Karen Quinlan, an Alleged Incompetent.* 137 N.J. Super. 227 (1975) 348 A.2d 801.

39. Lepore, *Mansion.*

40. Duff RS, Campbell AG. Moral and ethical dilemmas in the special-care nursery. *N Engl J Med.* 1973;289(17):890–94.

41. A right to die? Karen Ann Quinlan. *Newsweek.* November 3, 1975.

42. Powledge TM, Steinfels P. Following the news on Karen Quinlan. *Hastings Cent Rep.* 1975;5(6):5–6, 28.

43. Powledge and Steinfels, Following.

44. Rachels J. Active and passive euthanasia. In: Humber JM, Almeder RF, eds. *Biomedical Ethics and the Law.* Springer US; 1979:511–16.

45. McFadden RD. Kenneth C. Edelin, doctor at center of landmark abortion case, dies at 74. *New York Times.* December 30, 2013.

46. *Commonwealth v. Kenneth Edelin.* 371 Mass. 497. Suffolk County; 1976.

47. *In the Matter of Karen Quinlan, an Alleged Incompetent.*

48. Beresford HR. The Quinlan decision: problems and legislative alternatives. *Ann Neurol.* 1977;2(1):74–81.

49. Cohn J. Sick. *New Republic.* May 28, 2001.

50. Palmer T. Patients' rights: hospitals finding it's more than bedside manner. *Chicago Tribune.* March 10, 1985.

51. Rabkin MT, Gillerman G, Rice NR. Orders not to resuscitate. *N Engl J Med.* 1976;295(7):364–66.

52. Optimum care for hopelessly ill patients. A report of the Clinical Care Committee of the Massachusetts General Hospital. *N Engl J Med.* 1976;295(7): 362–64.

53. Puchalski CM, Vitillo R, Hull SK, Reller N. Improving the spiritual dimension of whole person care: reaching national and international consensus. *J Palliat Med.* 2014;17(6):642–56.

54. Jabre P, Belpomme V, Azoulay E, Jacob L, Bertrand L, Lapostolle F, et al. Family presence during cardiopulmonary resuscitation. *N Engl J Med.* 2013;368(11): 1008–18.

55. Stapleton RD, Ehlenbach WJ, Deyo RA, Curtis JR. Long-term outcomes after in-hospital CPR in older adults with chronic illness. *Chest.* 2014;146(5):1214–25.

56. Ehlenbach WJ, Barnato AE, Curtis JR, Kreuter W, Koepsell TD, Deyo RA, et al. Epidemiologic study of in-hospital cardiopulmonary resuscitation in the elderly. *N Engl J Med.* 2009;361(1):22–31.

HOW DEATH WAS REDEFINED

1. Nolan JP, Morley PT, Vanden Hoek TL, Hickey RW, Kloeck WG, Billi J, et al. Therapeutic hypothermia after cardiac arrest: an advisory statement by the ad-

vanced life support task force of the International Liaison Committee on Resuscitation. *Circulation.* 2003;108(1):118–21.

2. Fernandez L. Friends believe Jahi McMath, "quiet leader," is alive. NBC Bay Area. www.nbcbayarea.com/news/local/Jahi-McMath-Brain-Death-Tonsillectomy -EC-Reems-Academy-Friends-Believe-Alive-239629891.html. 2014.

3. Narang I, Mathew JL. Childhood obesity and obstructive sleep apnea. *J Nutr Metab.* 2012;2012:134202.

4. Fernandez L. Catholic organization says Jahi McMath "with Jesus Christ." NBC Bay Area. www.nbcbayarea.com/news/local/Catholic-Organization-Says-Jahi -McMath-With-Jesus-Christ-239314591.html. 2014.

5. Klingensmith SW. Child animism; what the child means by alive. *Child Dev.* 1953;24(1):51–61.

6. Driver R, Squires A, Rushworth P, Wood-Robinson V. *Making Sense of Secondary Science: Research into Children's Ideas.* Routledge; 1993.

7. Sheehan NW, Papalia-Finlay DE, Hooper FH. The nature of the life concept across the life span. *Int J Aging Hum Dev.* 1980;12(1):1–13.

8. Anderson N. Living nonliving things: 4th grade. Pages accessed at Ohio State University and the National Science Foundation at gk-12.osu.edu/Lessons/02-03 /LivingNonliving_Web.pdf.

9. Benner SA. Defining life. *Astrobiology.* 2010;10(10):1021–30.

10. Deamer D. *First Life: Discovering the Connections between Stars, Cells, and How Life Began.* Berkeley, CA: Reports of the National Center for Science Education; 2011.

11. Oparin A. *Origin of Life.* Macmillan; 1938.

12. Benner, Defining life.

13. Deamer D. *Origins of Life: The Central Concepts.* Jones & Bartlett Publishers; 1994.

14. Jabr F. Why nothing is truly alive. *New York Times.* March 12, 2014.

15. Mullen L. Forming a definition for life: interview with Gerald Joyce. *Astrobiology.* July 25, 2013.

16. Hamlin H. Life or death by EEG. *JAMA.* 1964;190:112–14.

17. Seeley LJ. Electroencephalographic recording of a death due to nontoxic causes. *JAMA.* 1954;156(17):1580.

18. Wertheimer P, Jouvet M, Descotes J. Diagnosis of death of the nervous system in comas with respiratory arrest treated by artificial respiration [in French]. *Presse Med.* 1959;67(3):87–88.

19. Matis G, Chrysou O, Silva D, Birblis T. Brain death: history, updated guidelines and unanswered questions. *Internet Journal of Neurosurgery.* 2012;8(1).

20. Tentler RL, Sadove M, Becka DR, Taylor RC. Electroencephalographic evidence of cortical death followed by full recovery; protective action of hypothermia. *JAMA.* 1957;164(15):1667–70.

21. Hamlin, Life or death.

22. Löfstedt S, von Reis, G. Intrakraniella lesioner med bilateralt upphävd kontrast-passage i a. carotis interna [Intracranial lesions with abolished passage of x-ray contrast through the internal carotid arteries]. *Opusc Med.* 1956;202:1199–202.

23. Kinnaert P. Some historical notes on the diagnosis of death—the emergence of the brain death concept. *Acta Chir Belg.* 2009;109(3):421–28.

24. Haas LF. Hans Berger (1873–1941), Richard Caton (1842–1926), and electroen-cephalography. *J Neurol Neurosurg Psychiatry.* 2003;74(1):9.

25. Beecher HK. Experimentation in man. *JAMA.* 1959;169(5):461–78.

26. Harkness J, Lederer SE, Wikler D. Laying ethical foundations for clinical research. *Bull World Health Organ.* 2001;79(4):365–66.

27. Beecher HK. Ethics and clinical research. *N Engl J Med.* 1966;274(24):1354–60.

28. Beecher HK. Ethical problems created by the hopelessly unconscious patient. *N Engl J Med.* 1968;278(26):1425–30.

29. A definition of irreversible coma. Report of the ad hoc committee of the Harvard Medical School to examine the definition of brain death. *JAMA.* 1968;205(6): 337–40.

30. McCoy AW. Science in Dachau's shadow: Hebb, Beecher, and the development of CIA psychological torture and modern medical ethics. *J Hist Behav Sci.* 2007;43(4):401–17.

31. Giacomini M. A change of heart and a change of mind? Technology and the redefinition of death in 1968. *Soc Sci Med.* 1997;44(10):1465–82.

32. Vovelle M. Rediscovery of death since 1960. *Ann Am Acad Pol Soc Sci.* 1980; 447:89–99.

33. *Black's Law Dictionary.* 488. (4th ed. 1968).

34. In Re Estate of Pyke. 427 P.2d 67 (Kan. 1967).

35. Kennedy IM. The Kansas statute on death—an appraisal. *N Engl J Med.* 1971; 285(17):946–50.

36. Mills DH. The Kansas death statute: bold and innovative. *N Engl J Med.* 1971;285(17):968–69.

37. United States President's Commission for the Study of Ethical Problems in Med-icine and Biomedical and Behavioral Research. *Defining Death: A Report on the Medical, Legal and Ethical Issues in the Determination of Death.* 1981.

38. Charron W. Death: a philosophical perspective on the legal definitions. *Wash-ington University Law Review.* 1975;1975(4).

39. Veatch R, Ross LF. Part One: Defining Death. In: *Transplantation Ethics.* 2nd ed. Georgetown University Press; 2000.

40. United States President's Commission, Defining Death. 1981.

41. Youngner SJ, Landefeld CS, Coulton CJ, Juknialis BW, Leary M. "Brain death" and organ retrieval. A cross-sectional survey of knowledge and concepts among health professionals. *JAMA.* 1989;261(15):2205–10.

42. Kramer AH, Zygun DA, Doig CJ, Zuege DJ. Incidence of neurologic death among

patients with brain injury: a cohort study in a Canadian health region. *CMAJ.* 2013;185(18):E838–45.

43. Smith M. Brain death: time for an international consensus. *Br J Anaesth.* 2012; 108(suppl 1):i6–9.

WHEN THE HEART STOPS

1. Saba MM, Ventura HO, Saleh M, Mehra MR. Ancient Egyptian medicine and the concept of heart failure. *J Card Fail.* 2006;12(6):416–21.

2. Serageldin I. Ancient Alexandria and the dawn of medical science. *Global Cardiology Science and Practice.* 2013;4(47).

3. Stanton JA. Aesculapius: a modern tale. *JAMA.* 1999;281(5):476–77.

4. Cheng TO. Hippocrates and cardiology. *JAMA.* 2001;141(2):173–83.

5. Quinsy J. *The American Medical Lexicon, on the Plan of Quincy's Lexicon Physico-Medicum, with Many Retrenchments, Additions, and Improvements; Comprising an Explanation of the Etymology and Signification of the Terms Used in Anatomy, Physiology, Surgery, Materia.* Reprint ed. Forgotten Books; 2013.

6. Powner DJ, Ackerman BM, Grenvik A. Medical diagnosis of death in adults: historical contributions to current controversies. *Lancet.* 1996;348(9036):1219–23.

7. Death or coma? *BMJ.* 1885;2(1296):841–42.

8. Poe EA. *The Premature Burial.* Reprint ed. Quill Pen Classics; 2008.

9. Gairdner W. Case of lethargic stupor or trance. *Lancet.* 1884;123(3150):56–58.

10. Williamson J. Premature burial. *Scientific American.* May 9, 1896.

11. Anabiosis—life in death. *Literary Digest.* August 22, 1914:304.

12. Baldwin JF. Premature burial. *Scientific American.* October 24, 1896:315.

13. To stop premature burial; bill introduced yesterday in the assembly by Mr. Redington of New York. *New York Times.* January 19, 1899.

14. Alexander M. "The Rigid Embrace of the Narrow House": premature burial & the signs of death. *Hastings Cent Rep.* 1980;10(3):25–31.

15. Beecher, Ethical problems [see "How Death Was Redefined," note 28].

16. What and when is death? *JAMA.* 1968;204(6):539–40.

17. Watson CJ, Dark JH. Organ transplantation: historical perspective and current practice. *Br J Anaesth.* 2012;108(suppl 1):i29–42.

18. Merrill JP, Murray JE, Harrison JH, Guild WR. Successful homotransplantation of the human kidney between identical twins. *JAMA.* 1956;160(4):277–82.

19. Machado C. The first organ transplant from a brain-dead donor. *Neurology.* 2005;64(11):1938–42.

20. Powner et al., Medical diagnosis.

21. Iltis AS, Cherry MJ. Death revisited: rethinking death and the dead donor rule. *J Med Philos.* 2010;35(3):223–41.

22. DeVita MA, Snyder JV. Development of the University of Pittsburgh Medical Center policy for the care of terminally ill patients who may become organ donors after death following the removal of life support. *Kennedy Inst Ethics J.* 1993;3(2):131–43.

23. Institute of Medicine. *Non-Heart-Beating Organ Transplantation. Practice and Protocols. Committee on Non-Heart-Beating Transplantation II: The Scientific and Ethical Basis for Practice and Protocols.* Washington, DC: Institute of Medicine; 2000.

24. Halazun KJ, Al-Mukhtar A, Aldouri A, Willis S, Ahmad N. Warm ischemia in transplantation: search for a consensus definition. *Transplant Proc.* 2007; 39(5):1329–31.

25. Institute for Health Metrics and Evaluation, The state of US health [see "How Life (and Death) Were Prolonged," note 9].

26. John 11:1–45.

27. Sheth KN, Nutter T, Stein DM, Scalea TM, Bernat JL. Autoresuscitation after asystole in patients being considered for organ donation. *Crit Care Med.* 2012; 40(1):158–61.

28. Krarup NH, Kaltoft A, Lenler-Petersen P. Risen from the dead: a case of the Lazarus phenomenon—with considerations on the termination of treatment following cardiac arrest in a prehospital setting. *Resuscitation.* 2010;81(11):1598–99.

29. Shewmon DA. *Mental Disconnect: "Physiological Decapitation" as a Heuristic For Understanding Brain Death.* Scripta Varia 110. Vatican City: Pontifical Academy of Sciences; 2007.

30. White RJ, Wolin LR, Massopust LC Jr, Taslitz N, Verdura J. Cephalic exchange transplantation in the monkey. *Surgery.* 1971;70(1):135–99.

31. Lizza JP. Where's Waldo? The "decapitation gambit" and the definition of death. *J Med Ethics.* 2011;37(12):743–46.

32. www.neurology.org/content/82/10_Supplement/P4.285

33. www.washingtontimes.com/news/2015/may/10/jury-doctor-who-had-affair-with-patient-must-pay-h/

34. United States President's Commission for the Study of Ethical Problems in Medicine and Biomedical and Behavioral Research. *Defining Death: A Report on the Medical, Legal and Ethical Issues in the Determination of Death.* 1981.

WHEN DEATH TRANSCENDS

1. Levy DE, Caronna JJ, Singer BH, Lapinski RH, Frydman H, Plum F. Predicting outcome from hypoxic-ischemic coma. *JAMA.* 1985;253(10):1420–26.

2. Wijdicks EF, Hijdra A, Young GB, Bassetti CL, Wiebe S. Practice parameter: prediction of outcome in comatose survivors after cardiopulmonary resuscitation (an evidence-based review): report of the Quality Standards Subcommittee of the American Academy of Neurology. *Neurology.* 2006;67(2):203–10.

3. Culotta E. On the origin of religion. *Science.* 2009;326(5954):784–87.

4. Henshilwood CS, d'Errico F, Watts I. Engraved ochres from the Middle Stone Age levels at Blombos Cave, South Africa. *J Hum Evol.* 2009;57(1):27–47.

5. Vandermeersch B. The excavation of Qafzeh. *Bulletin du Centre de recherche français à Jérusalem.* 2002;10:65–70.

6. Culotta, On the origin of religion.

7. Barrett JL. Exploring the natural foundations of religion. *Trends Cogn Sci.* 2000; 4(1):29–34.

8. Povinelli DJ, Preuss TM. Theory of mind: evolutionary history of a cognitive specialization. *Trends Neurosci.* 1995;18(9):418–24.

9. Kelemen D. Why are rocks pointy? Children's preference for teleological explanations of the natural world. *Dev Psychol.* 1999;35(6):1440–52.

10. Kelemen D, Rosset E. The human function compunction: teleological explanation in adults. *Cognition.* 2009;111(1):138–43.

11. Harris P. On not falling down to earth: children's metaphysical questions. In: Rosegren K, Johnson C, Harris P, eds. *Imagining the Impossible: Magical, Scientific, and Religious Thinking in Children.* Cambridge University Press; 2000.

12. Sosis R. Religious behaviors, badges, and bans: signaling theory and the evolution of religion. In: McNamara P, ed. *Where God and Science Meet: How Brain and Evolutionary Studies Alter Our Understanding of Religion.* Vol. 1. Praeger; 2006:61–86.

13. Sosis R, Bressler, ER. Cooperation and commune longevity: a test of the costly signaling theory of religion. *Cross Cultural Research.* 2003;37:211–39.

14. Bering JM, Blasi CH, Bjorklund DF. The development of afterlife beliefs in religiously and secularly schooled children. *Br J Dev Psychol.* 2005;23(4):587–607.

15. Becker E. *The Denial of Death.* Reprint ed. Free Press; 1987.

16. Rosenblatt A, Greenberg J, Solomon S, Pyszczynski T, Lyon D. Evidence for terror management theory, I: the effects of mortality salience on reactions to those who violate or uphold cultural values. *J Pers Soc Psychol.* 1989;57(4):681–90.

17. Rosenblatt et al., Evidence.

18. Pyszczynski T, Abdollahi A, Solomon S, Greenberg J, Cohen F, Weise D. Mortality salience, martyrdom, and military might: the great satan versus the axis of evil. *Pers Soc Psychol Bull.* 2006;32(4):525–37.

19. Landau MJ, Solomon S, Greenberg J, Cohen F, Pyszczynski T, Arndt J, et al. Deliver us from evil: the effects of mortality salience and reminders of 9/11 on support for President George W. Bush. *Pers Soc Psychol Bull.* 2004;30(9):1136–50.

20. Yum YO, Schenck-Hamlin W. Reactions to 9/11 as a function of terror management and perspective taking. *J Soc Psychol.* 2005;145(3):265–86.

21. Jong J, Halberstadt J, Bluemke M. Foxhole atheism, revisited: the effects of mortality salience on explicit and implicit religious belief. *J Exp. Med.* 2012;48(5):983–89.

22. Dezutter J, Soenens B, Luyckx K, Bruyneel S, Vansteenkiste M, Duriez B, et al. The role of religion in death attitudes: distinguishing between religious belief and style of processing religious contents. *Death Studies.* 2009;33(1):73–92.

23. Pyne D. A model of religion and death. *J Exp. Med.* 2010;39(1):46.

24. Kübler-Ross E. *On Death and Dying.* Simon and Schuster; 1969:479–83.

25. Branson R. The secularization of American medicine. *Stud Hastings Cent.* 1973;1(2):17–28.

26. Gallup. Religion. 2014. www.gallup.com/poll/1690/religion.aspx.

27. Koenig HG. Religious attitudes and practices of hospitalized medically ill older adults. *Int J Geriatr Psychiatry.* 1998;13(4):213–24.

28. Roberts JA, Brown D, Elkins T, Larson DB. Factors influencing views of patients with gynecologic cancer about end-of-life decisions. *Am J Obstet Gynecol.* 1997;176(1 Pt 1):166–72.

29. Breitbart W, Gibson C, Poppito SR, Berg A. Psychotherapeutic interventions at the end of life: a focus on meaning and spirituality. *Can J Psychiatry.* 2004; 49(6):366–72.

30. Vachon M, Fillion L, Achille M. A conceptual analysis of spirituality at the end of life. *J Palliat Med.* 2009;12(1):53–59.

31. Shahabi L, Powell LH, Musick MA, Pargament KI, Thoresen CE, Williams D, et al. Correlates of self-perceptions of spirituality in American adults. *Ann Behav Med.* 2002;24(1):59–68.

32. Halstead MT, Fernsler JI. Coping strategies of long-term cancer survivors. *Cancer Nurs.* 1994;17(2):94–100; Gall TL. The role of religious coping in adjustment to prostate cancer. *Cancer Nurs.* 2004;27(6):454–61; VandeCreek L, Rogers E, Lester J. Use of alternative therapies among breast cancer outpatients compared with the general population. *Altern Ther Health Med.* 1999;5(1):71–76.

33. Yates JW, Chalmer BJ, St James P, Follansbee M, McKegney FP. Religion in patients with advanced cancer. *Med Pediatr Oncol.* 1981;9(2):121–28.

34. Smith TB, McCullough ME, Poll J. Religiousness and depression: evidence for a main effect and the moderating influence of stressful life events. *Psychol Bull.* 2003;129(4):614–36.

35. McClain CS, Rosenfeld B, Breitbart W. Effect of spiritual well-being on end-of-life despair in terminally-ill cancer patients. *Lancet.* 2003;361(9369):1603–7.

36. Koffman J, Morgan M, Edmonds P, Speck P, Higginson IJ. "I know he controls cancer": the meanings of religion among Black Caribbean and White British patients with advanced cancer. *Soc Sci Med.* 2008;67(5):780–89.

37. Morgan PD, Fogel J, Rose L, Barnett K, Mock V, Davis BL, et al. African American couples merging strengths to successfully cope with breast cancer. *Oncol Nurs Forum.* 2005;32(5):979–87.

38. Okon TR. Spiritual, religious, and existential aspects of palliative care. *J Palliat Med.* 2005;8(2):392–414.

39. Balboni TA, Vanderwerker LC, Block SD, Paulk ME, Lathan CS, Peteet JR, et al. Religiousness and spiritual support among advanced cancer patients and associations with end-of-life treatment preferences and quality of life. *J Clin Oncol.* 2007;25(5):555–60; True G, Phipps EJ, Braitman LE, Harralson T, Harris D, Tester W. Treatment preferences and advance care planning at end of life: the

role of ethnicity and spiritual coping in cancer patients. *Ann Behav Med.* 2005;30(2):174–79; Johnson KS, Elbert-Avila KI, Tulsky JA. The influence of spiritual beliefs and practices on the treatment preferences of African Americans: a review of the literature. *J Am Geriatr Soc.* 2005;53(4):711–19.

40. Phelps AC, Maciejewski PK, Nilsson M, Balboni TA, Wright AA, Paulk ME, et al. Religious coping and use of intensive life-prolonging care near death in patients with advanced cancer. *JAMA.* 2009;301(11):1140–47.

41. Powell LH, Shahabi L, Thoresen CE. Religion and spirituality. Linkages to physical health. *Am Psychol.* 2003;58(1):36–52.

42. PRRI, Pre-Election American Values Survey. publicreligion.org/research/2012 /10/american-values-survey-2012/. 2012.

43. Phelps et al., Religious coping.

44. Jacobs LM, Burns K, Bennett Jacobs B. Trauma death: views of the public and trauma professionals on death and dying from injuries. *Arch Surg.* 2008; 143(8):730–35.

45. Silvestri GA, Knittig S, Zoller JS, Nietert PJ. Importance of faith on medical decisions regarding cancer care. *J Clin Oncol.* 2003;21(7):1379–82.

46. BBC. Mother dies after refusing blood. news.bbc.co.uk/2/hi/uk_news/england /shropshire/7078455.stm. 2007.

47. Tulsky JA, Chesney MA, Lo B. How do medical residents discuss resuscitation with patients? *J Gen Intern Med.* 1995;10(8):436–42.

48. Engelhardt HT Jr, Iltis AS. End-of-life: the traditional Christian view. *Lancet.* 2005;366(9490):1045–49.

49. Pope Pius XII, *The Prolongation of Life* [see "How We Learned Not to Resuscitate," note 39].

50. Pope John Paul II (1995) Evangelium Vitae, March 25, www.vatican.va.

51. Unitarian Universalist Association. The Right to Die with Dignity. 1988 General Resolution. www.uua.org/statements/statements/14486.shtml.

52. The Holy Synod of the Church of Greece, Bioethics Committee (2000) Press release, August 17. Basic positions on the ethics of transplantation and euthanasia. www.bioethics.org.gr.

53. Steinberg A, Sprung CL. The dying patient: new Israeli legislation. *Intensive Care Med.* 2006;32(8):1234–7; Weiss RB. Pain management at the end of life and the principle of double effect: a Jewish perspective. *Cancer Invest.* 2007;25(4):274–47.

54. Rappaport ZH, Rappaport IT. Brain death and organ transplantation: concepts and principles in Judaism. *Adv Exp Med Biol.* 2004;550:133–37.

55. Dorff EN. End-of-life: Jewish perspectives. *Lancet.* 2005;366(9488):862–65.

56. Dorff, End-of-life.

57. Dorff, End-of-life.

58. Foreign Policy. The List: The world's fastest growing religions. www.foreignpolicy .com/articles/2007/05/13/the_list_the_worlds_fastest_growing_religions. May 2007.

59. Crabtree S. Gallup World. Religiosity highest in world's poorest nations. www .gallup.com/poll/142727/religiosity-highest-world-poorest-nations.aspx-1. August 31, 2010.

60. Padela AI, Arozullah A, Moosa E. Brain death in Islamic ethico-legal deliberation: challenges for applied Islamic bioethics. *Bioethics.* 2013;27(3):132–39.

61. Baeke G, Wils JP, Broeckaert B. "Be patient and grateful"—elderly Muslim women's responses to illness and suffering. *J Pastoral Care Counsel.* 2012;66(3–4):5.

62. Banning M, Hafeez H, Faisal S, Hassan M, Zafar A. The impact of culture and sociological and psychological issues on Muslim patients with breast cancer in Pakistan. *Cancer Nurs.* 2009;32(4):317–24.

63. Dein S, Swinton J, Abbas SQ. Theodicy and end-of-life care. *J Soc Work End Life Palliat Care.* 2013;9(2–3):191–208.

64. Pew Research Center. Religious groups' views on end-of-life issues. November 2013.

65. da Costa DE, Ghazal H, Al Khusaiby S. Do Not Resuscitate orders and ethical decisions in a neonatal intensive care unit in a Muslim community. *Arch Dis Child Fetal Neonatal Ed.* 2002;86(2):F115–9; Ebrahim AF. The living will (Wasiyat Al-Hayy): a study of its legality in the light of Islamic jurisprudence. *Med Law.* 2000;19(1):147–60.

66. Gupta R. Death beliefs and practices from an Asian Indian American Hindu perspective. *Death Stud.* 2011;35(3):244–66.

67. Firth S. End-of-life: a Hindu view. *Lancet.* 2005;366(9486):682–86.

68. Desai PN. Medical ethics in India. *J Med Philos.* 1988;13(3):231–55.

69. McClain-Jacobson C, Rosenfeld B, Kosinski A, Pessin H, Cimino JE, Breitbart W. Belief in an afterlife, spiritual well-being and end-of-life despair in patients with advanced cancer. *Gen Hosp Psychiatry.* 2004;26(6):484–86.

70. Matsumura S, Bito S, Liu H, Kahn K, Fukuhara S, Kagawa-Singer M, et al. Acculturation of attitudes toward end-of-life care: a cross-cultural survey of Japanese Americans and Japanese. *J Gen Intern Med.* 2002;17(7):531–39.

71. Pirutinsky S, Rosmarin DH, Pargament KI, Midlarsky E. Does negative religious coping accompany, precede, or follow depression among Orthodox Jews? *J Affect Disord.* 2011;132(3):401–5.

72. Pearson SD, Goldman L, Orav EJ, Guadagnoli E, Garcia TB, Johnson PA, et al. Triage decisions for emergency department patients with chest pain: do physicians' risk attitudes make the difference? *J Gen Intern Med.* 1995;10(10):557–64.

73. Pines JM, Hollander JE, Isserman JA, Chen EH, Dean AJ, Shofer FS, et al. The association between physician risk tolerance and imaging use in abdominal pain. *Am J Emerg Med.* 2009;27(5):552–7.

74. Bensing J, Schreurs K, De Rijk AD. The role of the general practitioner's affective behaviour in medical encounters. *Psychology and Health.* 1996;11(6):825–38.

75. Geller SE, Burns LR, Brailer DJ. The impact of nonclinical factors on practice variations: the case of hysterectomies. *Health Serv Res.* 1996;30(6):729–50.

76. Curlin FA, Lantos JD, Roach CJ, Sellergren SA, Chin MH. Religious characteristics of U.S. physicians: a national survey. *J Gen Intern Med.* 2005;20(7):629–34.

77. Curlin FA, Sellergren SA, Lantos JD, Chin MH. Physicians' observations and interpretations of the influence of religion and spirituality on health. *Arch Intern Med.* 2007;167(7):649–54.

78. Curlin FA, Chin MH, Sellergren SA, Roach CJ, Lantos JD. The association of physicians' religious characteristics with their attitudes and self-reported behaviors regarding religion and spirituality in the clinical encounter. *Med Care.* 2006; 44(5):446–53.

79. Curlin et al., Physicians' observations.

80. Wenger NS, Carmel S. Physicians' religiosity and end-of-life care attitudes and behaviors. *Mt Sinai J Med.* 2004;71(5):335–43.

81. Curlin FA, Nwodim C, Vance JL, Chin MH, Lantos JD. To die, to sleep: US physicians' religious and other objections to physician-assisted suicide, terminal sedation, and withdrawal of life support. *Am J Hosp Palliat Care.* 2008;25(2): 112–20.

82. Cohen J, van Delden J, Mortier F, Lofmark R, Norup M, Cartwright C, et al. Influence of physicians' life stances on attitudes to end-of-life decisions and actual end-of-life decision-making in six countries. *J Med Ethics.* 2008;34(4):247–53.

83. Asch DA, DeKay ML. Euthanasia among US critical care nurses. Practices, attitudes, and social and professional correlates. *Med Care.* 1997;35(9):890–900.

84. Sprung CL, Maia P, Bulow HH, Ricou B, Armaganidis A, Baras M, et al. The importance of religious affiliation and culture on end-of-life decisions in European intensive care units. *Intensive Care Med.* 2007;33(10):1732–39.

85. Romain M, Sprung CL. End-of-life practices in the intensive care unit: the importance of geography, religion, religious affiliation, and culture. *Rambam Maimonides Med J.* 2014;5(1):e0003.

86. Tierney E, Kauts V. "Do Not Resuscitate" (DNR) policies in the ICU—the time has come for openness and change. *Bahrain Medical Bulletin.* 2014;36(2).

87. Saeed F, Kousar N, Aleem S, Khawaja O, Javaid A, Siddiqui MF, et al. End-of-life care beliefs among Muslim physicians. *Am J Hosp Palliat Care.* 2014.

88. MacLean CD, Susi B, Phifer N, Schultz L, Bynum D, Franco M, et al. Patient preference for physician discussion and practice of spirituality. *J Gen Intern Med.* 2003;18(1):38–43.

89. Monroe MH, Bynum D, Susi B, Phifer N, Schultz L, Franco M, et al. Primary care physician preferences regarding spiritual behavior in medical practice. *Arch Intern Med.* 2003;163(22):2751–56.

90. MacLean et al., Patient preference.

91. Ellis MR, Vinson DC, Ewigman B. Addressing spiritual concerns of patients: family physicians' attitudes and practices. *J Fam Pract.* 1999;48(2):105–9.

92. Luckhaupt SE, Yi MS, Mueller CV, Mrus JM, Peterman AH, Puchalski CM, et al. Beliefs of primary care residents regarding spirituality and religion in clinical

encounters with patients: a study at a midwestern U.S. teaching institution. *Acad Med.* 2005;80(6):560–70.

93. Balboni TA, Paulk ME, Balboni MJ, Phelps AC, Loggers ET, Wright AA, et al. Provision of spiritual care to patients with advanced cancer: associations with medical care and quality of life near death. *J Clin Oncol.* 2010;28(3):445–52.

94. Balboni TA, Balboni M, Enzinger AC, Gallivan K, Paulk ME, Wright A, et al. Provision of spiritual support to patients with advanced cancer by religious communities and associations with medical care at the end of life. *JAMA. Intern Med.* 2013;173(12):1109–17.

95. Puchalski C, Romer AL. Taking a spiritual history allows clinicians to understand patients more fully. *J Palliat Med.* 2000;3(1):129–37.

96. Lo B, Kates LW, Ruston D, Arnold RM, Cohen CB, Puchalski CM, et al. Responding to requests regarding prayer and religious ceremonies by patients near the end of life and their families. *J Palliat Med.* 2003;6(3):409–15.

97. Sinclair S, Pereira J, Raffin S. A thematic review of the spirituality literature within palliative care. *J Palliat Med.* 2006;9(2):464–79.

98. PRRI, Pre-Election American Values Survey.

99. Norenzayan A, Gervais WM. The origins of religious disbelief. *Trends Cogn Sci.* 2013;17(1):20–25. 2012.

100. Zuckerman P. *Society without God.* New York University Press; 2008.

101. Norenzayan A, Gervais WM, Trzesniewski KH. Mentalizing deficits constrain belief in a personal God. *PLoS ONE.* 2012;7(5):e36880.

102. Paul GS. Religiosity tied to socioeconomic status. *Science.* 2010;327(5966):642.

103. Bulow HH, Sprung CL, Baras M, Carmel S, Svantesson M, Benbenishty J, et al. Are religion and religiosity important to end-of-life decisions and patient autonomy in the ICU? The Ethicatt study. *Intensive Care Med.* 2012;38(7): 1126–33.

104. Curlin et al., Religious characteristics.

105. Smith-Stoner M. End-of-life preferences for atheists. *J Palliat Med.* 2007;10(4): 923–28.

106. Dennett D. The bright stuff. *New York Times.* July 12, 2003.

107. Pew Research Center. How Americans Feel About Religious Groups. www .pewforum.org/2014/07/16/how-americans-feel-about-religious-groups/. July 16, 2014.

108. Jones JM. Some Americans reluctant to vote for Mormon, 72-year-old presidential candidates: Based on February 9–11, 2007, Gallup poll. Gallup News Service. www.gallup.com/poll/26611/some-americans-reluctant-vote-mormon -72yearold-presidential-candidates.aspx. 2007.

109. Edgell P, Gerteis J, Hartmann D. Atheists as "other": moral boundaries and cultural membership in American society. *ASR.* 2006;71(2):211–34.

110. Gervais WM, Shariff AF, Norenzayan A. Do you believe in atheists? Distrust is central to anti-atheist prejudice. *J Pers Soc Psychol.* 2011;101(6):1189–206.

111. Swan LK, Heesacker M. Anti-atheist bias in the United States: testing two critical assumptions. *Secularism and Nonreligion.* 2012;1:32–42.

112. Gervais WM. Everything is permitted? People intuitively judge immorality as representative of atheists. *PLoS ONE.* 2014;9(4):e92302.

113. Charles et al., Insights from studying prejudice [see "How We Learned Not to Resuscitate," note 37].

114. Zuckerman et al., Atheism [see "How We Learned Not to Resuscitate," note 38].

115. Shahabi et al., Correlates of self-perceptions.

116. Roberts et al., Factors influencing views of patients.

117. Collin M. The search for a higher power among terminally ill people with no previous religion or belief. *Int J Palliat Nurs.* 2012;18(8):384–89.

118. Smith-Stoner, End-of-life preferences.

119. Smith-Stoner, End-of-life preferences.

120. Baggini J, Pym M. End of life: the humanist view. *Lancet.* 2005;366(9492):1235–37.

121. Smith-Stoner, End-of-life preferences.

122. Wenger and Carmel, Physicians' religiosity; Cohen et al., Influence of physicians' life stances; Bulow et al., Are religion and religiosity important.

123. Vail KE III, Arndt J, Abdollahi A. Exploring the existential function of religion and supernatural agent beliefs among Christians, Muslims, atheists, and agnostics. *Pers Soc Psychol Bull.* 2012;38(10):1288–300.

124. The World Health Organization Quality of Life assessment (WHOQOL): position paper from the World Health Organization. *Soc Sci Med.* 1995;41(10):1403–9; JCAHO. Joint Commission on Accreditation of Healthcare Organizations. CAMH Refreshed Core, January, 1998.

WHEN GUARDIANS ARE BURDENED

1. Labbate LA, Benedek DM. Bedside stuffed animals and borderline personality. *Psychol Rep.* 1996;79(2):624–26.

2. Cervenka MC, Lesser R, Tran TT, Fortune T, Muthugovindan D, Miglioretti DL. Does the teddy bear sign predict psychogenic nonepileptic seizures? *Epilepsy Behav.* 2013;28(2):217–20; Schmaling KB, DiClementi JD, Hammerly J. The positive teddy bear sign: transitional objects in the medical setting. *J Nerv Ment Dis.* 1994;182(12):725.

3. Stern TA, Glick RL. Significance of stuffed animals at the bedside and what they can reveal about patients. *Psychosomatics.* 1993;34(6):519–21.

4. Adelman RD, Tmanova LL, Delgado D, Dion S, Lachs MS. Caregiver burden: a clinical review. *JAMA.* 2014;311(10):1052–60.

5. Liu Y, Kim K, Almeida DM, Zarit SH. Daily fluctuation in negative affect for family caregivers of individuals with dementia. *Health Psychol.* 2014.

6. Rabow MW, Hauser JM, Adams J. Supporting family caregivers at the end of life: "they don't know what they don't know." *JAMA.* 2004;291(4):483–91.

7. Lynn Feinberg SCR, Ari Houser, and Rita Choula. *Valuing the Invaluable: 2011 Update. The Growing Contributions and Costs of Family Caregiving.* AARP Public Policy Institute; 2011.

8. Feinberg et al., *Valuing.*

9. National Alliance for Caregiving and AARP. *Caregiving in the U.S.* www.caregiving.org/wp-content/uploads/2015/05/2015_CaregivingintheUS_Final-Report-June-4_WEB.pdf. 2015.

10. National Alliance for Caregiving and AARP, *Caregiving.*

11. National Alliance for Caregiving and AARP, *Caregiving.*

12. Feinberg et al., *Valuing.*

13. Hurd MD, Martorell P, Delavande A, Mullen KJ, Langa KM. Monetary costs of dementia in the United States. *N Engl J Med.* 2013;368(14):1326–34.

14. Hurd et al., Monetary costs.

15. Schulz R, Beach SR. Caregiving as a risk factor for mortality: the Caregiver Health Effects Study. *JAMA.* 1999;282(23):2215–19.

16. Pochard F, Azoulay E, Chevret S, Lemaire F, Hubert P, Canoui P, et al. Symptoms of anxiety and depression in family members of intensive care unit patients: ethical hypothesis regarding decision-making capacity. *Crit Care Med.* 2001;29(10): 1893–97.

17. Cochrane JJ, Goering PN, Rogers JM. The mental health of informal caregivers in Ontario: an epidemiological survey. *Am J Public Health.* 1997;87(12):2002–7.

18. Prigerson HG, Jacobs SC. Perspectives on care at the close of life. Caring for bereaved patients: "all the doctors just suddenly go." *JAMA.* 2001;286(11): 1369–76.

19. Christakis NA, Allison PD. Mortality after the hospitalization of a spouse. *N Engl J Med.* 2006;354(7):719–30.

20. Emanuel EJ, Fairclough DL, Slutsman J, Alpert H, Baldwin D, Emanuel LL. Assistance from family members, friends, paid care givers, and volunteers in the care of terminally ill patients. *N Engl J Med.* 1999;341(13):956–63.

21. Gallicchio L, Siddiqi N, Langenberg P, Baumgarten M. Gender differences in burden and depression among informal caregivers of demented elders in the community. *Int J Geriatr Psychiatry.* 2002;17(2):154–63.

22. Vincent C, Desrosiers J, Landreville P, Demers L, group B. Burden of caregivers of people with stroke: evolution and predictors. *Cerebrovasc Dis.* 2009;27(5):456–64; Salmon JR, Kwak J, Acquaviva KD, Brandt K, Egan KA. Transformative aspects of caregiving at life's end. *J Pain Symptom Manage.* 2005;29(2):121–29.

23. Steadman PL, Tremont G, Davis JD. Premorbid relationship satisfaction and caregiver burden in dementia caregivers. *J Geriatr Psychiatry Neurol.* 2007;20(2):115–19.

24. Burton AM, Sautter JM, Tulsky JA, Lindquist JH, Hays JC, Olsen MK, et al. Burden and well-being among a diverse sample of cancer, congestive heart failure, and chronic obstructive pulmonary disease caregivers. *J Pain Symptom Manage.* 2012;44(3):410–20.

25. van Exel J, Bobinac A, Koopmanschap M, Brouwer W. The invisible hands made visible: recognizing the value of informal care in healthcare decision-making. *Expert Rev Pharmacoecon Outcomes Res.* 2008;8(6):557–61.

26. Kelton Global. The Conversation Project National Survey. theconversationproject.org/wp-content/uploads/2013/09/TCP-Survey-Release_FINAL-9-18-13.pdf. 2013.

27. Daitz B. With poem, broaching the topic of death. *New York Times.* January 24, 2011.

28. Dying Matters Coalition Survey. comres.co.uk/poll/669/dying-matters-coalition-survey-of-gps-and-the-public.htm. 2012.

29. Forrow L. The "4 R's" of respecting patients' preferences. www.boston.com/lifestyle/health/mortalmatters/2013/09/the_4_rs_of_respecting_patients_preferences.html. 2013.

30. Kutner L. Due process of euthanasia: the living will, a proposal. *Indiana Law Journal.* 1969;44(4):539–54.

31. Annas GJ. The health care proxy and the living will. *N Engl J Med.* 1991; 324(17):1210–13.

32. La Puma J, Orentlicher D, Moss RJ. Advance directives on admission. Clinical implications and analysis of the Patient Self-Determination Act of 1990. *JAMA.* 1991;266(3):402–5.

33. Butler M, Ratner E, McCreedy E, Shippee N, Kane RL. Decision aids for advance care planning: an overview of the state of the science. *Ann Intern Med.* 2014; 161(6):408–18.

34. In re Martin. 538 NW2d 399; Mich. 1995.

35. Emanuel LL, Barry MJ, Stoeckle JD, Ettelson LM, Emanuel EJ. Advance directives for medical care—a case for greater use. *N Engl J Med.* 1991;324(13): 889–95.

36. Holley JL, Stackiewicz L, Dacko C, Rault R. Factors influencing dialysis patients' completion of advance directives. *Am J Kidney Dis.* 1997;30(3):356–60.

37. Morrison RS, Olson E, Mertz KR, Meier DE. The inaccessibility of advance directives on transfer from ambulatory to acute care settings. *JAMA.* 1995;274(6): 478–82.

38. Morrison et al., The inaccessibility of advance directives.

39. Omer ZB, Hwang ES, Esserman LJ, Howe R, Ozanne EM. Impact of ductal carcinoma in situ terminology on patient treatment preferences. *JAMA. Intern Med.* 2013;173(19):1830–31.

40. Ott BB. Advance directives: the emerging body of research. *Am J Crit Care.* 1999;8(1):514–19.

41. Danis M, Garrett J, Harris R, Patrick DL. Stability of choices about life-sustaining treatments. *Ann Intern Med.* 1994;120(7):567–73.

42. New York Bar Association. New York Living Will. www.nysba.org/WorkArea/DownloadAsset.aspx?id=26506. 2014.

43. Brett AS. Limitations of listing specific medical interventions in advance directives. *JAMA*. 1991;266(6):825–28.

44. NPR. Episode 521: The Town That Loves Death. Planet Money. www.npr.org/blogs /money/2014/02/28/283444163/episode-521-the-town-that-loves-death. 2014.

45. Hammes BJ, Rooney BL. Death and end-of-life planning in one midwestern community. *Arch Intern Med*. 1998;158(4):383–90.

46. United States Census Bureau. QuicksFacts: La Crosse County, Wisconsin. quick facts.census.gov/qfd/states/55/55063.html. 2014.

47. Puchalski CM, Zhong Z, Jacobs MM, Fox E, Lynn J, Harrold J, et al. Patients who want their family and physician to make resuscitation decisions for them: observations from SUPPORT and HELP. Study to Understand Prognoses and Preferences for Outcomes and Risks of Treatment. Hospitalized Elderly Longitudinal Project. *J Am Geriatr Soc*. 2000;48(5 suppl):S84–90.

HOW DEATH IS NEGOTIATED

1. Kumar A, Aronow WS, Alexa M, Gothwal R, Jesmajian S, Bhushan B, et al. Prevalence of use of advance directives, health care proxy, legal guardian, and living will in 512 patients hospitalized in a cardiac care unit/intensive care unit in 2 community hospitals. *Arch Med Sci*. 2010;6(2):188–91.

2. Kirkpatrick JN, Guger CJ, Arnsdorf MF, Fedson SE. Advance directives in the cardiac care unit. *Am Heart J*. 2007;154(3):477–81.

3. Escher M, Perrier A, Rudaz S, Dayer P, Perneger TV. Doctors' decisions when faced with contradictory patient advance directives and health care proxy opinion: a randomized vignette-based study. *J Pain Symptom Manage*. 2014.

4. Escher et al., Doctors' decisions.

5. Diekema DS. Revisiting the best interest standard: uses and misuses. *J Clin Ethics*. 2011;22(2):128–33.

6. Himmelstein DU, Thorne D, Warren E, Woolhandler S. Medical bankruptcy in the United States, 2007: results of a national study. *Am J Med*. 2009;122(8):741–46.

7. Senelick R. Get your doctor to stop using medical jargon. Huffington Post. www .huffingtonpost.com/richard-c-senelick-md/medical-jargon_b_1450797.html. 2012.

8. Fagerlin A, Schneider CE. Enough. The failure of the living will. *Hastings Cent Rep*. 2004;34(2):30–42.

9. Brickman P, Coates D, Janoff-Bulman R. Lottery winners and accident victims: is happiness relative? *J Pers Soc Psychol*. 1978;36(8):917–27.

10. Silver RL. *Coping with an Undesirable Life Event: A Study of Early Reactions to Physical Disability* [dissertation]. Northwestern University; 1982.

11. Schkade DA, Kahneman, D. Does living in California make people happy? A focusing illusion in judgments of life satisfaction. *Psychological Science*. 1998;9(5): 340–46.

12. Shalowitz DI, Garrett-Mayer E, Wendler D. The accuracy of surrogate decision makers: a systematic review. *Arch Intern Med*. 2006;166(5):493–97.

13. Danis et al., Stability of choices [see "When Guardians Are Burdened," note 41].

14. Suhl J, Simons P, Reedy T, Garrick T. Myth of substituted judgment. Surrogate decision making regarding life support is unreliable. *Arch Intern Med*. 1994; 154(1):90–96.

15. Coppola KM, Ditto PH, Danks JH, Smucker WD. Accuracy of primary care and hospital-based physicians' predictions of elderly outpatients' treatment preferences with and without advance directives. *Arch Intern Med*. 2001;161(3):431–40.

16. Vig EK, Starks H, Taylor JS, Hopley EK, Fryer-Edwards K. Surviving surrogate decision-making: what helps and hampers the experience of making medical decisions for others. *J Gen Intern Med*. 2007;22(9):1274–79.

17. Watson A, Sheridan B, Rodriguez M, Seifi A. Biologically-related or emotionally-connected: who would be the better surrogate decision-maker? *Med Health Care Philos*. 2014.

18. Emanuel EJ. Living wills: are durable powers of attorney better? *Hastings Cent Rep*. 2004;34(6):5–6; author reply 7.

19. Wastila LJ, Farber NJ. Residents' perceptions about surrogate decision makers' financial conflicts of interest in ventilator withdrawal. *J Palliat Med*. 2014; 17(5):533–39.

20. Rodriguez RM, Navarrete E, Schwaber J, McKleroy W, Clouse A, Kerrigan SF, et al. A prospective study of primary surrogate decision makers' knowledge of intensive care," *Crit Care Med*. 2008;36(5):1633–6; Azoulay E, Chevret S, Leleu G, Pochard F, Barboteu M, Adrie C, et al. Half the families of intensive care unit patients experience inadequate communication with physicians. *Crit Care Med*. 2000;28(8):3044–49.

WHY FAMILIES FALL

1. Quinn JR, Schmitt M, Baggs JG, Norton SA, Dombeck MT, Sellers CR. Family members' informal roles in end-of-life decision making in adult intensive care units. *Am J Crit Care*. 2012;21(1):43–51.

2. Hawkins NA, Ditto PH, Danks JH, Smucker WD. Micromanaging death: process preferences, values, and goals in end-of-life medical decision making. *Gerontologist*. 2005;45(1):107–17.

3. Puchalski et al., Patients who want [see "When Guardians Are Burdened," note 47].

4. Long AC, Curtis JR. The epidemic of physician-family conflict in the ICU and what we should do about it. *Crit Care Med*. 2014;42(2):461–62.

5. Beam C. Under the knife. *New Yorker*. August 25, 2014.

6. Warraich H. Pakistan: the final frontier for a polio-free world. *Lancet*. 2011; 377(9761):207–8; Warraich HJ. Religious opposition to polio vaccination. *Emerg Infect Dis*. 2009;15(6):978.

7. Studdert DM, Mello MM, Burns JP, Puopolo AL, Galper BZ, Truog RD, et al. Conflict in the care of patients with prolonged stay in the ICU: types, sources, and predictors. *Intensive Care Med.* 2003;29(9):1489–97.

8. Schuster RA, Hong SY, Arnold RM, White DB. Investigating conflict in ICUs—is the clinicians' perspective enough? *Crit Care Med.* 2014;42(2):328–35.

9. Breen CM, Abernethy AP, Abbott KH, Tulsky JA. Conflict associated with decisions to limit life-sustaining treatment in intensive care units. *J Gen Intern Med.* 2001;16(5):283–89.

10. Studdert et al., Conflict.

11. Silveira MJ, Kim SY, Langa KM. Advance directives and outcomes of surrogate decision making before death. *N Engl J Med.* 2010;362(13):1211–18.

12. Majesko A, Hong SY, Weissfeld L, White DB. Identifying family members who may struggle in the role of surrogate decision maker. *Crit Care Med.* 2012; 40(8):2281–86.

13. Marks MA, Arkes HR. Patient and surrogate disagreement in end-of-life decisions: can surrogates accurately predict patients' preferences? *Med Decis Making.* 2008;28(4):524–31.

14. Schenker Y, Crowley-Matoka M, Dohan D, Tiver GA, Arnold RM, White DB. I don't want to be the one saying "we should just let him die": intrapersonal tensions experienced by surrogate decision makers in the ICU. *J Gen Intern Med.* 2012;27(12):1657–65.

15. Parks SM, Winter L, Santana AJ, Parker B, Diamond JJ, Rose M, et al. Family factors in end-of-life decision-making: family conflict and proxy relationship. *J Palliat Med.* 2011;14(2):179–84.

16. Studdert et al., Conflict.

17. Breen et al., Conflict.

18. Salam R. How La Crosse, Wisconsin slashed end-of-life medical expenditures. *National Review.* www.nationalreview.com/agenda/372501/how-la-crosse-wisconsin-slashed-end-life-medical-expenditures-reihan-salam. 2014.

19. Fritsch J, Petronio S, Helft PR, Torke AM. Making decisions for hospitalized older adults: ethical factors considered by family surrogates. *J Clin Ethics.* 2013; 24(2):125–34.

20. Knickle K, McNaughton N, Downar J. Beyond winning: mediation, conflict resolution, and non-rational sources of conflict in the ICU. *Crit Care.* 2012;16 (3):308.

21. Kramer BJ, Kavanaugh M, Trentham-Dietz A, Walsh M, Yonker JA. Predictors of family conflict at the end of life: the experience of spouses and adult children of persons with lung cancer. *Gerontologist.* 2010;50(2):215–25.

22. Sherer RA. Who will care for elder orphans. *Geriatric Times.* 2004;5(1). Available at www.cmellc.com/geriatrictimes/g040203.html.

23. McPherson M, Lynn, S., Brashears, M. Social isolation in America: changes in core discussion networks over two decades. *ASR.* 2006;71(3):353–75.

24. Sessums LL, Zembrzuska H, Jackson JL. Does this patient have medical decision-making capacity? *JAMA*. 2011;306(4):420–27.

25. Holt-Lunstad J, Smith TB, Layton JB. Social relationships and mortality risk: a meta-analytic review. *PLoS Med*. 2010;7(7):e1000316.

26. Ettema EJ, Derksen LD, van Leeuwen E. Existential loneliness and end-of-life care: a systematic review. *Theor Med Bioeth*. 2010;31(2):141–69.

27. Meisel A, Jennings B., Ethics, end-of-life care, and the law: overview. In: Doka KJ, ed. *Living with Grief: Ethical Dilemmas at the End of Life*. Hospice Foundation of America; 2005:63–79.

28. Hornung CA, Eleazer GP, Strothers HS III, Wieland GD, Eng C, McCann R, et al. Ethnicity and decision-makers in a group of frail older people. *J Am Geriatr Soc*. 1998;46(3):280–86.

29. Meisel and Jennings, Ethics.

30. White DB, Curtis JR, Wolf LE, Prendergast TJ, Taichman DB, Kuniyoshi G, et al. Life support for patients without a surrogate decision maker: who decides? *Ann Intern Med*. 2007;147(1):34–40.

31. Norris WM, Nielsen EL, Engelberg RA, Curtis JR. Treatment preferences for resuscitation and critical care among homeless persons. *Chest*. 2005;127(6):2180–87.

32. Chawla N, Arora NK. Why do some patients prefer to leave decisions up to the doctor: lack of self-efficacy or a matter of trust? *J Cancer Surviv*. 2013;7(4):592–601.

33. Alemayehu E, Molloy DW, Guyatt GH, Singer J, Penington G, Basile J, et al. Variability in physicians' decisions on caring for chronically ill elderly patients: an international study. *CMAJ*. 1991;144(9):1133–38.

34. Phillips C, O'Hagan M, Mayo J. Secrecy hides cozy ties in guardianship cases. *Seattle Times*. April 21, 2010.

35. Colbert JA, Adler JN. Clinical decisions. Family presence during cardiopulmonary resuscitation—polling results. *N Engl J Med*. 2013;368(26):e38.

36. Jabre et al., Family presence [see "How We Learned Not to Resuscitate," note 56].

37. Kramer DB, Mitchell SL. Weighing the benefits and burdens of witnessed resuscitation. *N Engl J Med*. 2013;368(11):1058–59.

38. Hafner JW, Sturgell JL, Matlock DL, Bockewitz EG, Barker LT. "Stayin' Alive": a novel mental metronome to maintain compression rates in simulated cardiac arrests. *J Emerg Med*. 2012;43(5):e373–77.

39. Idris AH, Guffey D, Aufderheide TP, Brown S, Morrison LJ, Nichols P, et al. Relationship between chest compression rates and outcomes from cardiac arrest. *Circulation*. 2012;125(24):3004–12.

WHEN DEATH IS DESIRED

1. A piece of my mind. It's over, Debbie. *JAMA*. 1988;259(2):272.

2. It's almost over—more letters on Debbie. *JAMA*. 1988;260(6):787–89.

3. Gaylin W, Kass LR, Pellegrino ED, Siegler M. "Doctors must not kill." *JAMA*. 1988;259(14):2139–40.

4. Parachini A. AMA journal death essay triggers flood of controversy. *Los Angeles Times*. February 19, 1988.

5. Wilkerson I. Essay on mercy killing reflects conflict on ethics for physicians and journalists. *New York Times*. February 23, 1988.

6. It's almost over—more letters on Debbie.

7. It's almost over—more letters on Debbie.

8. Lundberg GD. "It's over, Debbie" and the euthanasia debate. *JAMA*. 1988; 259(14):2142–43.

9. Lundberg G. *Severed Trust: Why American Medicine Hasn't Been Fixed*. Basic Books; 2002:228.

10. Lundberg, "It's over, Debbie" and the euthanasia debate.

11. Van Guilder S. My right to die: a cancer patient argues for voluntary euthanasia. *Los Angeles Times*. June 26, 1988.

12. Lombardo PA. Eugenics at the movies. *Hastings Cent Rep*. 1997;27(2):43; Surgeon lets baby, born to idiocy, die. *New York Times*. July 25, 1917:11.

13. Vote to oust Haiselden; medical society's committee against Bollinger baby's physician. *New York Times*. December 15, 1915:9.

14. Vijayakumar L. Altruistic suicide in India. *Arch Suicide Res*. 2004;8(1):73–80.

15. A Divya. Why sati is still a burning issue. *Times of India*. timesofindia.indiatimes .com/Why-sati-is-still-a-burning-issue/articleshow/4897797.cms. August 16, 2009.

16. Judges 16:28–30 (NASB).

17. Crone DM. Historical attitudes toward suicide. *Duquesne Law Rev*. 1996; 35(1):7–42.

18. Celsus. *De Medicina*. Book 5. 26:1. First century BC.

19. Pliny the Elder. *The Natural History*. Bostock J and Riley HT, trans. Book 7: Man, His Birth, His Organization, and the Invention of the Arts. Chapter 50. 1855.

20. Hippocrates. Oath of Hippocrates. In: Chadwick J, Mann WN, trans. *Hippocratic Writings*. Penguin Books; 1950.

21. Papadimitriou JD, Skiadas P, Mavrantonis CS, Polimeropoulos V, Papadimitriou DJ, Papacostas KJ. Euthanasia and suicide in antiquity: viewpoint of the dramatists and philosophers. *J R Soc Med*. 2007;100(1):25–28.

22. Koop CE. Introduction (to a symposium on assisted suicide). *Duquesne Law Rev*. 1996;35(1):1–5.

23. Frum D. Who was the real Cato? *Daily Beast*. December 20, 2012.

24. Thorne MA. *Lucan's Cato, the Defeat of Victory, the Triumph of Memory* [dissertation]. University of Iowa. ir.uiowa.edu/etd/749. 2010.

25. Kaplan KJ, Schwartz MB. Zeno vs. Job: The Biblical Case against "Rational Suicide." In: *A Psychology of Hope: A Biblical Response to Tragedy and Suicide*. Revised and expanded ed. Wm B Eerdmans Publishing Co; 2008.

26. Crone, Historical attitudes.

27. Eberl JT. Aquinas on euthanasia, suffering, and palliative care. *Natl Cathol Bioeth Q.* 2003;3(2):331–54.

28. More T. *Utopia and Other Writings.* New American Library; 1984.

29. Baker R, reviewer. *Bulletin of the History of Medicine.* 2006;80(4):789–90. Review of: Dowbiggin I. *A Concise History of Euthanasia: Life, Death, God, and Medicine.*

30. Hume D. *Essays on Suicide and the Immortality of the Soul: The Complete Unauthorized Edition.* 1783.

31. Paterson C. *Assisted Suicide and Euthanasia: A Natural Law Ethics Approach.* Ashgate Publishing; 2012:23.

32. Locke J. *Two Treatises of Government.* Book II, chapter IV, section 23. 1689.

33. Brassington I. Killing people: what Kant could have said about suicide and euthanasia but did not. *J Med Ethics.* 2006;32(10):571–74.

34. Genesis 3:16 (KJV, Cambridge Edition).

35. Warren JC. *Etherization with Surgical Remarks.* William D Ticknor & Co; 1848: 36, 69–71.

36. Warren, *Etherization.*

37. Euthanasia. *Popular Science Monthly.* 1873;3:90–96.

38. Emmanuel L. *Regulating How We Die: The Ethical, Medical, and Legal Issues Surrounding Physician-Assisted Suicide.* Harvard University Press; 1998:185.

39. The moral side of euthanasia. *Journal of the American Medical Association.* 1885;5:382–83; Euthanasia. *Br Med J.* 1906;1:638–39.

40. Darwin C. *The Descent of Man, and Selection in Relation to Sex.* Volume 1, chapter 5, part 1. D Appleton; 1872:162.

41. Sofair AN, Kaldjian LC. Eugenic sterilization and a qualified Nazi analogy: the United States and Germany, 1930–1945. *Ann Intern Med.* 2000;132(4):312–19.

42. Gauvey SK, Shuger NB. The permissibility of involuntary sterilization under the parens patriae and police power authority of the state: In re Sterilization of Moore. *Univ Md Law Forum.* 1976;6(3):109–28.

43. Spriggs EJ. Involuntary sterilization: an unconstitutional menace to minorities and the poor. *Rev Law Soc Change.* 1974;4(2):127–51.

44. Sofair and Kaldjian, Eugenic sterilization.

45. Feeble-mindedness and the future [editorial]. *N Engl J Med.* 1933;208:852–53.

46. Sterilization and its possible accomplishments [editorial]. *N Engl J Med.* 1934; 211:379–80.

47. *Carrie Buck v. John Hendren Bell, Superintendent of State Colony for Epileptics and Feeble Minded.* 274 US 200. 1927.

48. *Carrie Buck v. John Hendren Bell.*

49. Marker RL, Smith WJ. The art of verbal engineering. *Duquesne Law Rev.* 1996;35(1):81–107.

50. Humphry D. *What's in a Word? The Results of a Roper Poll of Americans on How They View the Importance of Language in the Debate Over the Right to*

Choose to Die. Junction City, OR: Euthanasia Research and Guidance Organization; 1993:1–3.

51. Marker and Smith, The art of verbal engineering.

52. Davis A. Jack Kevorkian: a medical hero? His actions are the antithesis of heroism. *BMJ.* 1996;313(7051):228.

53. Roberts J, Kjellstrand C. Jack Kevorkian: a medical hero. *BMJ.* 1996;312(7044):1434.

54. *Vacco, Attorney General of New York, et al. v. Quill et al.* 521 US 793. 1997.

55. *Washington, et al., Petitioners v. Harold Glucksberg, et al.* 521 US 702. 1997.

56. Simons M. *Between Life and Death.* The Age; 2013.

57. Kissane DW, Street A, Nitschke P. Seven deaths in Darwin: case studies under the Rights of the Terminally Ill Act, Northern Territory, Australia. *Lancet.* 1998; 352(9134):1097–102.

58. Kissane DW. Case presentation: a case of euthanasia, the Northern Territory, Australia. *J Pain Symptom Manage.* 2000;19(6):472–73.

59. Sheldon T. Obituary: Andries Postma. *Br Med J.* 2007;334:320.

60. Van Der Maas PJ, Van Delden JJ, Pijnenborg L, Looman CW. Euthanasia and other medical decisions concerning the end of life. *Lancet.* 1991;338(8768):669–74.

61. Green K. Physician-assisted suicide and euthanasia: safeguarding against the "slippery slope"—The Netherlands versus the United States. *Indiana Int Comp Law Rev.* 2003;13(2):639–81.

62. Glick S. Euthanasia in The Netherlands. *J Med Ethics.* 1999;25(1):60.

63. van der Maas PJ, van der Wal G, Haverkate I, de Graaff CL, Kester JG, Onwuteaka-Philipsen BD, et al. Euthanasia, physician-assisted suicide, and other medical practices involving the end of life in the Netherlands, 1990–1995. *N Engl J Med.* 1996;335(22):1699–705.

64. Onwuteaka-Philipsen BD, van der Heide A, Koper D, Keij-Deerenberg I, Rietjens JA, Rurup ML, et al. Euthanasia and other end-of-life decisions in the Netherlands in 1990, 1995, and 2001. *Lancet.* 2003;362(9381):395–99.

65. Bilsen J, Cohen J, Chambaere K, Pousset G, Onwuteaka-Philipsen BD, Mortier F, et al. Medical end-of-life practices under the euthanasia law in Belgium. *N Engl J Med.* 2009;361(11):1119–21.

66. Watson R. Luxembourg is to allow euthanasia from 1 April. *BMJ.* 2009;338:b1248.

67. Steck N, Egger M, Maessen M, Reisch T, Zwahlen M. Euthanasia and assisted suicide in selected European countries and US states: systematic literature review. *Med Care.* 2013;51(10):938–44.

WHEN THE PLUG IS PULLED

1. Maynard B. My right to death with dignity at 29. CNN.com. www.cnn.com/2014 /10/07/opinion/maynard-assisted-suicide-cancer-dignity/. 2014.

2. Willems DL, Daniels ER, van der Wal G, van der Maas PJ, Emanuel EJ. Attitudes and practices concerning the end of life: a comparison between physicians from

the United States and from The Netherlands. *Arch Intern Med.* 2000;160(1):63–8; Meier DE, Emmons CA, Wallenstein S, Quill T, Morrison RS, Cassel CK. A national survey of physician-assisted suicide and euthanasia in the United States. *N Engl J Med.* 1998;338(17):1193–201.

3. Meier et al., A national survey of physician-assisted suicide and euthanasia in the United States. *N Engl J Med.* 1998;338(17):1193–201.

4. Lee MA, Nelson HD, Tilden VP, Ganzini L, Schmidt TA, Tolle SW. Legalizing assisted suicide—views of physicians in Oregon. *N Engl J Med.* 1996;334(5):310–15.

5. Meier et al., A national survey.

6. Asch DA. The role of critical care nurses in euthanasia and assisted suicide. *N Engl J Med.* 1996;334(21):1374–79.

7. Kolata G. 1 in 5 nurses tell survey they helped patients die. *New York Times.* May 23, 1996.

8. Emanuel EJ, Fairclough DL, Daniels ER, Clarridge BR. Euthanasia and physician-assisted suicide: attitudes and experiences of oncology patients, oncologists, and the public. *Lancet.* 1996;347(9018):1805–10.

9. Wilson KG, Scott JF, Graham ID, Kozak JF, Chater S, Viola RA, et al. Attitudes of terminally ill patients toward euthanasia and physician-assisted suicide. *Arch Intern Med.* 2000;160(16):2454–60.

10. Oregon Public Health Division, *Death with Dignity Annual Report—2013.* public .health.oregon.gov/ProviderPartnerResources/EvaluationResearch /DeathwithDignityAct/Documents/year16.pdf. January 28, 2014.

11. Battin MP, van der Heide A, Ganzini L, van der Wal G, Onwuteaka-Philipsen BD. Legal physician-assisted dying in Oregon and the Netherlands: evidence concerning the impact on patients in "vulnerable" groups. *J Med Ethics.* 2007; 33(10):591–97.

12. Levy MH. Pharmacologic treatment of cancer pain. *N Engl J Med.* 1996;335 (15):1124–32.

13. Marquet RL, Bartelds A, Visser GJ, Spreeuwenberg P, Peters L. Twenty five years of requests for euthanasia and physician assisted suicide in Dutch general practice: trend analysis. *BMJ.* 2003;327(7408):201–2.

14. Ganzini L, Goy ER, Dobscha SK. Why Oregon patients request assisted death: family members' views. *J Gen Intern Med.* 2008;23(2):154–57.

15. Maynard, My right.

16. Oregon Public Health Division, *Death with Dignity Annual Report.*

17. Tucker KL. State of Washington, third state to permit aid in dying. *J Palliat Med.* 2009;12(7):583–4; discussion 5.

18. Rich BA. Baxter v. Montana: what the Montana Supreme Court said about dying, dignity, and palliative options of last resort. *Palliat Support Care.* 2011;9(3): 233–37.

19. McCarthy M. Vermont governor agrees to sign bill on physician assisted suicide. *BMJ.* 2013;346:f3210.

20. Angell M. The Brittany Maynard effect: how she is changing the debate on assisted dying. *Washington Post.* October 31, 2014.

21. Bever L. Brittany Maynard, as promised, ends her life at 29. *Washington Post.* November 2, 2014.

22. Glass RM. AIDS and suicide. *JAMA.* 1988;259(9):1369–70.

23. Campo R. *The Final Show: What the Body Told.* Duke University Press; 1996.

24. Hermann C, Looney S. The effectiveness of symptom management in hospice patients during the last seven days of life. *J Hosp Palliat Nurs.* 2001;3(3); Georges JJ, Onwuteaka-Philipsen BD, van der Heide A, van der Wal G, van der Maas PJ. Symptoms, treatment and "dying peacefully" in terminally ill cancer patients: a prospective study. *Support Care Cancer.* 2005;13(3):160–68.

25. Morita T, Inoue S, Chihara S. Sedation for symptom control in Japan: the importance of intermittent use and communication with family members. *J Pain Symptom Manage.* 1996;12(1):32–38.

26. Mangan JT. An historical analysis of the principle of double effect. *Theol Studies.* 1949;10:41–61; Quill TE, Dresser R, Brock DW. The rule of double effect—a critique of its role in end-of-life decision making *N Engl J Med.* 1997;337(24):1768–71.

27. *Vacco, Attorney General of New York, et al. v. Quill et al.* 521 US 793. 1997; *Washington, et al., Petitioners v. Harold Glucksberg, et al.* 521 US 702. 1997.

28. Brief of the American Medical Association, et al., as amici curiae in support of petitioners, at 6, *Washington v. Glucksberg,* 117 S. Ct. 2258 (No. 96–110). 1997.

29. Billings JA, Block SD. Slow euthanasia. *J Palliat Care.* 1996;12(4):21–30.

30. Quill, TE. Death and dignity. A case of individualized decision making *N Engl J Med.* 1991;324(10):691–94.

31. Quill TE. The ambiguity of clinical intentions. *N Engl J Med.* 1993;329(14):1039–40.

32. Orentlicher D. The Supreme Court and terminal sedation: rejecting assisted suicide, embracing euthanasia. *Hastings Constit Law Q.* 1997;24(4):947–68.

33. Bruce A, Boston P. Relieving existential suffering through palliative sedation: discussion of an uneasy practice. *J Adv Nurs.* 2011;67(12):2732–40.

34. AMA. Opinion 2.201—Sedation to Unconsciousness in End-of-Life Care. 2008.

35. Sykes N, Thorns A. Sedative use in the last week of life and the implications for end-of-life decision making. *Arch Intern Med.* 2003;163(3):341–4; Thorns A, Sykes N. Opioid use in last week of life and implications for end-of-life decision making. *Lancet.* 2000;356(9227):398–99.

36. Claessens P, Menten J, Schotsmans P, Broeckaert B. Palliative sedation: a review of the research literature. *J Pain Symptom Manage.* 2008;36(3):310–33.

37. Patterson JR, Hodges MO. The rule of double effect. *N Engl J Med.* 1998; 338(19):1389; author reply 90.

38. Lo B, Rubenfeld G. Palliative sedation in dying patients: "we turn to it when everything else hasn't worked." *JAMA.* 2005;294(14):1810–16.

39. Johnson D. Questions of law live on after father helps son die. *New York Times.* May 7, 1989.

40. Johnson, Questions of law.

41. Mitchell C. On heroes and villains in the Linares drama. *Law Med Health Care.* 1989;17(4):339–46.

42. Man who unplugged son takes PCP. *Los Angeles Times.* June 2, 1989.

43. Fairman RP. Withdrawing life-sustaining treatment. Lessons from Nancy Cruzan. *Arch Intern Med.* 1992;152(1):25–27.

44. Busalacchi P. Cruzan: clear and convincing? How can they? *Hastings Cent Rep.* 1990;20(5):6–7.

45. Lewin T. Nancy Cruzan dies, outlived by a debate over the right to die. *New York Times.* December 27, 1990.

46. Prendergast TJ, Luce JM. Increasing incidence of withholding and withdrawal of life support from the critically ill. *Am J Respir Crit Care Med.* 1997;155(1):15–20.

47. Eddy DM. A piece of my mind. A conversation with my mother. *JAMA.* 1994; 272(3):179–81.

48. Miller FG, Meier DE. Voluntary death: a comparison of terminal dehydration and physician-assisted suicide. *Ann Intern Med.* 1998;128(7):559–62.

49. Orentlicher D. The alleged distinction between euthanasia and the withdrawal of life-sustaining treatment: conceptually incoherent and impossible to maintain. *Univ Ill Law Rev.* 1998;1998(3):837–59.

50. Sontheimer D. Suicide by advance directive? *J Med Ethics.* 2008;34(9):e4.

51. Kwok AC, Semel ME, Lipsitz SR, Bader AM, Barnato AE, Gawande AA, et al. The intensity and variation of surgical care at the end of life: a retrospective cohort study. *Lancet.* 2011;378(9800):1408–13.

52. Tschirhart EC, Du Q, Kelley AS. Factors influencing the use of intensive procedures at the end of life. *J Am Geriatr Soc.* 2014;62(11):2088–94.

53. Battin MP. Terminal sedation: pulling the sheet over our eyes. *Hastings Cent Rep.* 2008;38(5):27–30.

54. Bernstein N. A father's last wish, and a daughter's anguish. *New York Times.* September 25, 2014.

#WHENDEATHISSHARED

1. Angell R. The old man. *New Yorker.* February 17 & 24, 2014.

2. Chabra S. The diary of another nobody. *Oblomov's Sofa.* September 2014.

3. Erlanger S. A writer whose pen never rests, even facing death. *New York Times.* October 31, 2014.

4. Warraich H. The rituals of modern death. *New York Times.* September 16, 2015.

5. Lowney AC, O'Brien T. The landscape of blogging in palliative care. *Palliat Med.* 2012;26(6):858–59.

6. Smith B. Dying in the social media: when palliative care meets Facebook. *Palliat Support Care.* 2011;9(4):429–30.

7. Cha AE. Crowdsourcing medical decisions: ethicists worry Josh Hardy case may set bad precedent. *Washington Post.* March 23, 2014.

8. Wernick A. Social media is transforming the way we view death and grieving. PRI.org. www.pri.org/stories/2014-12-11/social-media-transforming-way-we-view -death-and-grieving. December 2014.

9. Miller D. Hospices—the potential for new media. www.ucl.ac.uk/anthropology /people/academic_staff/d_miller/mil-28. 2015.

10. Johnson I. Nobel renews debate on Chinese medicine. *New York Times.* October 10, 2015.

11. Borland S. How NHS dehumanises patients, by doctor, 32, who is dying of rare form of cancer. *Daily Mail.* June 6, 2014.

12. Miller, Hospices.

13. Davies C. The death café. Aeon. aeon.co/magazine/philosophy/death-has -become-too-sanitised/. September 11, 2013.

14. Hayasaki E. Death is having a moment. *Atlantic.* October 25, 2013.

15. Reese H. The college course that's all about death. *Atlantic.* January 14, 2014.

16. O'Connor K. The death-positive movement. *Pacific Standard Magazine.* May 16, 2013.

17. Blackie LE, Cozzolino PJ. Of blood and death: a test of dual-existential systems in the context of prosocial intentions. *Psychol Sci.* 2011;22(8):998–1000.

18. Vail KE III, Juhl J, Arndt J, Vess M, Routledge C, Rutjens BT. When death is good for life: considering the positive trajectories of terror management. *Pers Soc Psychol Rev.* 2012;16(4):303–29.

19. Aldwin CM, Molitor NT, Avron S III, Levenson MR, Molitor J, Igarashi H. Do stress trajectories predict mortality in older men? Longitudinal findings from the VA Normative Aging Study. *J Aging Res.* 2011;2011:896109.

20. Periyakoil VS, Neri E, Fong A, Kraemer H. Do unto others: doctors' personal end-of-life resuscitation preferences and their attitudes toward advance directives. *PLoS ONE.* 2014;9(5):e98246.

21. Gallo JJ, Straton JB, Klag MJ, Meoni LA, Sulmasy DP, Wang NY, et al. Life-sustaining treatments: what do physicians want and do they express their wishes to others? *J Am Geriatr Soc.* 2003;51(7):961–69.

INDEX